EVERYTHING IS INTERCONNECTED

TOWARDS A GLOBALIZATION WITH A HUMAN FACE AND AN INTEGRAL ECOLOGY

D1548282

EVERYTHING IS INTERCONNECTED

Towards a Globalization with a Human Face and an Integral Ecology

Edited by Joseph Ogbonnaya and Lucas Briola

MARQUETTE
UNIVERSITY

PRESS

ASSOCIATION
of UNIVERSITY
PRESSES

MARQUETTE UNIVERSITY PRESS
MILWAUKEE

The Association of Jesuit University Presses

Marquette Studies in Theology

No. 90

Lonergan Studies, International Institute for Method in Theology

Robert Doran and Joseph Ogbonnaya, General Editors

Book Design by Carol Sawyer

Library of Congress Cataloging-in-Publication Data

Names: Ogbonnaya, Joseph, 1968- editor. Briola, Lucas, 1991- editor.
Title: Everything is interconnected : towards a globalization with a human
    face and an integral ecology / Joseph Ogbonnaya and Lucas Briola, editors
Description: First [edition]. | Milwaukee : Marquette University Press, 2019. |
    Series: Marquette studies in theology; no. 90 | Includes bibliographical
    references and index. | Summary: "This collection of essays serves the calls
    of Catholic social teaching for a globalization with a human face (Pope John
    Paul II) and an integral ecology (Pope Francis). Aided by the thought of
    Bernard Lonergan and Robert Doran, the contributors take an interdisciplinary
    approach, focusing on questions pertaining to politics, economics, social
    theory, environmental studies, and theology"--Provided by publisher.
Identifiers: LCCN 2019022587 | ISBN 9781626007185 (paperback)
Subjects: LCSH: Globalization--Religious aspects--Catholic Church. |
    Christian sociology--Catholic Church.
Classification: LCC BX1795.G66 E98 2019 | DDC 261.8088/282--dc23
LC record available at https://lccn.loc.gov/2019022587

CONTENTS

Acknowledgments vii

Foreword ix
Robert M. Doran, S.J.

Introduction xi
Joseph Ogbonnaya and Lucas Briola

SECTION I

TOWARDS A GLOBALIZATION WITH A HUMAN FACE / 1

1. A Heuristic for the Critical Analysis of Globalization 3
   Paul St. Amour

2. Redeeming Global Finance from Neoliberal Ideology 23
   Nicolas J. Baumgartner

3. Scotosis and Structural Inequality: The Dangers of Bias
   in a Globalized Age 39
   Kate Ward

4. Solidarity and the Possibility of Global Human Rights 57
   Nicholas Olkovich

5. The Dynamics of Grace in the Humanization
   of Globalization 79
   Joseph Ogbonnaya

6. Communitarian Solutions to the Ecological Crisis:
   Michael Northcott, Bernard Lonergan, and Robert Doran
   in Dialogue 97
   Gerard Whelan, S.J.

SECTION II

Towards an Integral Ecology / 117

7. Hearing and Answering the One Cry of Earth and Poor:
   An Integral Ecology, Eucharistic Healing, and the Scale
   of Values..................................... 119
   Lucas Briola

8. The Original Green Campaign: Dr. Hildegard of Bingen's
   Viriditas as Complement to *Laudato Si'*............. 137
   John D. Dadosky

9. Interpreting *Laudato Si'*: What Does It Mean to
   Be Human?.................................... 159
   Thomas Hughson, S.J.

10. The Glory to be Revealed: Grace and Emergence in
    an Ecological Eschatology 179
    Benjamin J. Hohman

11. Ecological Conversion, Healing, and the Integral Ecology
    of *Laudato Si'*............................... 199
    Cristina Vanin

12. Educating for Ecological Responsibility: Bernard Lonergan,
    Pope Francis, and a Local Case Study Prompted by
    a Global Reality.............................. 215
    Jame Schaefer

13. Cities as Learning Ecosystems: Lonergan's Emergent
    Probability in Urban Spaces..................... 235
    Edward Dunar

14. Water Ethics Under Development: Help from Lonergan's
    Method...................................... 253
    Thomas C. McAuley

Contributors..................................... 273
Index 279

ACKNOWLEDGMENTS

We thank greatly all of our authors for their rich contributions to the volume. They are the ones who "made" the volume. So too would this effort be impossible without the assistance of Marquette University Press, especially Maureen Kondrick. We thank them. Finally, we remain eternally grateful for the thought, dedication, and energy of Fr. Robert Doran, SJ. In gathering us together in the International Institute for Method in Theology, he is the "first cause" of this project. We proudly dedicate this first publication of the Institute to him.

FOREWORD

Robert M. Doran (Marquette University)

I wish to thank Joseph Ogbonnaya and Lucas Briola for inviting me to write a brief foreword to this very fine book. Informative comments on each of the contributions to this volume appear in the introduction, and so I will limit myself to remarks on the place of this volume in the projected work of the International Institute for Method in Theology.

The Marquette Lonergan Project has sponsored one or two colloquia a year since 2009. The spring 2017 colloquium saw the launching of the Institute, under the joint sponsorship of the Marquette Lonergan Project, the Lonergan Research Institute at Regis College in the University of Toronto, and the theology faculty of the Gregorian University, Rome.

The Institute for Method in Theology is really the brainchild of Bernard Lonergan, who in the last few years of his life began to collect a library whose books were stamped "Institute for Method in Theology." These books are presently housed in the Lonergan Research Institute in Toronto. When in 1984 I proposed the idea of what became the LRI to the Reverend William Addley, S.J., then Provincial of the Jesuits of Upper Canada, I had two goals in mind: the publication of the Collected Works of Bernard Lonergan and the establishment of the Institute for Method in Theology.

It was clear that the Collected Works had to take precedence, but it was also clear that the Institute enjoyed equal billing in the long-range forecast of the steps that would be taken to preserve, promote, develop, and implement the work of Bernard Lonergan. Recent research in the archive of Frederick Crowe, my long-time collaborator in launching the LRI and getting the Collected Works off the ground, confirms that the Institute for Method in Theology was an integral part of the original plan.

As I drew toward the end of the task of overseeing the editing of Lonergan's Collected Works, I decided that it was time to organize the Institute for Method in Theology. The spring 2017 colloquium at Marquette marked the official beginning of this new venture, but I had already procured the collaboration of more than thirty scholars as original members of the Institute. I had divided the work of the new Institute into five research groups and had appointed a coordinator for each group: Systematic Theology (Darren Dias, University of St Michaels' College, Toronto), Philosophy (Brian Bajzek, now at Christ the King Seminary, Buffalo), Economics for Humane Globalization (Joseph Ogbonnaya, Marquette University), Ecological Culture (Lucas Briola, now at Saint Vincent College, Latrobe, PA), and Critical-realist Hermeneutics (Joseph Gordon, Johnson University). The five coordinators and representatives from the LRI (Eric Mabry, Interim Director at the time) and the Gregorian (Gerard Whelan) were present at the launching. Joseph Ogbonnaya and Lucas Briola almost immediately decided that their respective teams would work together to produce the present volume, which is the first in what I hope will be a long list of works coming from the research of the Institute. I am very proud that this volume is the first major production of the Institute.

In the meantime, the membership of the Institute has almost doubled. And the spring colloquium each year at Marquette will be devoted to the work of one or more of the research teams. I am hoping that new teams will spring up and that there will continue to be collaboration among the teams similar to that which produced the current volume.

Anyone who wants further information on the Institute is invited to check the homepage of either of the Marquette Lonergan websites: www.bernardlonergan.com and www.loneriganresource.com. There you will find a paper entitled "International Institute for Method in Theology: Newsletter 1." This first newsletter contains information on most of the current members of the Institute. In the meantime, just enjoy reading the present volume. It will be well worth your time.

INTRODUCTION

Joseph Ogbonnaya (Marquette University)
and Lucas Briola (Saint Vincent College)

We live in an interconnected age. Globalization, as the reality and intensification of worldwide interconnectedness made possible by information technology, has come to stay. The various forms of globalization—whether religious, economic, political, cultural, or environmental—all aim at creating a common ground for human interrelatedness, prosperity, and sustainable development. The extent and the impact of these many dimensions of globalization have been mixed however, and, unsurprisingly, globalization continues to provoke vigorous debate in its appraisals. Pope John Paul II brings some clarity to these conversations. As he declares, "Globalization, *a priori*, is neither good nor bad. It will be what people make of it. No system is an end in itself, and it is necessary to insist that globalization, like any other system, *must be at the service of the human person; it must serve solidarity and the common good.*"[1] That is, according to Catholic social teaching, globalization *can* and *must* have a human face and be a force for good. Rather than endlessly debate the merits and perils of globalization then, here Pope John Paul II reorients us instead to work towards the realization of this noble goal.

Today's ecological crisis stands as one significant indicator of the progress or, more accurately, the lack thereof made in this complex task. In *Laudato si'*, convinced that "everything is interconnected," Pope Francis remarks how "a true ecological

1. John Paul II, "Address of the Holy Father to the Pontifical Academy of Social Sciences," April 27, 2001, http://w2.vatican.va/content/john-paul-ii/en/speeches/2001/april/documents/hf_jp-ii_spe_20010427_pc-social-sciences.html. Emphasis added. See also Kenneth R. Himes, "Globalization with a Human Face: Catholic Social Teaching and Globalization," *Theological Studies* 69 (2008): 269–289.

approach *always* becomes a social approach" and vice-versa.[2] He accordingly prescribes an "integral ecology" as the cornerstone for caring for our common home and, in turn, as a pillar for a more humane globalization.[3] Against a "globalization of indifference" (*LS* 52) fostered by modernity's "excessive anthropocentrism" (*LS* 116), an integral ecology promotes a vision in which everything is in fact recognized and hallowed as interconnected.[4] Against the "globalization of the technocratic paradigm" that produces an uncritical, one-dimensional account of development (*LS* 106) and fragments reality through its hyper-specialization (*LS* 110, 138), an integral ecology seeks an interdisciplinary dialogue (*LS* 201) able to construct "another type of progress, one which is healthier, more human, more social, more integral" (*LS* 112). Since everything is connected, Pope Francis proposes that a genuine integral ecology catalyzes the type of globalization for which John Paul II called.

In the joined task of promoting a more humane globalization and an integral ecology, then, a central question becomes *how* in fact everything is connected. Inspired by Catholic social teaching, the essays in this collection submit that the thought of Bernard Lonergan—especially, though by no means exclusively, as interpreted through his commentator, Robert M. Doran—provides key conceptual tools for making these connections. As the following essays also demonstrate, such efforts likewise begin to sketch how one might live righteously in our interconnected world. This volume is timely, as the church strives to articulate its redemptive mission amid both a surge of

---

2. Francis, *Laudato Si'* [Encyclical on Care for Our Common Home], May 24, 2015, §49. Forms of the phrase, "everything is interconnected," appear no less than nine times in the encyclical (see *LS* 70, 91, 92, 117, 120, 137, 138, 142, 240).

3. As Kevin Irwin writes, "integral ecology" represents "the most distinctive contribution of the encyclical" and "the most important theological insight about ecology in the document" (*A Commentary on* Laudato Si': *Examining the Background, Contributions, Implementation, and Future of Pope Francis's Encyclical* (New York: Paulist Press, 2016), 102, 117). "Integral ecology" is referred to nine times in *Laudato si'*, and Pope Francis devotes its entire fourth chapter to developing the concept.

4. See Vincent J. Miller, "Integral Ecology: Francis's Spiritual and Moral Vision of Interconnectedness," in *The Theological and Ecological Vision of Laudato Si': Everything is Connected*, ed. Vincent J. Miller (New York: Bloomsbury T&T Clark, 2017), 11–28.

nationalist sentiments blaming fiscal crises on globalization and a multiplication of omens signaling the onset of environmental catastrophe. Lonergan himself hoped his work could help Catholic social teaching respond more effectively to the signs of the times.[5] For his part, Lonergan grasped the dynamics of globalization quite well. Specifically, he repudiated both the idea of infinite progress inherent in liberal capitalism and the Marxist notion that human history is oriented internally towards progress. On the contrary, he, like other Christian ethicists, held that history always remains open to both destruction and redemption. Lonergan accordingly fashioned an analysis of history with three categories, ones that guide this volume considerably: progress, decline, and redemption.[6] So too did he call for a radical criticism of economics as a human science in its three principal variants: the traditional market economy, the Marxist-inspired socialist economy, and the new transactional economy constituted by giant corporations.[7] In "Healing and Creating in History," Lonergan observed that globalization is characterized by global governance, the use of large capital, quests for cheap raw materials, a global market network, and stiff competition. He recognized the possible adverse effects of globalization on developing and developed countries due to multinational companies' quest for the maximization of profit.[8]

Nevertheless, Lonergan did not answer all of the questions that continue to arise from our interconnected world. For instance, certain dimensions of globalization—such as the many visions of development, the ethics and politics of change, the emergence of post-colonial and de-colonial discourses, and the new critical

---

5. See Patrick Brown, "'Aiming Excessively High and Far': The Early Lonergan and the Challenge of Theory in Catholic Social Thought," *Theological Studies* 72 (2011): 620–644.

6. Bernard J.F. Lonergan, "Analytic Concept of History," in *Method: Journal of Lonergan Studies*, vol. 11, no. 1 (Spring 1993): 1–36, at 14; cf. Joseph Ogbonnaya, *Lonergan, Social Transformation and Sustainable Human Development* (Eugene, OR: Wipf and Stock, 2013), 154.

7. Bernard J.F. Lonergan, "Moral Theology and the Human Sciences," in *Philosophical and Theological Papers, 1965–1980*, Collected Works of Bernard Lonergan (CWL), vol. 17, eds. Robert Croken and Robert Doran (Toronto: University of Toronto Press, 2004), 311.

8. Bernard J. F. Lonergan, "Healing and Creating in History," in *A Third Collection*, ed. Frederick Crowe (Mahwah, NJ: Paulist Press, 1985), 100–109.

traditions (e.g., feminist thought, etc.)—did not arrive until after Lonergan's time. He never engaged ecological questions either, despite their intersection with the questions surrounding globalization. Lonergan studies must therefore continue to engage the various discourses of globalization, development, and ecology.

One noteworthy attempt in this vein comes from Robert Doran. His writings, especially his *Theology and the Dialectics of History*, supply a fecund means to understand and serve the world's interconnectedness.[9] In response to today's global crises, Doran draws upon the notion of a "world cultural humanity" and develops an "integral scale of values." The essays that follow will unpack these concepts further. For now, suffice it to say, Doran's heuristic can not only counter the imperial, technocratic tendencies of stronger developed countries over developing ones, but also can preserve the fragile, dialectical relationships that constitute subjects, communities, and cultures. Fulfilling the intentions of Catholic social teaching, this framework can help mediate redemption to a distorted dialectics of history instead of dismissing societal breakdown as a portent of an "end of history," as frequently suggested by skewed postmodern conceptions of history. The challenge posed today, then, is coming to grips with the world's greater interconnectedness in such a way that promotes genuine progress without enabling a mechanistic instrumentalization of the human person and the rest of creation. Indeed, Doran's work serves as a fitting starting point for many of our contributors' attempts to foster a globalization with a human face and an integral ecology.

Overview of the Volume

In view of the interrelatedness of globalization and ecology, this work includes two sections: (1) the philosophical, ethical, cultural, political, and economic dimensions of globalization and (2) the theory behind and the concrete implementation of an integral ecology. Admittedly, this division is somewhat artificial, as the essays of each section frequently overlap both in the questions that they address and the sources that they employ.

---

9. Robert M. Doran, *Theology and the Dialectics of History* (Toronto: University of Toronto Press, 1990).

The first section seeks a heuristic that might allow for an insightful analysis of the dynamics of globalization and a non-ideological adjudication of these debates. Globalization can fragment and exclude various segments of society, leading to a distortion of the practical intelligence constitutive of society. At the cultural-political junction, the imperatives of globalization can coopt culture to serve merely economic ends and render cultural critiques of political dysfunction ineffective. At the political-economic junction, globalization, especially in its current neo-liberal form, can introduce certain "necessities" and "determinisms" into the political process, which seemingly render that process irrelevant (e.g., "market-driven" demands of multinational corporations to deregulate and cut taxes under the threat of moving operations elsewhere). There can occur "a race to the bottom," often most detrimental to the interests and rights of the most vulnerable persons. At the economic-technical junction, globalization tends to impose a mega-scale monolithic implementation of technology. This occurs in ways that are quasi-monopolistic and largely capital-intensive and therefore undermining competitive enterprise and innovation. Finally, at the technical-natural junction, globalization can result in profound environmental degradation.

The first three essays elaborate the philosophical, economic, and ethical foundations of globalization in light of Lonergan's philosophy and economics as well as Doran's structure of history. In "A Heuristic for the Critical Analysis of Globalization," Paul St. Amour describes how Lonergan's philosophical and economic writings afford a normative and explanatorily powerful heuristic for an analysis of globalization able to avoid its potentially dehumanizing outcomes. He argues that Lonergan's metaphysic of "emergent probability," especially as augmented by his macroeconomic circulation analysis, offers an analytical tool for understanding the normative relations between the cultural, political, economic, technical, and natural components of globalization.

Nicolas Baumgartner, in "Redeeming Global Finance from Neoliberal Ideology," next expounds the intricacies of neoliberal ideology, untangling it from capitalism. He argues that human development cannot be adequately apprehended and served by neoliberal theory, but that global capital still remains key to human development. Following Lonergan's understanding of "value" and guided by Catholic social teaching on the question, he considers the role of global capital in human development and how it can encourage decisions born from authenticity. Baumgartner's article helpfully offers an alternative to simplistic rejections of globalization that erroneously confuse capitalism with neoliberalism.

In "Scotosis and Structural Inequality: The Dangers of Bias in a Globalized Age," Kate Ward continues to investigate how the current social order advances disvalue and how it might instead mediate authentic value. In particular, Ward studies how economic inequality shapes the moral lives of persons and communities. Using Lonergan's notions of "scotosis" and "bias," she explores how economic inequality both results from and promotes a biased ignorance and, ultimately, a dehumanization of the Other. As an alternative, Ward advocates for increased financial transparency and a positive "globalization of solidarity" able to offset the social fragmentation that inhibits the imperatives made by an authentically interconnected world.

The next three essays discuss the implications of globalization for culture, anthropology, and the environment. Globalization tends towards a homogenizing imposition of a dominant American culture that undermines cultural diversity. The issue of human rights follows closely from these cultural concerns. Nicholas Olkovich, in "Solidarity and the Possibility of Global Human Rights," illustrates this point well. There, he articulates an ethic of intellectual and social solidarity capable of grounding an alternative account of global human rights. He does so through a critical examination of the work of Richard Rorty. From that conversation, Olkovich develops a form of cosmopolitanism capable of harmonizing insights from both sides of contemporary debates between cultural relativists and universalists concerning the possibility of a global ethic and global human rights. Through this reformed cosmopolitanism, he believes, can globalization better serve the human person.

Indeed, generally, globalization aims at improving human well-being, but unfortunately, it is limited by its materialistic anthropology. A truly integral human development instead must incorporate religious value. Drawing upon Doran's appropriation of Lonergan's scale of values, Joseph Ogbonnaya, in "The Dynamics of Grace in the Humanization of Globalization," accordingly aims to reposition globalization towards a more holistic social transformation. Ogbonnaya outlines a framework in which the religious values of God's love enable persons both to act with integrity and, as a result, to engender a critical global culture guided by soteriological value. This broader framework allows globalization to become a force for a world-cultural community inclusive of all humanity. So too, we are beginning to realize, must this community include all creation. In "Communitarian Solutions to the Ecological Crisis: Michael Northcott, Bernard Lonergan, and Robert Doran in Dialogue," Gerard Whelan starts to move in this direction. He conducts a dialectical analysis on the thought of environmental theologian Michael Northcott through Lonergan's and Doran's heuristic categories. More broadly, Whelan considers how, besides reacting to globalizing trajectories, communitarian movements also respond to the ecological crisis in a distinct way. He goes on to discern the presence of decline and progress within these current forms of localism. From his analysis, Whelan highlights the potential of Lonergan's thought for advancing a more communitarian economics able to respect both the insights of populist movements and the limits of the earth. The article underscores the overlapping questions raised by globalization and the ecological crisis; it thus serves as a fitting bridge to the next section of the volume.

Building on the insights of the first section, the essays in the volume's second section exhibit how the work of Lonergan and his followers (especially Doran) can help strengthen an integral ecology and a transformative response to the technocratic paradigm. The first five essays of the section critically ground the meaning of an integral ecology through theoretical reflection. Mindful of Pope Francis's constant admonition that "realities are greater than ideas" (*LS* 201), the next three essays apply this integral ecology to some concrete problems that plague our common, global, and interconnected home.

In "Hearing and Answering the One Cry of Earth and Poor: An Integral Ecology, Eucharistic Healing, and the Scale of Values," Lucas Briola explains the connections between social and environmental exigencies within the church's redemptive mission. To do so, he clarifies the meaning behind Pope Francis's emphasis on the twin "cries" of the earth and the poor in *Laudato si'* by transposing them onto Doran's scale of values. Besides solidifying the explanatory potential of Doran's work, this transposition enables one to more easily discern how, for the encyclical, the Eucharist mediates healing within our common home, answers the cries of the poor and the earth, and thus simultaneously promotes a humane globalization and an integral ecology.

In "The Original Green Campaign: Dr. Hildegard of Bingen's *Viriditas* as Complement to *Laudato Si*," John Dadosky further teases out the nature of an integral ecology. While laudatory of Pope Francis's efforts in *Laudato si'*, Dadosky argues that the encyclical missed a prime opportunity to incorporate the bold thought of Hildegard of Bingen. After expounding Hildegard's theology of "*viriditas*" ("the greening" life force of God), he indicates how her prophetic thought crystalizes Pope Francis's call for an integral ecology, whether in specifying the nature of "ecological conversion" (*LS* 217) or grounding the "gospel of creation" delineated in the second chapter of *Laudato si'*. Dadosky concludes by showing how Hildegard's original insights can enrich ecological theology today and, as a result, lay the foundations for a systematic theology befitting an integral ecology.

"Interpreting *Laudato Si'*: What Does It Mean to Be Human?," written by Thomas Hughson, begins to construct that systematic theology, similarly complementing the integral ecology outlined in *Laudato si'* along the way. Hughson focuses on the anthropological questions that Pope Francis raises in the encyclical, especially in light of evolution. As a response, Hughson turns to Lonergan's cognitional theory in an effort to ground a less anthropocentric and more relational conception of the human person. As a way to support his theoretical argument, Hughson discusses the findings of empirical paleoanthropological research regarding human evolution. He ends by returning to the Lonergan project, suggesting how his essay might further specify Doran's identification of "cosmological meaning" within the integral scale of values.

Benjamin Hohman, in "The Glory to be Revealed: Grace and Emergence in an Ecological Eschatology," likewise generates some dynamic categories for a systematic theology that supports an integral ecology. He concentrates on questions concerning eschatology, again supplementing the starting point provided by *Laudato si'*. By means of Lonergan's notion of "generalized emergent probability," Hohman answers several ecotheological questions raised in the encyclical's reception. In addressing these questions and supplying an emergent account of grace and eschatology, he forwards a vision of theological foundations that adroitly preserves the unity and integrity of creation and redemption. By so doing, Hohman shows how Lonergan's work can preserve the interconnected understanding of world order that must mark an integral ecology.

Cristina Vanin continues this line of thought in her "Ecological Conversion, Healing, and the Integral Ecology of *Laudato Si*." She uses Doran's notions of the "dialectics of history" and "psychic conversion" to tease out the meaning of "ecological conversion," a key category for an integral ecology (*LS* 217). Observing that the technocratic paradigm truncates cosmological meaning, she shows how Pope Francis's call to this conversion intends for us a recovery of connection and attentiveness to the relationships that surround us throughout all creation. Resonating deeply with several nature writers, Doran's stress on psychic conversion, Vanin proposes, elucidates the challenging profundity of this personal change. Only through this radical conversion can one recognize that "everything is connected" and so live out an integral ecology in everyday life. Indeed, like the essays that precede hers, Vanin confirms the enduring relevance and promise of the Lonergan project for theoretically grounding the integral ecology of *Laudato si'*. In focusing on ecological conversion, moreover, she begins to show how this theorizing naturally raises the question of how to implement an integral ecology concretely.

This practical focus distinguishes the next few essays. Drawing from Lonergan's own methodological analogy based on the image of a pair of scissors, these first five essays of the book's second part serve as a sharp "upper blade" of theory that shapes the way that one encounters, understands, and responds to concrete data. The three essays that follow, meanwhile, serve as the concomitant "lower blade" that brings that theory into contact with the richness of the world situation and so sharpens the cutting upper edge.[10] Hence, the first five theoretical essays frame the applications made in the next three essays, while those applications can simultaneously provide critical checks on the cogency of these theoretical proposals. In particular, this volume applies Lonergan's thought to questions within environmental education, urban development, and water ethics. Such topics are just a few of the many that constitute an integral ecology and so, by extension, are essential for a humane globalization as well.

In the last chapter of *Laudato si'*, Pope Francis asserts that an integral ecology requires an education that teaches us how to attend

---

10. Bernard J.F. Lonergan, *Insight: A Study of Human Understanding*, CWL 3, eds. Frederick E. Crowe and Robert M. Doran (Toronto: University of Toronto Press, 2005), 337.

to our interconnectedness. He underscores the need for a broad environmental education that promotes good environmental *habits*, not merely the dissemination of information (*LS* 211). In "Educating for Ecological Responsibility: Bernard Lonergan, Pope Francis, and A Local Case-Study Prompted by a Global Reality," Jame Schaefer accordingly builds upon Lonergan's fourth transcendental precept—to "Be Responsible"—in order to explain the theological-philosophical rationale for her Spring 2017 capstone seminar for the Interdisciplinary Environmental Ethics minor at Marquette University (which she founded). Specifically, she recounts how her students developed a practical tool to facilitate the switch from fossil fuels to renewable and efficient energy strategies at local levels. Through this process, as Schaefer confirms, her students learned and exercised habits of authentic ecological responsibility able to kindle an integral ecology.

Laudato si' also details how the squalor and chaos that commonly infect urban settings manifest the connection between today's social and ecological crises (*LS* 44). Edward Dunar, in "Cities as Learning Ecosystems: Lonergan's Emergent Probability in Urban Spaces," responds to this exigency. Also using Lonergan's notion of "emergent probability," Dunar suggests a way forward for navigating longstanding debates in urban design about the appropriateness of guiding design metaphors for the city. This account, he believes, can support a more robust articulation of what Kevin Lynch calls the "learning ecosystem" of urban life. Such an attempt helps answer Pope Francis's call for urban spaces more suited to an "ecology of daily life" (*LS* 150–153). Dunar indicates how, through the promotion of such an ecology, cities can become holy settings of redemptive agency and collective grace.

Pope Francis names water poverty and its commercialization as another primary obstacle towards developing an integral ecology, yet another issue that affects persons and the earth alike (*LS* 27–31). In this spirit, in "Water Ethics Under Development: Help from Lonergan's Method," Thomas McAuley draws from his over thirty years of experience as a water resources engineer to examine the ethical presuppositions often implicit in water management. McAuley uses specifically Lonergan's "generalized empirical method," "emergent probability," and "scale of values" to address questions arising both within the field of water ethics and from McAuley's own work for the Canadian portion of the International Joint Commission (an organization that adjudicates transboundary water disputes along the U.S.-Canadian border). Through this dialogue, the essay answers Pope Francis's clarion call for a management of water that is subject to the common, cosmic good rather than "the dictates of an efficiency-driven paradigm of technocracy" (*LS* 189). Like the rest of the contributors in the volume, McAuley effectively displays how Lonergan's thought can guide the intertwined task of nurturing an integral ecology and a globalization with a human face.

Conclusion

Lonergan understood quite presciently the challenges that our interconnected world poses. In *Insight: A Study of Human Understanding*, convinced that "the world lies in pieces before [humanity] and pleads to be put together again," he hoped "to seek a common ground on which [people] of intelligence might meet."[11] Later, in *Method of Theology*, Lonergan reiterated his intentions to establish "a method . . . for integrating theology with scholarly and scientific human studies. The aim of such integration is to generate well-informed and continuously revised policies and plans for promoting good and undoing evil both in the church and in human society generally."[12] The essays cumulatively hope to continue Lonergan's integrating intentions here by outlining and mediating the broad scope of redemption demanded by our interconnected world.

These essays intend to supplement previous efforts in applying Lonergan's thought to these matters. Moreover, by no means are the topics covered here exhaustive. Needless to say, a collection of essays simply cannot match the breadth of today's global crises. The range of topics in this volume thus stands as an invitation for further interdisciplinary dialogue, both within and beyond the field of Lonergan studies. We join hands with all efforts aimed at "seeking common ground, "promoting good," and "undoing evil" in a world where everything is interconnected.

---

11. Lonergan, *Insight*, 552, 7.

12. Bernard J.F. Lonergan, *Method in Theology* (New York: Herder and Herder, 1972), 366.

SECTION I

Towards a Globalization with a Human Face

CHAPTER ONE

A Heuristic for the Critical Analysis of Globalization

Paul St. Amour (Saint Joseph's University)

I n *Globalization and Its Discontents Revisited*, Nobel laureate
Joseph Stiglitz argues incisively that globalization has fallen
short of its initial promises. While from the outset most economists recognized there would be both winners and losers accompanying the global expansion of commerce and finance, promoters
of globalization tended to be overly optimistic that globalization
would improve the lives of all. Benefits were highlighted while costs
were ignored, and it was not made sufficiently clear that the benefits
would accrue disproportionately to owners and upper management
of multinational corporations. While globalization has undeniably raised the standard of living in some regions (most notably in
Asia), the poor in many parts of the developing world find their lives
unimproved. More recently, discontent has spread to developed
nations as well, which are currently undergoing a wave of anti-
globalization sentiment, some of which has found political expression in a resurgence of right-wing nationalism. As Stiglitz concludes,
"For millions of people globalization has not worked. Many have
actually been made worse off, as they have seen their jobs destroyed
and their lives become more insecure. They have felt increasingly
powerless against forces beyond their control. They have seen their
democracies undermined, their cultures eroded."[1]

While Stiglitz does not advocate blanket withdrawal from
globalization, he argues that meaningful reform must acknowledge
that globalization has been mismanaged and deep-seated problems

---

1. Joseph E. Stiglitz, *Globalization and Its Discontents Revisited: Anti-
Globalization in the Era of Trump* (New York: W.W. Norton & Co., 2018), 336.

remain to be addressed. The following are just a few concerns he elucidates. First, trade negotiations have effectively advanced the interests of multinational corporations and the global financial industry, but have procedurally excluded significant stakeholders: developing nations, the poor, advocates for the environment, and workers. Second, there has been a history of ill-fated foreign investment in developing countries, in which resolution focused excessively on repayment of Western creditors and was achieved by compromising national sovereignty, undermining democratic process, and imposing austerity programs. Third, the mobility of capital and corporate access to international labor markets have generated relentless competitive pressures tending toward the minimization of wages, regulation, and corporate taxation. As governments compete to attract foreign investment, workers globally feel their jobs threatened by foreign workers willing to work for less. This well-documented "race to the bottom" is detrimental in many ways. Lower incomes and weaker job protections (especially in manufacturing) negatively impact the lives of workers and their families as well as drag on consumer demand. A weakening of the tax base threatens the capacity of governments to provide public goods and sustain social welfare. Deregulation potentially threatens everything from environmental sustainability, to worker safety, to financial stability. Fourth, in some regions, globalization has induced job destruction in excess of job creation, leading to higher unemployment rates. Fifth, globalization has been accompanied by higher income and wealth inequality.[2]

The Challenge of Humanizing Globalization

Acknowledging the failures of globalization as it has been practiced in recent decades, if accompanied by a countervailing appreciation for globalization's potential benefits if practiced more wisely, prompts a question: how might globalization be reformed, reoriented in a progressive manner, humanized? The question intends more than mere improvement in the economic good of order. Properly economic goods (for example, economic growth, maintenance of full employment, financial and monetary stability, sustainable public

---

2. See also Joseph E. Stiglitz, *The Price of Inequality* (New York: W.W. Norton & Co., 2013).

financing, and balanced trade) are all important—not least because they underpin material conditions for the recurrence of vital, social, cultural, personal, and religious goods. It is understood, furthermore, that attainment of such economic goods is rendered more precarious in the new global context. Nevertheless, might we also hold expectations for globalization that extend beyond purely economic considerations and critically analyze globalization in light of these ulterior expectations? Is it not reasonable to expect globalization to be conducted in a manner that affirms and supports principles of human rights, democratic rule, subsidiarity, equality of opportunity, and environmental sustainability? Might it be possible for globalization to be practiced in a way that is more democratic, more human in scale, and more permeated by a widespread, equitable participation in free enterprise? I intend to propose a heuristic for thinking about globalization that could help advance such ends. Before doing so however, it is necessary to repudiate two prevalent but unhelpful mindsets: first, globalization regarded abstractly, and second, globalization regarded deterministically.

First, the merits of globalization cannot be debated adequately if discourse is confined to abstract and purely economic considerations.[3] While such considerations do legitimately constitute a theoretical core for understanding, what a narrow focus tends to neglect is the actual *history* of globalization in concrete practice. The "global market" is not some abstract disembodied medium, but rather always concretely constituted by some set of *politically* established institutions, laws, regulations, and agreements. The particular details of these social arrangements matter greatly, and ultimately determine the qualitative fabric of the global market that actually exists. While purely abstract economic conceptualizations have been marshalled to promote globalization as inherently full of promise, a broader attention to concrete history discloses the less jejune conclusion that the outcomes of globalization have ranged from very good to very bad. Hence, it is important to regard globalization not primarily as an abstract concept, but rather as a spectrum of concrete possibilities, not all of which are desirable. Necessary is a willingness to consider

---

3. For instance, one recalls models originating in Adam Smith and David Ricardo that demonstrate mutually advantageous trade based on specialization and comparative advantage.

the actual history of globalization as it has been concretely practiced thus far and a comprehensive framework for responsibly guiding global interdependence.

Second, perhaps because globalization is something of a juggernaut—a complex worldwide phenomenon seemingly beyond the control even of individual nation states—one can tend to regard it with a kind of fatalistic complacency, as something about which little can be done, as obviously "a reality that is here to stay." As a corrective to this deterministic attitude, it is worth recalling the anti-globalization movement. To the extent its representatives gain political power and are efficacious in exercising that power, it is possible that there may occur at least a partial withdrawal from globalization or perhaps a modification of its existing institutions, laws, regulations, and agreements. Such modifications may or may not represent improvements. It depends, of course, on what those modifications actually are and how they are concretely implemented. At the same time, a nationalist-inspired withdrawal from globalization is liable to be counterproductive in several ways. For consumers, available goods and services would likely be restricted in variety, lower in quality, and more expensive in price. Producers would face losing economies of scale, constricting supply chains, and narrowing of their markets. Labor and free enterprise related to export and import opportunities would be forfeited. The flow of technology and ideas, which has been a catalyst for economic growth in the developing world, would be impeded. Finally, a common basis for international cooperation (so essential for resolving global problems and for avoiding war) would be partially undermined. Thus, a case could be made that globalization, if not "here to stay" as a permanent matter of fact, at least *ought* to stay, as a matter of economic expedience. Yet, note that this is a judgment of value, not a judgment of fact. If a decision to preserve globalization in some form stems from a judgment of value, this entails that real choices remain regarding what particular form is most tolerable. What kind of globalization is desirable? What institutional, legal, regulatory framework would be best, most just, and most in the service of humanity? Granted, such decisions cannot be made by any single nation and will require widespread collaboration. Yet it neither follows from this, nor from the juggernaut nature of globalization itself, that ethical complacency is justified. The dialectic of history requires ongoing intelligent and responsible guidance, and the phenomenon of globalization is not exempt from this imperative.

Central to Bernard Lonergan's philosophy was an explanation of human history as dialectical—as constituted not merely by progress, but also by decline. Progress follows from the recurrent exercise of attentive, intelligent, reasonable, and responsible cognitional operations by individuals as well as by institutions that mediate their cooperation. Decline follows from the absence of such operation and cooperation—from inattentiveness, stupidity, unreasonableness, irresponsibility, bias, indifference, or hatred.

It seems there has been considerable difficulty not only in anticipating significant problems of globalization beforehand, but even fully noticing them after they arise. (Of course, anticipating or noticing problems is a precondition for understanding and possibly correcting them.) Part of the difficulty is that many of globalization's problems are experienced in developing nations, primarily by the poor. These voices have largely been excluded from the debate about globalization. The environment likewise has no voice of its own and has not been adequately represented. Furthermore, the notion that there has occurred anything like a genuine "debate" about globalization in the first place is dubious. Neoliberalism has been remarkably influential in systematically arguing for unfettered markets and the minimization of political intervention in economic matters. Under its influence, there has been cultivated an incapacity to appreciate the fact that markets are sometimes inefficient and, consequently, a general unwillingness to examine symptoms of market failure or proposals for reforms.[4] The anti-globalization movement (and demagogues who would exploit its aspirations for their own purposes) now thrust the obvious failures of globalization forward for belated consideration. Still, nationalist withdrawal is liable to induce a significant economic setback and interjects considerable new geopolitical risks as well. Hence, it is timely to pose the question: How are we to understand the complex reality of globalization in a non-ideological manner? If globalization is to continue, but on a reformed and more humanized basis, how might current failings be systematically examined and new possibilities be more comprehensively envisioned? I propose that a heuristic for the critical analysis of globalization is needed and Lonergan's account of emergent probability establishes a theoretical foundation for this task.

---

4. See John Cassidy, *How Markets Fail: The Logic of Economic Calamities* (New York: Picador, 2010).

Emergence: The Theoretical Foundation for the Heuristic

Through his metaphysics, Lonergan sought to understand natural and human reality in an evolutionary fashion, as an emerging series of distinct levels of conditions, each making possible higher kinds of action and interaction and each transforming possibilities at the underlying levels.[5] In this account and in Lonergan's macroeconomic writings, economics is not presented as a conceptualistically isolated domain. While the economy can be understood in terms of its own proper internal terms and relations, it must also be understood in relation to extrinsic natural, technical, social, political, and cultural schemes of recurrence. Moreover, while the sub-human levels of world-order (the physical, chemical, botanical, and zoological) are merely *intelligible*, the human level is constituted by operations of *intelligence* by which we establish, maintain, and transform the conditions for our own living. Human reality, including economic activity, is self-constituted. It is mediated by meaning and motivated by value.

Emergent technical, economic, political, and cultural levels of human self-constitution can be successively differentiated. In his account of human intelligence, Lonergan explicated "common sense" knowing as knowing for the sake of making and doing. Evolutionarily, it is likely to have manifested initially in tool making. "At first, there appears little to differentiate man from the beasts, for in primitive fruit-gathering cultures, hunger is linked to eating by a simple sequence of bodily movements. But primitive hunters take time out from hunting to make spears, and primitive fishers take time out from fishing to make nets."[6] Spearmaking and netmaking are instances of practical intelligence, indeed of *technological* innovation functioning in an incipient context of economic capital formation. The manufacture and subsequent use of spears and nets generate and sustain a more amenable set of living conditions—some combination of more food, more leisure, and more people who can be fed. *Economic* activity is emergent upon the exercise of human intelligence at the technical level.

---

5. For a fuller account of emergent probability, see Bernard Lonergan, *Insight: A Study of Human Understanding*, Collected Works of Bernard Lonergan (CWL), vol. 3, eds. Frederick E. Crowe and Robert M. Doran (Toronto: Toronto University Press, 1992), 138–51, 234–7.

6. Lonergan, *Insight*, 233.

Production is in fact an important mode of human self-constitution. By insights, creativity, and action at the technical and economic levels, human beings set the material conditions under which they will live. Economic activity transforms the potentialities of nature (e.g., wood, metal, plant fibers) into a standard of living (e.g., nutritious food and commodious housing). Ongoing insights into the limitations of the productive process yield ever further technological innovations, which in turn evoke ever further expansions of capital. Lonergan writes, "As inventions accumulate, they set problems calling forth more inventions. The new inventions complement the old only to suggest further improvements, to reveal fresh possibilities, and eventually to call forth in turn the succession of mechanical and technological higher viewpoints that mark epochs in man's material progress."[7]

This expansion of technological innovation and capital formation in turn sets conditions for the emergence of new patterns of social relations. In proportion to its complexity, the expansion requires the performance of a bewildering variety of specialized tasks, the development of skills necessary for the efficient execution of those tasks, and some manner of eliciting cooperation among all involved. As requisite patterns of cooperation must be recurrent and ongoing, capital expansion establishes an exigence for an orderly and stable framework for cooperation. As Lonergan describes this process, "It calls forth some economic system, some procedure that sets the balance between the production of consumer goods and new capital formation, some method that settles what quantities of what goods and services are to be supplied, some device for assigning tasks to individuals and for distributing among them the common product."[8]

While a functioning economic system presupposes complex routines of cooperation, the act of establishing or transforming an economic system is not itself an economic but rather a *political* act. "Each step in the process of technological and economic development is an occasion on which minds differ, new insights have to be communicated, enthusiasm has to be roused, and a common decision must be reached."[9] Given this recurrent need for effective agreement, there arises a further exigence for a political specialization of common

---

7. Lonergan, *Insight*, 233.

8. Lonergan, *Insight*, 234.

9. Lonergan, *Insight*, 234.

sense. Political order is emergent upon economic order. "As technology evokes the economy, so the economy evokes the polity."[10] Political orders, in turn, are themselves promoted or criticized, built up or abandoned, in light of a yet-higher level of human activity, that is, the apprehension of *cultural* meanings and values.

Hence Lonergan differentiated emerging natural, technical, economic, political, and cultural schemes and clarified how these are related through a series of successive sublations. Lower levels of order set conditions of possibility for higher levels. The presence of fish and hungry people evokes the possibility of making nets. Beginning to make nets generates questions about who makes the nets and how many, who fishes and for how long, and who gets to eat the fish. Once an established economic system is in place, such questions will tend to be answered in a routine and seemingly self-evident manner. Nevertheless, economic systems are not naturally given (as is the weather, for example). They arise and are transformed through the political discourse that the exigence for economic cooperation itself evoked. Economic and political events in turn—especially negative experiences of tragedy, breakdown, or conflict—can evoke a yet higher level of cultural reflection. Economic or political failure can engender the reconsideration of political authority or the envisioning of a less dysfunctional political order. Reflection in the wake of tragedy can also awaken questions of fundamental human identity—questions that can be explored freely only at the level of culture—through drama and dance, music and poetry, painting and sculpture, literature and philosophy.

Implicit in Lonergan's emergent conception of human reality is an understanding of the *normative relation of theory to praxis*. As lower levels of praxis concretely establish an exigence for higher orders of reflection, such reflection (and the decisions arising from it) reorders the underlying praxis—and generally in a progressive manner. Normally, cultural reflection and creativity ought to exercise a critical function with respect to deficiencies disclosed in the established political order. The political order ought to enable and regulate economic activity, such that it can be optimally efficient, sustainable, and just. The economic order, when it functions as it ought, both engages in production that makes optimal use of available technological innovations and ensures sustainable conditions of monetary circulation

---

10. Lonergan, *Insight*, 234.

necessary for the long-term elevation of a community's standard of living.[11] Technology itself is a multi-layered supervening of practical human intelligence upon the potentialities of nature. Finally, natural ecologies have a fragile reality of their own which can be disregarded only at the risk of their (and our) destruction.

Unfortunately, this normative conception of how theory relates to praxis is neither widely understood nor appreciated and is frequently subverted. Although culture possesses *de jure* a critical function, political regimes have *de facto* perennially resisted such criticism of their transgressions against religious, personal, cultural, political, social, and vital values. By an exercise of power, this criticism can be suppressed. Yet, a political order that remains closed to culture's envisioning of higher human aspirations will rob itself of the self-awareness and motivation necessary for self-correction and improvement. It will invite decay. A political "order" that would attempt to domesticate culture—that would subjugate its poets, musicians, artists, authors, and free press to brute power—blinds itself to the values that those cultural agents might otherwise have disclosed and lowers itself into the decadent routines of the typical tyranny.

Likewise, *de jure*, the political order exists partly to enable and regulate economic activity. Contrary to neoliberal ideology, markets do not exist in some sort of apolitical vacuum and can fail. The establishment of institutional, legal, and regulatory frameworks necessary for the existence and functioning of markets is itself a political achievement. Market inefficiencies in the production of public goods (such as affordable health care) as well as the market generation of negative externalities (such as pollution and unemployment) require prudential political initiatives that implement practical insights tending toward more optimal, sustainable, and equitable economic systematization. The notion that political ordering of economic activity is unnecessary or generally counterproductive stems either from a dubious optimism regarding the "invisible hand of the market" or an overblown cynicism regarding the incompetence or corruption of government.

---

11. This is the central thrust of Lonergan's writings on macroeconomics. See Bernard Lonergan, *Macroeconomic Dynamics: An Essay in Circulation Analysis*, CWL 15, eds. Frederick G. Lawrence, Patrick H. Byrne, and Charles C. Hefling, Jr. (Toronto: Toronto University Press, 1999); and Bernard Lonergan, *For a New Political Economy*, CWL 21, ed. Philip J. McShane (Toronto: Toronto University Press, 1998).

Nevertheless, for nearly five decades, neoliberalism has been quite effective in convincing politicians to abdicate their responsibility for economic oversight and in unfettering commerce and finance from "intrusive" regulation and taxation.[12]

Application to the Analysis of Globalization

My general thesis is that when higher-order reflection is suppressed, ignored, or met with intolerance, there tends to occur an illegitimate subordination of the higher by the lower. Though higher-order reflection should be normative, when it is not, opportunities for progress are forgone and the development of the common good is stunted. Vital, social, cultural, personal, and religious values are undermined in subtle or dramatic ways. To the extent that the established "good of order" deteriorates, particular goods generated by that order also fail to materialize, diminish in quality, or are less widely and equitably distributed.[13] In short, ideology precipitates objective decline.

My thesis specifically regarding globalization is that the expansion of commerce and finance from a national to a global scale certainly complicates matters and possibly abets a deleterious subordination of the political to the economic order. Even for economies relatively closed at the national level (such as in a pre-globalized, minimal-foreign-trade context), fostering and maintaining conditions for growth, financial sustainability, and social justice is difficult enough. Globalization superimposes complex additional challenges

---

12. The inconsistency of neoliberalism becomes glaringly apparent when purportedly efficient and self-regulating markets break down (as they dramatically did during the Great Depression, the Asian Crisis, and the Global Financial Crisis). In this context, the scene of former free-market ideologues clamoring for government bailouts is more than a little ironic. A heavy price is paid in these episodes and, typically, not by those who had benefited from the unfettering of markets.

13. For Lonergan's conception of the structure of the human good see Lonergan, *Insight*, 237–9; Lonergan, *Method in Theology* (New York: Herder and Herder, 1972), 47–55; and Bernard Lonergan, *Topics in Education: The Cincinnati Lectures of 1959 on the Philosophy of Education*, CWL 10, eds. Robert M. Doran and Frederick E. Crowe (Toronto: Toronto University Press, 1993), 26–48. Also note that "particular goods" include concrete goods of every sort (e.g., religious, social, vital). Accordingly, while particular goods include "goods" in the narrow economic sense (i.e., as contrasted to services), they should not be construed as limited to these.

and introduces a host of new vulnerabilities. Technical innovations in transportation, data processing, and communications have allowed the delocalization of capital, labor markets, and markets for consumer and producer goods. Because capital can be shifted easily from one region to another, transnational corporations are free to exploit the new global markets by gravitating toward those regions where profits can be maximized with minimal regulatory intervention. If local pressures are placed on a transnational concerning wages, labor practices, environmental regulations, taxation, or any other form of public accountability to local stakeholders that the transnational deems unpalatable, operations can be shifted with relative ease to an alternative location where these pressures are deemed less onerous.

While the economic order is in fact distinct from the political and cultural, neoliberalism and its imperatives of a minimally regulated global economy have tended to conflate these three levels. When local and national communities risk the sudden evaporation of their economic base should they assert their ethically legitimate stakeholder interests, such communities are severely pressured, for the sake of economic competitiveness, to conform their political and cultural identities to the economic exigencies of the transnationals. A tragic incapacity to preserve cultural diversity and political autonomy effectively results over time. In the worst instances, the common good is sacrificed to what is actually an economic *disorder*.[14]

Prior to the unleashing of globalization, there should have occurred extensive and systematic research, debate, and democratic deliberation centered upon understanding and evaluating globalization's anticipatable effects upon all stakeholders.[15] If the problems and

---

14. To be more precise, the disorder stems largely from the "group bias" of multinational corporations, their owners, and politicians who are excessively dependent upon them. Coupled with a cultural climate characterized by widespread anti-intellectualism, a practicality opposed to theory, and indifference to long-term problems (which Lonergan diagnosed under the rubric of "general bias"), group bias combines with general bias in a pernicious manner to give rise to a "longer cycle of decline." See Lonergan, *Insight*, 247–57.

15. Stiglitz claims that significant *economic* research was presented at the outset, but that promoters of globalization emphasized the benefits, and downplayed the costs and risks. I suggest that a broad range of analysis is required, to address not merely economic considerations, but the full spectrum of globalization's cultural, political, economic, technical, and natural ramifications.

vulnerabilities that have now become apparent in the unfolding of this bold experiment are not remedied soon, globalization will increasingly (and rightly) be regarded as anti-progressive and dehumanizing. The anti-globalization movement—both in the developing world and more recently in developed nations—is seeking political redress to its grievances. Under the assumption that a nationalist retreat from globalization would be detrimental overall, and sharing the hope of many that globalization might be reformed, I offer the following sketch of a heuristic for the critical analysis of globalization.

The Heuristic Itself

Although globalization is a phenomenon driven primarily by economic interests, its ramifications are pervasive and affect every level of human reality, from the integrity of the environment to the practice of religion. Obviously, it is imperative that globalization be correctly understood and managed in its properly economic dimensions. However, it must also be understood, critically analyzed, and freely deliberated upon from a perspective far more comprehensive than has generally been adopted so far.[16] A heuristic to examine this perspective could be based upon the theoretic foundation presented above, of a cascade of higher-order reflection normatively transforming lower orders of praxis. A heuristic is a technique that facilitates understanding or discovery by methodically specifying the unknown that is intended.[17] The heuristic I propose is quite simple. Rather than basing research and policy deliberation upon narrow and abstract

---

16. Joseph Stiglitz pointed out that even a focus specifically upon economic factors can be conducted in a far too constricted manner. While he generally praised the World Bank for taking a broader view of problems confronting developing countries, he criticized the International Monetary Fund for its narrow focus on interest and currency exchange rates (factors most relevant to the repayment of Western creditors) to the neglect of other factors (such as employment and growth) more relevant to the economic well-being of ordinary citizens (Stiglitz, *Globalization and Its Discontents Revisited*, 284–302).

17. Algebraic understanding is facilitated by using variables such as x and y. Classical scientific method anticipates correlations between measurable variables, e.g., $f=ma$ or $e=mc^2$. Statistical method anticipates frequencies. See Lonergan, *Insight*, 57–92; and Joseph Flanagan, *Quest for Self-Knowledge: An Essay in Lonergan's Philosophy* (Toronto: University of Toronto Press, 1997), 32–68.

purely economic models alone, attention should also be directed more broadly, toward four "junctions" of interaction: first, the cultural-political junction; second, the political-economic junction; third, the economic-technical junction; and, four, the technical-natural junction. Each junction is a locus of concrete events, problems, and vulnerabilities at which specific issues concerning globalization might be identified. For Lonergan, human progress fundamentally requires asking and answering further relevant questions. The systematic consideration of each junction would tend to generate further relevant questions which otherwise might go unasked. The foundational theory of a normative hierarchical patterning of emergent levels (in descending order: cultural, political, economic, technical, natural) alerts us to the possibility of illegitimate inversions, of the subordination of the higher by the lower (and especially of the political by the economic). The possibility of practical reversals of these inversions may be suggestive of viable remedies. While it is not possible to utilize the heuristic thoroughly in this present context, we can briefly highlight each junction and indicate the range of questions the heuristic evokes for responsible consideration.

Globalization has undeniably disrupted preexisting cultural and social arrangements, often in ways described as destructive by those who actually underwent the changes. There occurred far too little political deliberation beforehand about the changes globalization would likely bring, far too little protection during the changes, and far too ineffective remediation afterwards. Admittedly, the clock cannot be turned back, but how might there be better cultural and social outcomes in the future? Concretely, "a culture is a set of meanings and values informing a common way of life."[18] Culture is that by which particular political orders are established and maintained, criticized and transformed. Normatively, the political order exists to exercise guidance over the lower economic good of order and to protect higher cultural, personal, and religious rights that might otherwise be vulnerable. When unfettered globalization subverts the political order, however, cultural goods are sacrificed to the imperatives of a minimally-regulated global economy. Consequently, globalization should be critically analyzed at the *cultural-political junction*. Examples of questions that might be explored at this junction include:

---

18. Lonergan, *Method in Theology*, 301.

- How are the lives of workers affected by trade liberalization? Are adequate social "safety nets" in place to protect and retrain unemployed workers? How might the negative social consequences of unemployment (i.e., alienation, anxiety, unenrollment of children from school, etc.) be mitigated?

- How might globalization alter or weaken local communities?[19] How does urbanization and the loss of rural society threaten cultural identity and potentially undermine traditional values?[20] How is the character of local community changed by the displacement of local stores, small businesses, and restaurants by more efficient foreign competitors?[21] Does globalization's reinforcement of the dominance of languages such as English threaten the vitality of native languages? Under what conditions does the pace of change become too rapid to allow sufficient time for cultural adaptation?[22]

- Might there be undesirable consequences to the global dominance of the American entertainment industry? Is it culturally healthy for trade agreements to prohibit nations from subsidizing their own domestic movie industries?[23] What are the cultural and political dangers accompanying the concentration of media power, increasing media ownership by multinational corporations, and foreign control of media?[24]

- What are the adverse effects of intellectual property rights agreements with respect to issues such as the affordability of life-saving medications, access to knowledge and facilitation of research, maintenance of privacy and personal data ownership, and biopiracy?[25]

- What are the perceived or actual inequities inherent in the globalization process, and how might these undermine mutual trust and social cohesion?[26] How does globalization contribute

---

19. Stiglitz, *Globalization and Its Discontents Revisited*, xxii–xxiv, 154–62.

20. Stiglitz, *Globalization and Its Discontents Revisited*, 334–5.

21. Stiglitz, *Globalization and Its Discontents Revisited*, 163–8.

22. Stiglitz, *Globalization and Its Discontents Revisited*, 106.

23. Stiglitz, *Globalization and Its Discontents Revisited*, 82.

24. Stiglitz, *Globalization and Its Discontents Revisited*, 255.

25. Stiglitz, *Globalization and Its Discontents Revisited*, 4, 40–3, 333.

26. Stiglitz, *Globalization and Its Discontents Revisited*, 308.

to the problem of income and wealth inequality?[27] What might be done to promote fairness and greater equality of opportunity?

• Has the implementation of global economic imperatives led to political repression, violations of human rights, the curtailment of freedom of speech, or other civil liberties?

While, *de jure*, the political order exercises legitimate guidance over the economic order, globalization under the sway of neoliberal ideology assumed that markets are efficient and self-regulating and pressured for minimal government oversight—indeed, for minimal government altogether. Insofar as markets are not in fact perfectly efficient and self-regulating,[28] and insofar as weak government is detrimental for other reasons that transcend economics, globalization has possibly been distortive and should be critically analyzed at the *political-economic junction*. Examples of questions that might be explored at this junction include:

• How has globalization contributed to the growth and increasing power of multinational corporations?[29] Do multinational corporations exercise power in a manner consistent with the principles of democracy, responsible citizenship, and environmental stewardship?

• How has globalization's framework for the international mobility of capital and access to global labor and consumer markets enabled a "race to the bottom" in terms of avoiding regulations, reducing wages and worker protections, and minimizing corporate taxation?[30] What are the consequences of the "market-driven" demands of multinational corporations to deregulate and cut taxes under threat of moving operations elsewhere—for workers, for communities, for the environment, and for a government's ability to provide public goods?

• To what extent have multinational corporations effectively become *trans*-national corporations, ultimately not loyal to any

---

27. Stiglitz, *Globalization and Its Discontents Revisited*, 4; and Stiglitz, *Price of Inequality*, 73–80.

28. See John Cassidy, *How Markets Fail: The Logic of Economic Calamities* (New York: Picador, 2010).

29. Stiglitz, *Globalization and Its Discontents Revisited*, 4.

30. Stiglitz, *Globalization and Its Discontents Revisited*, 38–40.

particular nation, but accountable merely to shareholders and the profit maximization they ostensibly demand?[31] Ought trade and investment agreements contain provisions that discourage or prohibit governments from enacting regulations necessary for the protection of health, safety, and the environment?[32]

- How has the deregulation and globalization of finance in particular contributed to more frequent, deeper, or more pervasive financial crises?[33] What has been the *public* cost of resolving these crises? What are the future risks? How might global finance be managed more prudentially?

- The International Monetary Fund, World Bank, and World Trade Organization have been criticized for imposing ineffective or destructive policies, for disregarding democratic process and national sovereignty, for hypocrisy and unaccountability, and for representing the interests of developed nations and multinational corporations over developing nations, ordinary citizens, and the poor. To what extent are these criticisms justified? If needed, how might these institutions be reformed?

- In *The Globalization Paradox: Democracy and the Future of the World Economy*, Dani Rodrick argues that there is a trilemma surrounding globalization; namely, that unfettered globalization, national sovereignty, and democracy cannot all be preserved. Two may be maintained, but only if one of the others is compromised. If this argument is cogent, what choice ought to be made?[34]

Long-term economic progress involves successive transformations of the means of production. This process has financial and technological conditions. Current consumption must be deferred to create savings, and savings must be invested intelligently to implement newly available technological innovations that improve production. Ideally,

---

31. See Richard J. Barnet and Ronald E. Muller, *Global Reach: The Power of the Multinational Corporations* (New York: Simon and Schuster, 1974); and Lonergan, *Macroeconomic Dynamics*, 99–100.

32. Stiglitz, *Globalization and Its Discontents Revisited*, 37, 305.

33. See Carmen M. Reinhart and Kenneth S. Rogoff, *This Time is Different: Eight Centuries of Financial Folly* (Princeton: Princeton University Press, 2009).

34. Dani Rodrik, *The Globalization Paradox: Democracy and the Future of the World Economy* (New York: W.W. Norton & Co., 2011).

the process is guided by the best available insights contributed by a wide variety of participants engaged in free enterprise. Globalization, however, involves a considerable concentration of financial power and complicates production relative to how it would otherwise occur if bound nationally. Consequently, globalization should be critically analyzed at the *economic-technical junction*. Examples of questions that might be explored at this junction include:

- To what extent does globalization's pressure toward maximum efficiency tend to require a mega-scale implementation of technology and encourage a "winner-take-all" competitive environment? Does extremely capital-intensive industry tend thereby to become quasi-monopolistic? If so, what are the long-term consequences for consumers and workers?[35] Ought the scale of production, and technologies employed be determined solely on the basis of profit maximization?[36]

- Rapid trade liberalization has resulted in the destruction of local small businesses by larger foreign firms.[37] Barring blanket protectionism, might there be creative solutions to foster and preserve distinctive and economically viable domestic small businesses? Might such efforts be justifiable on the basis of values that transcend raw economic efficiency and on conceptions of the human good unimagined by standard "textbook economics"? Given the indispensability of bank lending to small businesses and farmers in particular, should additional precautions be taken to prevent large foreign financial institutions from displacing smaller domestic banks?[38]

---

35. In discussing the Antigonish Movement, Lonergan wrote: "Why does the proletariat today include almost everyone? Why is control of industry in the hands of fewer and fewer? Radically it is our own fault. We leave our affairs to others, because we are too indolent and too stupid to get to work and run them ourselves. The results are palpably ruinous: our system of free enterprise cannot survive if only a few practice free enterprise." in Bernard Lonergan, *Shorter Papers*, CWL 20, ed. Robert C. Croken, Robert M. Doran, and H. Daniel Monsour (Toronto: Toronto University Press, 2007), 144.

36. See Joseph Pearce, *Small Is Still Beautiful: Economics as if Families Mattered* (Wilmington, DE: ISI Books, 2006).

37. Stiglitz, *Globalization and Its Discontents Revisited*, 163, 114.

38. Stiglitz, *Globalization and Its Discontents Revisited*, 127, 164–5.

- Might standard provisions in international trade and investment agreements that restrict the assistance governments can offer to domestic industry actually impede the necessary structural transformation of national economies?[39]

- Can producers be provided with better ways to mitigate global macroeconomic risks that threaten their businesses but which are not controllable at the firm or even national level (such as, the volatility of import and export prices, interest rates, and foreign exchange rates)?[40] To what extent has the establishment of extensive and complex global supply chains weakened the productive process?[41] Given the existential importance of food and energy in particular, has globalization perhaps devalued self-sufficiency and lulled the world into complacency with regard to issues of food and energy security?[42]

- Capital market liberalization has facilitated uncontrolled flows of cross-border short-term speculative investment. These flows have proven repeatedly to be destabilizing. Hot money on the way in exacerbates a boom-to-bust business cycle; on the way out, it typically triggers a drop in the exchange rate and a spike in interest rates, potentially resulting in financial crisis and crippling the economy. Might reasonable capital controls standardly be implemented to prevent this known phenomenon from recurring?[43]

- Increased international trade and lending have exacerbated the problem of some nations accruing unsustainable long-term trade deficits. What might be done to ensure more balanced and sustainable foreign trade?

Human economic activity effects a technological transformation of the potentialities of nature into a standard of living. In this process, the integrity and finite limits of natural ecologies ought to be respected. A global economy that lacks suitable regulations, technologies, and scales of production, however, contributes to profound

---

39. Stiglitz, *Globalization and Its Discontents Revisited*, 93.

40. Stiglitz, *Globalization and Its Discontents Revisited*, 10, 353.

41. Stiglitz, *Globalization and Its Discontents Revisited*, xxxiv, 378.

42. Stiglitz, *Globalization and Its Discontents Revisited*, 73–4.

43. Stiglitz, *Globalization and Its Discontents Revisited*, 33–5, 105–6, 115, 161, 194–5, 216–7, 324–5.

and potentially irreversible ecological and climactic degradation. Consequently, globalization should be critically analyzed at the *technical-natural junction*. Examples of questions that might be explored at this junction include:

- Has globalization made it too easy to move production to jurisdictions that impose only minimal environmental regulation? Have provisions for transnational corporations—to move production elsewhere when they deem existing or proposed regulations to be onerous—resulted in excessive bargaining power vis-à-vis governments that would otherwise seek greater environmental protections?

- Has globalization's tendency to increase the size of multinational corporations and the scale of their production potentially increased environmental harms relative to what these otherwise would have been under a larger number of smaller and more nationally-rooted firms operating at smaller scales of production?[44]

- Unfair subsidies are generally prohibited by global trade agreements. If a particular government refuses to impose proportionate costs upon domestic corporations that pollute or inflict environmental damage (for instance, if the U.S. withdraws from the Paris Agreement and does not charge for carbon emissions), are those corporations in effect unfairly receiving an implicit subsidy?[45]

- At the World Trade Organization, "it is the voices of trade that are heard" and "little attention is often paid to concerns about the environment."[46] How might global trade and investment agreements incorporate routine procedures that include voices genuinely representing the environment?

Conclusion

The responsible guidance of the global economy can neither occur under the spell of narrow ideologies, nor by overlooking and neglecting real problems, nor in the mode of *ad hoc* crisis management. The

---

44. See Pearce, *Small Is Still Beautiful*, 151–240.

45. Stiglitz, *Globalization and Its Discontents Revisited*, 17.

46. Stiglitz, *Globalization and Its Discontents Revisited*, 314.

intent of the foregoing heuristic is to remedy the tragic state of affairs described by Stiglitz, that "the advocates of globalization had overstated the benefits, underestimated the costs, and *paid little attention to how globalization affected people*—with the corporations getting a disproportionate share of the benefits and ordinary citizens bearing a disproportionate share of the costs—so much so that many, in some cases a majority, were worse off."[47]

Problems on the scale of the global economy may seem hopelessly complex and overwhelming. Yet, Lonergan would remind us that human beings are for themselves "the executor of the emergent probability of human affairs."[48] Understood as concretely embedded in a world-order of emergent probability, even the juggernaut of the global economy can be apprehended as a field of human self-constitution and as compatible with human liberty and responsibility. While the preservation of natural ecologies must be acknowledged as setting a lower material bound for human activity, insofar as there emerge successive supervening technical, economic, political, and cultural schemes of recurrence, "less and less importance attaches to the probabilities of appropriate constellations of circumstances. More and more importance attaches to the probabilities of the occurrence of insight, communication, persuasion, agreement, decision."[49] The humanization of the global economy will require persons who ask and answer a broad range of questions, who have insights grasping possible schemes of recurrence, who motivate themselves and others to bring about conditions rendering alternative schemes at first possible, and then probable, and at last actual. If the adoption of a heuristic for rethinking globalization would allow this difficult process to be approached in a more methodical and comprehensive manner, this might be propitious for the emergence of a more creative, holistic, and just stewardship over the global economy.

---

47. Stiglitz, *Globalization and Its Discontents Revisited*, 31. Emphasis mine.

48. Lonergan, *Insight*, 252.

49. Lonergan, *Insight*, 236.

CHAPTER TWO

Redeeming Global Finance from Neoliberal Ideology

Nicolas J. Baumgartner (*Durham University*)

Introduction

Mainstream financial theory posits that profit-risk optimization ought to be the only consideration when making an investment decision, with market mechanisms enabling an efficient allocation of capital. Yet, having faith in those market mechanisms is ultimately trusting the decision-making process of individuals, with supply and demand as aggregates of discrete choices. The free-market paradigm, as espoused by Michael Novak, advances that liberal institutions and enlightened self-interest are the surest ways to achieve development through globalization. But the Catholic Church, while recognizing the value of global capital in such a task and acknowledging a certain need to pursue profitable activities,[1] decries neoliberalism[2] as an ideology that works against a humane globalization, leaving many—the poor in particular—behind.

Admittedly, the strength of neoliberalism and mainstream financial theory is that they are easy to understand and help make sense of

---

1. John Paul II, *Centesimus Annus* [Encyclical on the Hundredth Anniversary of *Rerum Novarum*], May 1, 1991, §35. John Paul II acknowledges "the legitimate *role of profit* as an indication that a business is functioning well" but equally that "profitability is not the only indicator of a firm's condition"; its employees, the firm's "most valuable asset" can still be "humiliated and their dignity offended."

2. John Paul II, *Ecclesia in America* [Post-Synodal Apostolic Exhortation on the Encounter with the Living Jesus Christ: The Way to Conversion, Communion and Solidarity in America], January 22, 1999, §56. John Paul II offers here a definition of neoliberalism absent from other, especially earlier, papal encyclicals and exhortations: "based on a purely economic conception of man, this system considers profit and the law of the market as its only parameters, to the detriment of the dignity of and the respect due to individuals and peoples."

23

complex realities; at the root of the moral surd of neoliberal ideology are the limits of human cognition and the need to simplify our understanding of the economic forces at play. The quasi-religious reliance on markets and the totem of profit maximization make sense when it is clear that cultural and societal values are not easily ordered within existing theory. New approaches must be developed to cope with larger amounts of data to observe emergent probabilities that encompass such values together with financial sustainability. Macroeconomic and financial theory must also shift to a more profound dialectic with empirical data. Until grace becomes central to the task of redeeming history and naturalism is rejected, globalization will likely never be fully humane.

The Precepts of Mainstream Financial Theory: Profit Maximization and Trust in Markets

According to mainstream financial theory,[3] markets efficiently allocate resources, with individual(s) (entities) solely deciding between different risk-return profiles. Arbitrage—where an individual can benefit from returns higher than the market rate given a particular risk profile—is eliminated through fully functioning markets. In somewhat simpler terms, investments always constitute a certain risk: the company may go bankrupt, wiping out equity, or experience difficulties in repaying its loan, with investors experiencing financial losses. When negotiating the cost of capital and the returns the investor will receive over time, market rates determine—through the laws of supply and demand—the returns to be expected in relation to a particular level of risk. In short: there is a financial reward for taking higher risks, and reward and risk are correlated thanks to market mechanisms.

From a neoliberal perspective, efficient allocation of capital therefore demands liberalized and transparent markets. External interventions or limitations risk skewing this process and therefore risk a mismatching of risk and returns. It is best to leave markets

---

3. Mainstream financial theory finds its roots in Harry Markowitz's 1952 essay, for which he was awarded, together with his lifetime work, the 1990 Nobel Memorial Prize in Economic Sciences. Worth noting is that one of his thesis supervisors was Milton Friedman, putting him firmly in the Chicago School tradition. See Harry Markowitz, "Portfolio Selection," *The Journal of Finance* 7, no. 11 (1952): 77–91.

to "do their thing" than seek to manipulate them. It is then just one more step between trusting markets and seeking profit maximization; if the market allocates capital efficiently, then individuals only must make one set of decisions, what returns they are seeking and what level of risk they will take. Any other consideration, particularly ethical, can only be secondary by default.

Michael Novak, Democratic Capitalism, and Trust in Markets

A strong defender of liberalism within the Catholic tradition is Michael Novak. In his exposition of democratic capitalism, Novak enlists Lonergan's work to support his argument.[4] By allowing individuals to have as much freedom as possible to make self-interested choices, the spirit of liberalism can be unleashed and the right values will emerge. This allows history to progress:

> [M]arkets as free as possible from governmental and religious command best serve the common good. Such a system frees the intelligence, imagination, and enterprise of individuals to explore the possibilities inherent in world process, which [Lonergan] conceived of . . . as a universe of emergent probabilities.[5]

Novak argues that democratic capitalism possesses an inbuilt capacity for the good to emerge over time: "the laws of free economic markets are such that the real interests of individuals are best served in the long run by a systematic refusal to take short-term advantage."[6] In a similar argument to that of Milton Friedman, for whom the only corporate social responsibility of businesses is to maximize their profit,[7] "a firm aware of its long-term fiduciary responsibility to its

---

4. Michael Novak, *The Spirit of Democratic Capitalism* (New York: Simon and Shuster, 1982), 72. Novak notes the generality of Lonergan's theory and explicitly acknowledges that he applies it to support his argument.

5. Novak, *The Spirit of Democratic Capitalism*, 79.

6. Novak, *The Spirit of Democratic Capitalism*, 92.

7. Fulton Friedman, "A Friednzan Doctrine," *The New York Times*, September 13, 1970, https://www.nytimes.com/1970/09/13/archives/a-friedman-doctrine-the-social-responsibility-of-business-is-to.html.

shareholders must protect its investments for generations" and "must maintain a reputation for reliability, integrity and fairness."[8] And the aggregation of individual decisions, for Novak, is to be more rational than any plan imposed from above by knowledgeable agents; "the rationality of a market is not commanded."[9]

Pursuing profits and the ensuing emergence of commercial values is, for Novak, to be welcomed because they provide the necessary fabric for democratic governance to flourish: the cooperative spirit that arises from economic transactions, the self-determination of individuals and the social energy that emerges and the imagination and industry it demands. All these values are indications of a society empowered to strive for the common good, and "[i]t is a system in tune with emergent probability, the limitations of human intelligence, and the unreliability of the human heart."[10]

This approach is problematic on two levels. First, it is myopic in failing to identify the necessity to trust in the markets as profoundly ideological. As will be explored below, Catholic Social Teaching, while not offering an alternative economic system, clearly speaks against such an ideology. Second, trust in market mechanisms is ultimately trust in aggregated economic decisions which may result from flawed choices. Yet, the healing and creating of history—and, by extension, using global capital for a more humane development—can only happen when individuals can make better (economic) decisions.

Catholic Social Teaching and the Church's Rejection of Neoliberal Ideology

The Catholic Church speaks for using capital in a globalized world to support poverty alleviation.[11] Yet, it clearly rejects neoliberalism. For the church, that ideology leaves individuals and developing countries in poverty and must be challenged. As early as 1931,

---

8. Novak, *The Spirit of Democratic Capitalism*, 92.

9. Novak, *The Spirit of Democratic Capitalism*, 115.

10. Novak, *The Spirit of Democratic Capitalism*, 117.

11. Paul VI, *Populorum Progressio* [Encyclical On the Development of Peoples], March 26, 1967, §47. Paul VI acknowledges a panoply of approaches to development including "loans and investments."

Pius XI warned that "the right ordering of economic life cannot be left to a free competition of forces." For him, trust in market forces has led to "the errors of individualist economic teaching" that "[destroy] through forgetfulness or ignorance the social and moral character of economic life [and through holding] that economic life must be considered and treated as altogether free from and independent of public authority." The issue with such an economic system is that it is built on "a principle of self-direction which governs it much more perfectly than would the intervention of any created intellect." It is therefore "most necessary that economic life be again subjected to and governed by a true and effective directing principle."[12] In 1961, John XXIII takes this critique further, highlighting the limits of a naturalistic understanding of economic behavior, one "which denie[s] any correlation between economics and morality," where "[p]ersonal gain [is] considered the only valid motive for economic activity," and where "[e]very precaution [is] to be taken to prevent the civil authority from intervening in any way in economic matters."[13]

John XXIII's successor, Paul VI, also attacked the tenets of an "unbridled liberalism" that "results in the tyranny of the 'international imperialism of money'" that hails "profit as the chief spur to economic progress, free competition as the guiding norm of economics, and private ownership of the means of production as an absolute right, having no limits nor concomitant social obligations."[14] He later also declared that Christians cannot adhere to a liberal ideology "which believes it exalts individual freedom by withdrawing it from every limitation, by stimulating it through exclusive seeking of interest and power, and by considering social solidarities as more or less automatic consequences of individual initiatives."[15]

In 1987, John Paul II introduced a key concept that shed more light on why sole trust in the markets, and therefore the aggregate

---

12. Pius XI, *Quadragesimo Anno* [Encyclical on Reconstruction of the Social Order], May 15, 1931, §88.

13. John XXIII, *Mater et Magistra* [On Christianity and Social Progress], May 15, 1961, §11.

14. *Populorum Progressio*, §26.

15. Paul VI, *Octogesima Adveniens* [Apostolic Letter on the Occasion of the Eightieth Anniversary of the Encyclical *Rerum Novarum*], May 14, 1971, §26.

economic decisions of individual actors, can be problematic. For him, structural sin is the result of aggregated personal failures to maintain responsible behavior, where the "all-consuming desire for profit" and the "thirst for power, with the intention of imposing one's will upon others . . . at any price" prevent humane development. As he writes, "the true nature of evil which faces us with respect to the development of peoples [is] a question of a moral evil, the fruit of many sins which lead to 'structures of sin.'" Structures of sin can only be conquered with the help of divine grace, through a commitment to the good of one's neighbor and by losing oneself for the sake of the other instead of exploiting him. For John Paul II, economic development is inherently a spiritual pursuit and cannot be sufficiently resolved through a purely naturalistic framework.[16]

Writing in the immediate aftermath of the 2007–2008 financial crisis, Pope Benedict XVI amplifies the idea that development is a spiritual matter, with charity as the guiding norm in the "*de facto* interdependence of people and nations." He posits, "[o]nly in *charity, illuminated by the light of reason and faith* is it possible to pursue development goals that possess a more humane and humanizing value." Again, echoing his predecessors, he remarks, "the market can be a negative force, not because it is so by nature, but because a certain ideology can make it so." He also adds that "every economic decision has a moral consequence."[17] A few years later, Pope Francis likewise rejects "trickle-down theories which assume that economic growth, encouraged by a free market, will inevitably succeed in bringing about greater justice and inclusiveness in the world," noting that such an opinion has never been confirmed by the facts. Rather, it "expresses a crude and naïve trust in the goodness of those wielding economic power and in the sacralized working of the prevailing economic system. Meanwhile, the excluded are still waiting." Francis is particularly concerned by the accelerating gap in prosperity between a happy few and the majority of the population. For him, "[t]his imbalance is the result of ideologies which defend the absolute autonomy of the market

---

16. John Paul II, *Sollictudo Rei Socialis* [Encyclical for the Twentieth Anniversary of *Populorum Progressio*], December 30, 1987, §37, 41.

17. Benedict XVI, *Caritas in Veritate* [Encyclical on Integral Human Development in Charity and Truth], June 29, 2009, §9, 36–7.

place and financial speculation" and thus "[w]e can no longer trust in the unseen forces and the invisible hand of the market." Like his predecessors, Francis reiterates how "[e]ach meaningful economic decision made in one part of the world has repercussions everywhere else," and while it is addressed mainly to macroeconomic and trade policies of governments, the thought remains the same: every economic decision, and ultimately whom or what we trust, has a moral dimension.[18]

Ideological Blindness, Naturalism and (the End of) History

Novak argues that trust in market processes, rather than in well-meaning but erroneous state interventionism can lead to the common good through the emergence of commercial values and the pursuit of profit.[19] As has been clear, Catholic Social Teaching continually casts this in doubt, however, and what Novak sees as a necessary institutional framework for the common good to emerge is understood by successive popes as constituent of a misguided ideology. On one level, Novak ought to be credited for his pragmatism in seeking to show how an existing economic system could work towards the common good, particularly since the Vatican documents do not actually offer an alternative. Equally, Novak can be accused of too readily defending liberalism and failing to acknowledge its limits. This relative blindness puts him at odds with Lonergan. He too easily overlooks insights that point to the limits of a system he defends. Lonergan himself highlights profit maximization in his essay "Healing and Creating in History":

> [Multinational corporations] aim at maximizing profit, and that has been the aim of economic enterprise since the mercantile, the industrial, the financial revolutions ever more fully and thoroughly took charge of our affairs. The alternative to making a profit is bankruptcy. The alternative to

---

18. Francis, *Evangelii Gaudium* [Apostolic Exhortation on the Proclamation of the Gospel in Today's World], November 24, 2013, §54, 56, 204, 206.

19. Michael Novak, *Free Persons and the Common Good* (Lanham, MD: Madison Books, 1989), 89–92.

maximizing profit is inefficiency. . . . [Yet it] remains that the long-accepted principles are inadequate. They suffer from radical oversights. Their rigorous application on a global scale . . . heads us for disaster.[20]

We don't know what we don't know, and we are often blind to the limits of our thinking because we find it difficult to question assumptions that have served us well so far. Such lack of insight can clearly happen despite a liberal institutional framework. Lonergan calls on the creative process to remedy the limitations of accepted principles and theories, acknowledging that such an endeavour is an "uphill climb." It is already a challenging task to realize how one is influenced by a problematic ideology, but it is a particularly difficult one to suggest an alternative theoretical approach because we cannot easily escape the ideology that has conditioned our thinking. This group bias and our inability to think beyond the precepts of an ideology is too well exemplified by Novak's defense of democratic capitalism, which morphs into apologetics.

Trusting in market mechanisms is ultimately putting trust in the constitutive discrete decisions of individuals. It is unlikely, though, that individuals, regardless of their (in)ability to foresee supply and demand, can make good decisions, especially if they are called only to maximize profits. Yet, Novak defends this view, arguing that Adam Smith's invisible hand requires the "better judgement" rather than just the "interests" of individuals.[21] He writes:

> If each economic agent acts with maximal practical intelligence in the matter close at hand, better known to him than anyone else, the probability of the entire economic order being suffused with maximal practical intelligence is very high. It is higher, indeed than if only a handful of economic directors, however brilliant, were to attempt to impose an economic order upon all.[22]

---

20. Bernard J.F. Lonergan, *Macroeconomic Dynamics: An Essay in Circulation Analysis*, Collected Works of Bernard Lonergan (CWL) 15, eds. Patrick H. Byrne, Frederick G. Lawrence and Charles Hefling, Jr. (Toronto: University of Toronto Press, 1999), 100.

21. Novak, *Free Persons and the Common Good*, 103.

22. Novak, *Free Persons and the Common Good*, 99.

Novak does not argue that individuals should simply act selfishly but rather that they should make an enlightened choice. Still, this is not enough. Fred Lawrence highlights how, for Lonergan, "[a] healthy and vibrant economy demands that a critical mass of people be committed to the authenticity of attentiveness, intelligence, reasonableness, and responsibility." Lonergan was more aware than Novak of the limits of a naturalistic enlightened choice: "the overall lack of ingenuity and inquisitiveness on the part of . . . liberal capitalism [as with socialism] causes the general stagnation of an unintelligible social situation grounded in dramatic, egoistic, group, and general biases."[23]

Novak's recourse to an institutional framework to promote virtue again places too much faith in market mechanisms. While acknowledging that one way to defeat sin, even structural sin, is to convert individual hearts and another is to impose virtue by force, he argues instead for a third way, a doctrine of unintended consequences. Such a doctrine "turns the eyes of the political economist away from the moral intentions of individuals and toward the final social consequences of their actions" and argues that "the hopes for a good, free, and just society are best reposed in a system which gives high status to commerce and industry."[24] It relies on a self-interest that "far exceeds self-regard, selfishness, acquisitiveness, and greed," which can help a system "designed for sinners" to achieve "as much moral good as individuals and communities can generate under conditions of ample liberty."[25] Novak rightly rejects that humans are depraved but, as highlighted above, falls too easily prey to naturalism. Trust in market mechanisms, therefore, is a trust in the aggregation of decisions made by individuals deemed able to find the good by themselves, provided they are given the freedom to do so. However, such an ideology is problematic from a Christian perspective because it implicitly rejects the necessity of grace and instead relies solely on nature. Although Novak would himself not reject the necessity of grace, the political economy he promotes does just that. The outcome of "democratic-capitalist" market processes for global capital can only be as good as the aggregation of its underlying decisions.

---

23. Frederick Lawrence, "Editor's Introduction," in *Macroeconomic Dynamics,* lxix–lxx.

24. Novak, *The Spirit of Democratic Capitalism,* 89.

25. Novak, *The Spirit of Democratic Capitalism,* 94–5.

This faith in liberal institutions also means that Novak's understanding of history is closer to that of Francis Fukuyama than it is to Lonergan's.[26] In particular, for Novak, "[t]he insight that human beings can gain some control over the economic system on which they depend as a good of order appeared very late in human history. Adam Smith may be regarded as the genius chiefly responsible (although by no means solely) for the expression of this insight."[27] But for Lonergan, history is not a naturalistic process with democratic capitalism as its end. Rather, it is inherently unstable and dynamic, and without a foreseeable end in sight. History is not necessarily synonymous with progress but is rather liable to decline, not the least because it relies on the quality of individual decisions that constitute economic exchanges.[28] Therefore, a liberal political economy is not history's final destination that just needs a little bit of fixing, as Novak would have it. Rather, history demands a much more active and deeper engagement in the form of a creative task where "insights . . . coalesce, . . . complement and correct one other, . . . influence policies and programs, . . . reveal their shortcoming in their concrete results". These insights then in turn "give rise to further correcting insights, corrected policies, corrected programs, that gradually accumulate into the all-round, balanced, smoothly functioning system that from the start was needed but at the start was not yet known."[29] Clearly, exercising creating and healing in history must go beyond Novak's demonstration of democratic capitalism as a happy end. It must surpass the latter's naturalism and requires a deeper level of reflection behind individual (economic) decisions than what Novak permits.

Values and the Necessity of Grace

The recently published Vatican document, *Oeconomicae et pecuniarae quaestiones*, observes that "[t]he health of a system depends on the health of every single action performed" and "wherever profit

---

26. Francis Fukuyama, *The End of History and the Last Man* (New York: Avon Books, 1992).

27. Novak, *The Spirit of Democratic Capitalism*, 77.

28. Lonergan, *Macroeconomic Dynamics*, 4–5.

29. Lonergan, *Macroeconomic Dynamics*, 100.

is placed at the summit of the culture of a financial enterprise, and the actual demands of the common good are ignored, every ethical claim is really perceived as irrelevant." Further, "in order to function well, the market needs anthropological and ethical prerequisites that it is neither capable of giving for itself, nor producing on its own." Therefore, pursuing profit cannot be the sole guiding principle of capital allocation decisions; investments must also seek to promote the integrity of the human person, the universal destination of goods, and the preferential option for the poor.[30] Here, the church's teachings again depart strongly from Novak's liberalism; not as much good is to be expected from market processes themselves or the values that would emerge from those. Rather, values are the product of individual choices.

The question, then, is how these desirable values can emerge. The idea of an omniscient economic planner is dismissed by both Novak and Lonergan. Whereas Novak foresees no external intervention to help people make better decisions, there is for Lonergan such a necessity. Market processes cannot by themselves maximize human satisfaction, unless "the less fortunate [are] able to demand more than they can supply [and] the more fortunate supply more than they demand."[31] The reliance on an ideal based on sentiments, rather than on intelligence, can only lead to a dictated economy. Instead, this demands a certain moral intentionality by all economic actors for the good to emerge.

For Lonergan, "[t]he task will be vast, so vast that only the creative imagination of all individuals in all democracies will be able to construct at once the full conception and the full realization of the new order."[32] Individual responsibility and an explicitly moral dimension in decision-making plays a larger role in Lonergan's vision of political economy than Novak could allow. This also explains why Lonergan's own understanding and treatment of finance was subject

---

30. Congregation for the Doctrine of the Faith and the Dicastery for Promoting Integral Human Development, *Oeconomicae et Pecuniariae Quaestiones* [Considerations for an Ethical Discernment Regarding Some Aspects of the Present Economic-Financial System], January 6, 2018, §10, 19, 23.

31. Bernard J.F. Lonergan, *For a New Political Economy*, CWL 21, ed. Philip J. McShane (Toronto: University of Toronto Press, 1998), 36.

32. Lonergan, *For a New Political Economy*, 37.

to his broader theory of political economy. Finance was to be instrumental in balancing economic flows and this long-term consideration would have to prevail above and beyond the short-term goal of individual profit.[33] This means economic players would need to gain a much more complex picture of financial movements through theory than the mainstream precepts of profit and risk could ever consider.

Educating individuals to make intelligent choices is an active task required of both economic theorists and moral theologians, an aim that cannot be left to markets. As Lawrence notes, for Lonergan, the survival of democracy and by extension a democratic economy "cannot be identified merely with the Enlightenment's projects of steering public opinion from unenlightened to enlightened self-interest. Instead, [he] envisaged a vast and long-term educational effort" that would "encompass not only growing understanding and knowledge, but the objective surd of sin, and the redemptive potentialities of God's grace."[34] The values that would emerge as a result would therefore not be those that Novak reckons are the product of market mechanisms and the pillars of a functioning democratic capitalism.[35] They would need to be something more than just profit and commercial values.

Epistemological Simplicity and Cognitive Limitations as the Roots of Neoliberalism's Moral Surd

Neoliberalism and, by extension, mainstream financial theory share one singular quality: they are easy to understand, and mathematical language makes their computation relatively simple. Financial theory can focus on two variables that can be fairly easily quantified. The rate of return—that is, the return on investment ("ROI")—is simple arithmetic.[36] Risk calculation (probability of default) is statistics. They are isomorphic and share the same quantitative language. Additionally, relying on market processes to allocate capital is arguably not so much a rejection of moral intentionality than a simplification of decision-making;

---

33. Lonergan, *For a New Political Economy*, 41.

34. Lawrence, "Editor's Introduction," in *Macroeconomic Dynamics*, lxxi; cf. Lonergan, *Macroeconomic Dynamics*, 94–95.

35. Novak, *The Spirit of Democratic Capitalism*, 116–121.

36. ROI = (Gain from Investment - Cost of Investment) / Cost of Investment.

capital can be very easily allocated because there is only one set of variables, namely profit and risk. As with Novak's defense of liberalism, mainstream financial theory can be credited for its pragmatism, enabling the rapid allocation of capital on a global scale. The difficulty with adding other considerations than profit is that they complicate decision-making with competing values, and individuals face more difficult choices. The difficulty is not solely ethical—what goods should be prioritized—but also methodological. There is possibly no correlation between profit-making and humane development, solely coincidence, unless a strong assumption is made—as with Friedman and Novak—that businesses must consider social and environmental factors to be profitable in the long-term. But such an assumption is purely epistemological and is not easily demonstrated; the correlation may simply be spurious. Only in-depth statistical research requiring substantial data could highlight possible causal relationships.

Faced with overwhelming data, uncertainty, and emerging probabilities that at first do not seem to be isomorphic, individuals are incapable of making clear decisions unless the number of variables is kept low and on a unidimensional plane—that is, causally related even if not necessarily correlated. This simplification is likely to be the source of the moral surd in how capital is used globally. It cannot achieve a humane development because considering further considerations than profit is, by design, difficult. This may also explain why Catholic Social Teaching cannot readily offer a solution but only a critique of ideology and the limits of its simplification. Here theology can play its role: not by offering ready-made political and economic solutions, but rather considerations that are inherently metaphysical and methodological.

The Challenges of the Task Ahead

How, then, are we to rise above the conditioned pattern of our experience not only by insight but also by decision, free from coercion? How do we surpass the reduction of reality inherent to the liberalism and naturalism of the likes of Novak?[37] How do we become freer to make economic decisions that will lead to a more humane

---

37. See Robert M. Doran, *Theology and the Dialectics of History* (Toronto: University of Toronto Press, 1990), 40.

globalization in the face of enormous amounts of data to consider beyond risk and returns? How can we mend an economic system "where the function of capital is the maximization of profit, rather than use values of the whole community?"[38] How can a system work for the well-being of many even if religious, moral, and intellectual conversion are not widely spread? In short: when can we begin to rely on the aggregation of discrete economic decisions to benefit all beyond a simplistic faith in market mechanisms?

The task is enormous, and the church's social teachings are only a first step in the right direction by discerning the limits of neoliberal ideology and, by extension, mainstream financial theory.[39] Also needed is an in-depth statistical analysis of how values other than the precepts of returns and risk can lead to a humane globalization without assuming the determinism often derived from econometric analysis. Such a task will necessitate a theory of finance that accepts a normative order of inquiry and that is methodologically critical and dialectical.[40] Only then can an understanding of financial mechanisms emerge that can lead to an improvement of the lives of many, and this beyond purely economic considerations. This undertaking must acknowledge the work of grace in inquiry, which "effects a release from the vicious circles of disorder and distortion responsible for the prevailing situation, and promotes the mentality that could inform a global network of human communities capable of providing a genuine alternative to present possibilities."[41]

Lonergan's unfinished work on macroeconomic theory may likewise need to be seen within a historical perspective. The lack of computational powers—those we possess now—led economists to build theoretical models that served as great simplifications of macroeconomic reality, with Lonergan offering his own. While Lonergan advocated for a political economy, rather than a mere

---

38. See Doran, *Theology and the Dialectics of History*, 104.

39. Cf. Doran, *Theology and the Dialectics of History*, 107: "The ministry of the church . . . consists in the promotion, through prophetic witness, sacramental worship, and pastoral service of many kinds, of the integral scale of values that would constitute the new law on earth that it is the servant's mission to bring."

40. Doran, *Theology and the Dialectics of History*, 106.

41. Doran, *Theology and the Dialectics of History*, 525.

scientific exercise in economics,[42] his broader body of work also clearly engages empiricism, not the least to move beyond the problematic classical deductivism extant in both theology and mathematical economics.[43] The theoretical scaffolding that Lonergan built through his macroeconomic work can thus orient the categorization and interpretation of data, but will equally need to be, in time, reviewed by the emerging probabilities observed through that data, shifting from a logical to a statistical and dialectical methodology.

Technological Progress and New Scientific Insights to Continue Lonergan's Work

Technological progress and advances in behavioral sciences means that some ideas proposed by Lonergan can be actualized, given those developments. Two issues in particular are worth addressing: first, the cognitional limitations of individual decision-makers, as well as that of economic theorists and moral theologians; and second, the ethical challenge of helping individuals make better decisions without taking away their freedom of choice. In recent years, two developments are worth noting for their ability to support a departure from ideology and so encourage a more humane globalization.

The first one is the development of artificial intelligence, particularly its ability to observe statistical patterns and work through substantial amounts of data that would otherwise be impossible for humans. This may help both economic theorists and moral theologians in moving away from theoretical and deductivist models to ones that are empirically based.[44] Such an approach will be most helpful in developing economic models closer to reality and embrace a fuller set of variables and values.

The second one, a recent development in behavioral sciences, can enable individuals to make better decisions—namely, "boosting." This fosters people's competence to make their own choice and

---

42. Lonergan, *For a New Political Economy*, 1–10.

43. See Bernard J.F. Lonergan, *Method in Theology* (London: Darton, Longman, and Todd, 1972).

44. Cf. Lonergan, *Macroeconomic Dynamics*, 105.

exercise their own agency.[45] If we acknowledge that individuals are not always able to be attentive, intelligent, reasonable and responsible, we may seek to help them along the way. Lonergan's desire for economic education from the bottom up, not the least because people's cognitive limitations can be replaced—given such scientific progress—by policies and approaches that facilitate, rather than nudge, individuals to make better (economic) decisions.

Conclusion

The issue at the heart of mainstream financial theory and, by extension, neoliberalism is also what makes it so attractive: the simplification of economic choice-making to the maximization of profit, given a certain level of risk, by trusting markets to allocate capital efficiently. In such a case, individuals are not cognitively overwhelmed by other considerations, such as societal and cultural values. Meanwhile, Catholic social teaching, even if it highlights the limitations of ideology, struggles to offer an alternative economic theory, exemplifying the difficulty of providing more useful principles that can be applied as easily. With this in mind, Novak's defense of democratic liberalism ought to be acknowledged for its pragmatism.

By examining it more closely, however, its substantial deviation from Lonergan's thought becomes clear. Novak's naturalist move not only removes the necessity of grace but also departs from Lonergan's understanding of history. What is therefore needed for a more humane globalization is a deep engagement with the theories that underpin and constitute neoliberal ideology. By offering an alternative understanding of macroeconomic flows and the role of finance, within a broader set of values and guiding principles for decision-making, Lonergan's work can be continued. Although such a task will be challenging, new insights will now be more readily accessible through technological and scientific advancements that were not available at the time of Lonergan's writings.

---

45. See Ralph Hertwig and Till Grüne-Yanoff, "Nudging and Boosting: Steering or Empowering Good Decisions," *Perspectives on Psychological Science* 12, no. 6 (2017): 973–986.

CHAPTER THREE

Scotosis and Structural Inequality

The Dangers of Bias in a Globalized Age

Kate Ward (Marquette University)

Today's vast economic inequalities are widely believed to signal moral deficits, whether in wealthy individuals, public decision makers, or entire societies. In fact, the connection between economic inequality and moral failure is so widely taken for granted that it is common to hear speakers present statistics on gross inequality as if in themselves they constituted a moral argument. While I am far from averse to pointing out the scandal with a statistic—as will shortly become clear—a problem as widespread and influential as contemporary economic inequality demands more sustained investigation into its moral geneses and harms.[1] This essay will investigate an underdiscussed aspect of economic inequality: its impact on the moral lives of persons and communities. I begin by showing how inequality harms communities and perpetuates itself. Using Bernard Lonergan's understanding of bias and scotosis, I then explore how economic inequality both results from and promotes a biased ignorance of the Other, particularly those who are poor. I will draw on previous theological studies of globalization to propose a positive "globalization of solidarity" with the potential to counter inequality's pernicious moral and practical aspects.

Background on Inequality

Extreme economic inequality is present both within and across national boundaries and continues to grow.[2] To invoke a morally

---

1. Both income inequality and wealth inequality are significant for the purposes of this essay. I use "economic inequality" as a general term to refer to either or both.

2. Pedro Olinto and Jaime Saavedra, "An Overview of Global Income Inequality Trends," *World Bank: Inequality in Focus* 1, no. 1 (2012): 1–4, at 3;

salient statistic, Oxfam International reports that 8 men own the same amount of wealth as the poorest half of the world's population.[3] The U.S. is on track to set a record for inequality by the year 2030, when the top 10 percent of earners could take home 60 percent of national income, with less than 15 percent going to the poorest half of the population.[4] Increasingly, we have come to understand that today's extreme rates of global inequality are not natural or inevitable, but rather are traceable to choices made in societies about whether and how to intervene in markets.[5]

Amid today's vast inequalities, globalization has been portrayed as a harbinger of justice. It is true that countries like China and India are gaining in national income relative to the U.S. and Western Europe. Some understand this increase as a positive force that promises U.S. standards of living to Indian and Chinese workers.[6] Nevertheless, the reality is less encouraging. Within many of these formerly poor nations now gaining wealth, patterns of inequality appear to mimic those in the U.S.[7] The growth globalization brings can accumulate at the top, leaving the majority of workers who contribute to the growth behind.[8] Globalization has increased average income in many nations, but inequality within growing nations continues to increase as well.[9]

Greg Morcroft, "Global Income Inequality: The Story in Charts," International Business Times, December 24, 2013, http://www.ibtimes.com/global-income-inequality-story-charts-1519376.

3. "Just 8 Men Own Same Wealth as Half the World," Oxfam International, January 1, 2016, https://www.oxfam.org/en/pressroom/pressreleases/2017-01-16/just-8-men-own-same-wealth-half-world.

4. Thomas Piketty, *Capital in the Twenty-First Century*, trans. Arthur Goldhammer (Cambridge, MA: Harvard University Press, 2014), 264.

5. Piketty, *Capital in the Twenty-First Century*, 20.

6. Tyler Cowen, "Income Inequality Is Not Rising Globally, It's Falling," *The New York Times*, July 19, 2014, http://www.nytimes.com/2014/07/20/upshot/income-inequality-is-not-rising-globally-its-falling-.html.

7. Piketty, *Capital in the Twenty-First Century*, 326.

8. "Why Globalisation May Not Reduce Inequality in Poor Countries," *The Economist*, September 2, 2014, https://www.economist.com/blogs/economist-explains/2014/09/economist-explains-0.

9. "Theorist Eric Maskin: Globalization Is Increasing Inequality," World Bank, June, 23, 2014, http://www.worldbank.org/en/news/feature/2014/06/23/theorist-eric-maskin-globalization-is-increasing-inequality.

Should theologians and philosophers accordingly regard inequality as a problem? Some have argued that it makes more sense to focus on addressing poverty, even implying that concerns with how much the wealthy have are nothing more than thinly veiled resentment.[10] However, these arguments collapse in the face of a wealth of scholarship demonstrating that inequality itself correlates to and even causes many significant social problems.

We tend to think of issues like crime, incarceration, drug abuse, worse overall health, and lower average lifespan as problems of poverty. However, in their book, *The Spirit Level*, public health scholars Kate Pickett and Richard Wilkinson showed that these social ills are more closely associated with inequality than they are with poverty. For example, levels of crime and drug abuse rise when inequality increases in a given society, even if the living standard of the poor also improves.[11]

Unequal societies display what is called a "health gradient," meaning that poor health and early death are disproportionately concentrated in the lives of the poor.[12] Remarkably, however, while inequality does tend to increase such evils *disproportionately* among the poor, by no means is its harm extended *only* to the poor. Middle-class and wealthy people also experience more health problems in highly unequal societies than they do in more egalitarian ones. In unequal societies, say Pickett and Wilkinson, "the effects of inequality are not confined just to the least well-off: instead, they affect the vast majority of the population [. . . In a society with a socioeconomic health gradient, you] could take away all the health problems of the poor and leave most of the problem of health inequalities untouched."[13] Reducing inequality, and its attendant social dysfunctions, stands to benefit middle-class and wealthy people as well. Pickett and Wilkinson summarize:

---

10. See Andrew M. Yuengert, "What Is 'Sustainable Prosperity for All' in the Catholic Social Tradition?," in *The True Wealth of Nations: Catholic Social Thought and Economic Life*, ed. Daniel K. Finn (New York: Oxford University Press, 2010), 37–62.

11. Kate Pickett and Richard Wilkinson, *The Spirit Level: Why Greater Equality Makes Societies Stronger* (New York: Bloomsbury, 2011), 310–11.

12. Pickett and Wilkinson, *The Spirit Level*, 12.

13. Pickett and Wilkinson, *The Spirit Level*, 181.

Among the rich developed countries and among the fifty states of the United States, most of the important health and social problems of the rich world are more common in more unequal societies. . . . If—for instance—a country does badly on health, you can predict with some confidence that it will also imprison a larger proportion of its population, have more teenage pregnancies, lower literacy scores, more obesity, worse mental health, and so on. Inequality seems to make countries socially dysfunctional across a wide range of outcomes.[14]

Again, in every case Pickett and Wilkinson examined, inequality of wealth or income predicted these social evils *better* than poverty rates. This is true whether the societies studied were as large as countries or as small as U.S. zip codes.

Another reason to worry about inequality is that it perpetuates itself. As economist Thomas Piketty famously demonstrated, inequality self-perpetuates through the formula $r > g$; that is, investments over time grow more quickly than economies as a whole. $R > g$ means that those who have wealth to invest will always gain wealth faster than those starting from a poorer place. This increases inequality and threatens societal peace and stability.[15]

Inequality also self-perpetuates by reducing economic mobility. The more unequal a society, the less likely a poor person is to move up in income or a wealthy person is to move down.[16] Finally, inequality self-perpetuates by increasing the political voice and power of wealthy people relative to poor and middle-class ones. This makes it difficult for lower-income people to defend their own interests relative to those of the wealthy.[17] To return to my earlier question, yes, inequality is a problem worthy of concern in its own right, because

14. Pickett and Wilkinson, *The Spirit Level*, 174.

15. Piketty, *Capital in the Twenty-First Century*, 10.

16. "Inequalities in economic status are quite persistent across generations, especially among children of low-income parents and, most especially, in the United States" (Timothy M. Smeeding, Markus Jäntii, and Robert Erikson, "Introduction," in *Persistence, Privilege, and Parenting: The Comparative Study of Intergenerational Mobility* (New York: Russell Sage Foundation, 2011), 2).

17. Kay Lehman Schlozman, Sidney Verba, and Henry E. Brady, *The Unheavenly Chorus: Unequal Political Voice and the Broken Promise of American Democracy* (Princeton, NJ: Princeton University Press, 2012).

it self-perpetuates and because of its strong causal relationship with many serious social ills.

Inequality harms human flourishing and that alone recommends it to theologians' attention.[18] It shapes the physical destiny of persons in societies, often for the worse. That suggests it may shape our moral destinies as well. A theological perspective might usefully ask: what does the existence of today's vast inequalities say about the state of a society's moral life?

The question has been asked before. In his apostolic exhortation, *Evangelii gaudium*, Pope Francis diagnosed inequality as both symptom and cause of a morally fatal indifference to the poor.[19] My own current book project explains how inequality affects virtue formation by exacerbating the moral impacts of wealth and poverty. As I mentioned earlier, a theological intuition clearly suggests that vast inequality must be the result of moral failure. Still, we have not yet fully understood how present inequality shapes moral development. In what follows, I will show how Bernard Lonergan's work can help us better grasp the moral impact of inequality on persons and societies.

Lonergan on Bias

For Lonergan, the quest for insight is a signal feature of meaningful human life. But the process of reasoned discourse and testing of ideas that should lead to insight is neither naturally nor automatically successful. Indeed, it is frequently disrupted by bias, which takes four forms: individual, dramatic, group, and general bias.

In individual bias, the subject experiences free intellectual searching, but only in the quest for solutions that benefit herself,

---

18. Addressing inequality's harmful effects, Protestant theologian and economist Douglas Hicks said inequality is excessive when it obstructs meaningful participation in society, and Pope Benedict XVI called inequality a "scandal" opposed to human dignity. Douglas A. Hicks, *Inequality and Christian Ethics* (New York: Cambridge University Press, 2000), 232; and Benedict XVI, *Caritas in Veritate* [Encyclical on Integral Human Development in Charity and Truth], June 29, 2009, §22. See also Kate Ward and Kenneth R. Himes, "'Growing Apart': The Rise of Inequality," *Theological Studies* 75, no. 1 (March 1, 2014): 118–32.

19. Kate Ward, "Pope Francis' *Evangelii Gaudium* in Context: Theological Responses to Inequality," September 15, 2014, unpublished paper available upon request.

failing to pursue solutions that benefit the whole of society. She is conscious of her use of reason and of her self-imposed limitations on the conclusions that reason can reach.[20] Group bias, Lonergan says, "leads to a bias in the generative principle of a developing social order." Insights accepted by the group are those that "either meet with no group resistance or else find favor with groups powerful enough to overcome what resistance there is."[21] In the same way that individuals sort the information they absorb to reach personally convenient conclusions, "so also the group is prone to have a blind spot for the insights that reveal its well-being to be excessive or its usefulness at an end."[22] In other words, insights that would encourage the group to voluntarily accept a lower status or a lowered opinion of itself are conveniently ignored.

Dramatic bias describes the way the self manipulates new information to conform it to pre-existing, personally important understandings.[23] At this level of bias, Lonergan says subjects suffer from scotosis, an unconscious process through which individuals exclude knowledge that challenges their own common-sense, limited understanding of self and the world.[24] A scotoma or blind spot results from the self's own efforts to consciously or subconsciously reject information that would expand its worldview in ways that feel threatening or challenging.[25]

Finally, the general bias of common sense focuses on practical methods to the exclusion of broader issues and higher goals.[26] M. Shawn Copeland explains: "With its penchant for the 'quick-fix'

---

20. Bernard J.F. Lonergan, *Insight: A Study of Human Understanding*, Collected Works of Bernard Lonergan, vol. 3, eds. Frederick E. Crowe and Robert M. Doran (Toronto: University of Toronto Press, 2005), 244–7.

21. Lonergan, *Insight*, 249.

22. Lonergan, *Insight*, 248.

23. Lonergan, *Insight*, 214–5.

24. Lonergan, *Insight*, 215. An example is the failure of white Catholics to treat Black Catholics as fellow full members of the Body of Christ or for white theologians to take the contributions of Black Catholic theologians seriously. M. Shawn Copeland, "Guest Editorial," *Theological Studies* 4, no. 61 (December 2000): 605.

25. Lonergan, *Insight*, 215.

26. Lonergan, *Insight*, 198–202, 250–1.

and the short-term solution, the *general bias of common sense* colludes with group bias to disregard innovative and good ideas that might come from non-privileged groups. General bias regulates social arrangements to the immediate well-being of the dominant racial group and thereby despoils the common good."[27] While directed specifically to racial injustice, Copeland's analysis aptly describes general bias as a broader phenomenon.

It should be clear that bias in Lonergan's thought is not simply a matter of individual prejudice. Since developing insight is a communal process which bias disrupts, bias insinuates itself into the structures of society. Now we will explore how economic inequality both results from and contributes to group bias, dramatic bias, and general bias.

How Inequality Results from Bias and Scotosis

It is fairly self-evident how processes of scotosis and group bias can contribute to economic inequality. Theologians and social scientists alike have observed this process in action. Inequality can result from preexisting moral blind spots, including the failure to recognize others as human. Aspects of today's global inequality date as far back in history as colonization, a process driven by persistent group and general biases of European people against the peoples of Africa, Asia and the Americas. [28] Sebastian Kim, a theologian in the United Kingdom, rightly notes that the church's history of missionary expansion accompanied and is inseparable from this colonial legacy. He says the church "shares the responsibility for [today's global] inequality when it is either silent on the issue, or when it accumulates wealth at the expense of others."[29] Racism and dehumanization along racial lines contribute to inequality as well. Piketty shows the roots of

---

27. M. Shawn Copeland, *Enfleshing Freedom: Body, Race, and Being* (Minneapolis: Fortress Press, 2010), 14. Copeland wrote "the dominant racial group." Without intending to distort her words out of their intended meaning, I believe the general bias of common sense can be applied more broadly—for example, to defend the interests of the wealthy at the expense of those who are not.

28. Piketty, *Capital in the Twenty-First Century*, 70–71, 121.

29. Sebastian Kim, "Editorial," *International Journal of Public Theology* 7 (2013): 1–4.

contemporary U.S. inequality in the Atlantic slave trade, when the purportedly egalitarian U.S. maintained levels of inequality similar to those of socially stratified Europe.[30]

Several theologians have explored how economic inequality has a root cause in dehumanizing bias. Paulinus Odozor, a theologian from Nigeria teaching in the U.S., finds that factors internal and external to African society contribute to high levels of inequality in many African countries. External factors include destructive trade and development policies from Western countries. Internal cultural tendencies perpetuating inequality include government misallocation of resources and a persistent failure to recognize the humanity of outsiders or others.[31] Failing to recognize the humanity of others also contributes to economic inequality in the U.S., argues Mary Elizabeth Hobgood, when systemic racism distracts white U.S. Americans from the extent and causal factors of their own "economic disempowerment."[32] Similarly, Bryan Massingale argues that racism, individualism, and consumerism shape a "cultured indifference to the poor" unique to the U.S. context.[33]

Lonergan himself explicitly details how group bias results in stratified societies where the best and worst off enjoy radically different opportunities and qualities of life.[34] This is because those excluded by group bias will struggle to have their own insights accepted by the broader society. Hobgood paints a vivid picture of

---

30. Piketty, *Capital in the Twenty-First Century*, 152. Piketty acknowledges that this is a disturbing calculation to make but believes that it serves the cause of justice today to understand the historical U.S. economy, and modern U.S. duplicity about our own history, as accurately as possible. I agree on all counts.

31. Paulinus I. Odozor, "Truly Africa, and Wealthy! What Africa Can Learn from Catholic Social Teaching about Sustainable Economic Prosperity," in *The True Wealth of Nations*, 267–87.

32. Mary E. Hobgood, "White Economic and Erotic Disempowerment: A Theological Exploration in the Struggle against Racism," in *Interrupting White Privilege*, eds. Laurie M. Cassidy and Alex Mikulich (Maryknoll, NY: Orbis Books, 2007), 48.

33. Bryan N. Massingale, "An Ethical Reflection upon 'Environmental Racism' in the Light of Catholic Social Teaching," in *Challenge of Global Stewardship: Roman Catholic Responses*, eds. Maura A. Ryan and Todd David Whitmore (Notre Dame, IN: University of Notre Dame Press, 1997), 234–50.

34. Lonergan, *Insight*, 249.

how well-off people in unequal societies exercise bias to justify their own advantages. She writes:

> It becomes easy to justify our positions and the unearned privileges we enjoy, as well as the suffering of the lazy or unlucky 'unfortunate' others. We learn that self-discipline and hard work usually pay off, and due to our own hard work and individual merit, we are entitled to things that other people do not have. . . . The ideology protecting our privileges in the upper tiers of the working class conditions us to deny attention and feeling to those we have learned are unworthy.[35]

Group bias and scotosis are both operative when those who benefit from inequality accept their unearned privilege and ignore the harm, even the deadly harm, inequality deals to the less fortunate. General bias, privileging views that appear to be common sense, tempts those who benefit from inequality as well as those who are harmed by it to believe that the current economic situation is natural and inevitable, even desirable, rather than probing further to realize that economic structures are created by human societies and can be shaped to promote more just outcomes.

How Inequality Promotes Bias

Inequality is shaped by human choice, including choices about whether and when to intervene in markets. It also shapes human behavior in categories as basic as trust, health, and crime and punishment. Inequality is to a certain extent a creature of bias, but as it impacts societies, inequality can promote and foster bias as well. It warps our cognition and understanding, insinuating itself into social structures to shape what those in power regard as common sense. Inequality increases violence and punitive behavior within societies and contributes significantly to what Pope Francis has dubbed "the globalization of indifference."[36] Unequal societies are those whose structures encourage the development of group bias and scotosis by

---

35. Mary E. Hobgood, *Dismantling Privilege: An Ethics of Accountability* (Cleveland, OH: Pilgrim Press, 2000), 82.

36. Francis, *Evangelii Gaudium* [Apostolic Exhortation on the Proclamation of the Gospel in Today's World], November 24, 2013, §54.

keeping different "Others" out of sight and out of mind from those with power.

Pickett and Wilkinson suggest that inequality is responsible for increasing violence, sensitivity to shame, and fear of others in society. They found that violence is more common in societies with higher levels of inequality.[37] Summarizing a variety of sociological findings to explain why this might be, they write:

> Although everybody experiences disrespect and humiliation at times, they don't all become violent; we all experience loss of face but we don't turn round and shoot somebody. In more unequal societies more people lack these protections and buffers. Shame and humiliation become more sensitive issues in more hierarchical societies; status becomes more important, status competition increases and more people are deprived of access to markers of status and social success.[38]

The impact of inequality on violence begins in childhood. In more unequal societies, children are likelier to report being the victims of bullying, to get in physical fights, and to feel their peers are not "kind and helpful."[39]

Further evidence that inequality promotes bias is found in the higher incarceration rates of more unequal nations. Pickett and Wilkinson continue,

> In societies with greater inequality, where the social distances between people are greater, where attitudes of 'us and them' are more entrenched . . . public and policy makers alike are more willing to imprison people and adopt punitive attitudes towards the 'criminal elements' of society. . . . And as prison is not particularly effective for either deterrence or rehabilitation, then a society must only be willing to maintain a high rate (and high cost) of imprisonment for reasons unrelated to effectiveness.[40]

---

37. Pickett and Wilkinson, *The Spirit Level*, 140–41.

38. Pickett and Wilkinson, *The Spirit Level*, 140–41.

39. Pickett and Wilkinson, *The Spirit Level*, 139.

40. Pickett and Wilkinson, *The Spirit Level*, 155.

As evidenced by variance in incarceration rates, inequality in society accompanies a lack of empathy and a punitive mindset on the part of the powerful toward those without power. This indicates a failure to incorporate relevant information, or bias.

Pope Francis acknowledges the way inequality can create a destructive spiral of violence, punitive repression, and more violence. He writes in *Evangelii gaudium*, "Until exclusion and inequality in society and between peoples are reversed, it will be impossible to eliminate violence" (*EG* 59). He goes on to say, "When a society—whether local, national or global—is willing to leave a part of itself on the fringes, no political programmes or resources spent on law enforcement or surveillance systems can indefinitely guarantee tranquility" (*EG* 59).

Inequality in society leads to a blithe exclusion, a widespread social scotosis through which the wealthy forget the poor and, in the process, themselves become less human. This claim is beautifully demonstrated by the Nigerian theologian, Olubiyi Adeniyi Adewale, in his essay on the parable of Lazarus (Lk 16:19–31). Adewale's African perspective adds incisive detail to Jesus' criticism of the rich man's behavior in the parable. Lazarus's suffering and need were compounded by an illness so dire that, in Luke's telling, "dogs came and licked his sores." Adewale says that in an African worldview, the saliva of dogs can be helpful for healing and notes that Jews in Jesus' time believed this as well. So, the dogs who licked Lazarus's sores were actually helping him. Meanwhile, the rich man did not help him at all. Mired in scotosis by his obsession with money, the rich man unwittingly reveals himself as less human than the dogs.

Adewale compares Christians in wealthy societies to the rich man in the parable. As globalization facilitates instant communication, he says, "like the biblical Lazarus, the poor in Africa have been laid at the gate of the rich brethren of the developed countries. . . . Unfortunately, to date, a large percentage of the believers in the developed countries seem to have decided not to 'see' their covenant brethren in distress."[41] Even when globalized media allow for the encounter with new information that should facilitate insight, those who benefit from

---

41. Olubiyi Adeniyi Adewale, "An Afro-Sociological Application of the Parable of the Rich Man and Lazarus (Luke 16:19–31)," *Black Theology* 4, no. 1 (Jan 2006): 27–43, at 40.

global inequality maintain their scotosis, like the rich man who feigns ignorance of Lazarus's name until he himself is in need.

Evoking the parable, shocking anecdotes from several wealthy countries suggest that today's rates of social inequality have bred a disturbing lack of empathy for those in poverty. In Spain, soaring unemployment has led to an increase in hungry people "dumpster diving" in trash bins to find food. Officials in one city diagnosed such practices as offensive to human dignity and fixed the problem by installing locks on municipal trash cans.[42] A management company in London installed metal spikes on sheltered areas of its property, treating people experiencing homelessness like animal pests.[43] The National Coalition for the Homeless has documented over 50 U.S. cities where policies punish or restrict sharing food with homeless persons in public places.[44] The rich man's scotosis—his indifference to Lazarus—courses throughout wealthy societies.

As these disturbing anecdotes suggest, unequal societies are ones where wealthy people think so little of poor persons that they prefer not to see or encounter them at all. How apropos is Lonergan's statement that "to prevent insights, repression will have to inhibit demands for images."[45] Economic segregation—rich and poor people living in different, separate areas—increases as inequality increases. This harms economic mobility as poor people lose opportunities to connect with those better off and damages quality of life in many other ways. As Pickett and Wilkinson write, "The concentration of poor people in poor areas increases all kinds of stress, deprivation

---

42. Suzanne Daley, "Hunger on the Rise in Spain," *The New York Times*, September 24, 2012, http://www.nytimes.com/2012/09/25/world/europe/hunger-on-the-rise-in-spain.html.

43. Ben Quinn, "Anti-Homeless Spikes Are Part of a Wider Phenomenon of 'Hostile Architecture,'" *The Guardian*, June 13, 2014, http://www.theguardian.com/artanddesign/2014/jun/13/anti-homeless-spikes-hostile-architecture.

44. The National Coalition for the Homeless and The National Law Center on Homelessness and Poverty, "A Place at the Table: Prohibitions on Sharing Food with People Experiencing Homelessness," July 2010, http://nationalhomeless.org/publications/foodsharing/Food_Sharing_2010.pdf; and Mary Emily O'Hara, "More US Cities Are Cracking Down on Feeding the Homeless," VICE News, June 8, 2014, https://news.vice.com/article/more-us-cities-are-cracking-down-on-feeding-the-homeless.

45. Lonergan, *Insight*, 216.

and difficulty—from increased commuting times for those who have to leave deprived communities to find work elsewhere, to increased risk of traffic accidents, worse schools, poor levels of services, exposure to gang violence, pollution and so on."[46] Another way that economic segregation degrades the common good comes through a phenomenon economist Robert Reich calls "the secession of the successful."[47] Wealthy elites, able to pay privately for access to goods such as education and security, withdraw from the commons and frequently withdraw their support for the public funding of these goods, harming those who cannot afford to pay for them.

The racial and economic segregation fostered by inequality is a social structure that enables widespread scotosis. Keeping the poor separate from wealthier populations ensures that those with access to economic and social power will not think about the poor, their needs, or their suffering. Inequality perpetuates its own continued growth by making the status quo seem like common sense. As Copeland explains, under the influence of bias, "members of the privileged group are conditioned to withdraw from unnecessary experiential contact with 'other' non-privileged members of society, thereby depriving themselves of the potential of human and humane relationships."[48]

Inequality influences social structures and persons within them, encouraging bias against those in poverty. As Pope Francis movingly describes the "globalization of indifference":

> Almost without being aware of it, we end up being incapable of feeling compassion at the outcry of the poor, weeping for other people's pain, and feeling a need to help them, as though all this were someone else's responsibility and not our own. The culture of prosperity deadens us; we are thrilled if the market offers us something new to purchase. In the meantime all those lives stunted for lack of opportunity seem a mere spectacle; they fail to move us (*EG* 54).

---

46. Pickett and Wilkinson, *The Spirit Level*, 163.

47. Robert B. Reich, "Secession of the Successful: How the New U.S. Emphasis on 'Community' Legitimizes Economic Inequality," *Other Side* 31, no. 4 (July 1995): 20–26.

48. Copeland, *Enfleshing Freedom*, 14.

Morally significant processes of knowledge formation are bound up with economic structures. Economic inequality both results from and promotes biased horizons of knowing. However, created by God as free, humanity never fully loses that freedom, even if our freedom is certainly conditioned and determined by surrounding circumstances.[49] Solutions for the relationship of inequality and bias do exist. Since inequality is both a structural and moral problem, I will propose one structural and one moral solution.

Structural Solutions

On a structural level, the first step in fighting the inequality created by scotosis is greater financial transparency within and among nations. OXFAM credited transparent, accountable governments for reduced inequality in Latin America in recent years, while inequality rose elsewhere.[50] Piketty's proposal for a modest global tax on capital, intended to slow inequality's rapid growth through $r > g$, drew immense attention when his book was published.[51] What often got lost in the discussion around this provocative proposal is how much of Piketty's justification for a global wealth tax had to do with transparency. Piketty pointed out how the limitations of public reporting hamper our understanding of inequality. For example, it can be difficult to accurately surmise just how large the fortunes in the highest tax bracket are. A global tax on capital would help. It would especially benefit poorer countries, which are likelier to suffer from corruption,[52] and would aid in prosecuting those who "rake off" profits gained in trade by concealing assets from taxation.[53]

If bias manifests itself when we reject information that is detrimental to our self-understanding, transparency fights it. I have

---

49. See Lonergan's discussion of effective and essential freedom in *Insight*, 631–647. Thanks to Lucas Briola for this recommendation.

50. Ricardo Fuentes-Nieva and Nicholas Galasso, "Working for the Few: Political Capture and Economic Inequality," Oxfam International, January 20, 2014, http://www.oxfam.org/sites/www.oxfam.org/files/bp-working-for-few-political-capture-economic-inequality-200114-en.pdf, 24–25.

51. Piketty, *Capital in the Twenty-First Century*, 471.

52. Piketty, *Capital in the Twenty-First Century*, 539.

53. Piketty, *Capital in the Twenty-First Century*, 522.

explained how inequality self-mystifies; it makes it easier for the wealthy to ignore the poor and to ignore the harms caused by inequality itself. A Harvard Business School study showed that most Americans underestimate the true extent of national inequality: they think the U.S. is significantly more egalitarian than is in fact the case. Encouragingly, most U.S. people would prefer the economy to be more equal than they already think it is, that is, far more egalitarian than the reality.[54] This shows the value of challenging our assumptions. Transparency is not a complete solution to willed bias, but it is the first step in a process inviting persons and societies to authentic insight, to confronting the many harms of globalized inequality.

Lonergan describes how bias limits our horizons and our ability to know and gain insight, but holds out hope that moral conversion is possible. Conversion is envisioned not as a one-time "road to Damascus" moment, but an ongoing process throughout one's life. It follows religious conversion, a response of "yes" to God's offer of love—whether or not this "yes" is consciously understood as religious belonging.[55] Moral conversion means conversion from selfish goals, from a horizon limited by individual and group bias, to a horizon or set of goals that includes the interests of others, particularly different others.[56] As Robert Doran has proposed, it entails conversion to collective responsibility, each for the good of all.[57]

Moral Solution: A Globalization of Solidarity

I have discussed how economic inequality both issues from and promotes bias and scotosis. As a structural and moral problem, the impact of economic inequality on bias demands structural and

---

54. Michael I. Norton and Dan Ariely, "Building a Better America— One Wealth Quintile at a Time," *Perspectives on Psychological Science* 6, no. 1 (2011): 9–12; and Elizabeth Gudrais, "Loaded Perceptions: What We Know about Wealth," Harvard Magazine, December 2011, http://harvardmagazine. com/2011/11/what-we-know-about-wealth.

55. Robert M. Doran, "What Does Bernard Lonergan Mean by 'Conversion'?," 2011, https://www.loneganresource.com/pdf/lectures/What%20Does%20 Bernard%20Lonergan%20Mean%20by%20Conversion.pdf, 7–8.

56. Doran, "What Does Bernard Lonergan Mean by 'Conversion'?," 15–16.

57. Doran, "What Does Bernard Lonergan Mean by 'Conversion'?," 18.

moral solutions. To conclude, I'll return to a theme of this volume, a humane globalization, and discuss what moral conversion to the poor Other would look like concretely. Pope John Paul II popularized the term, the "globalization of solidarity," which Pope Francis has enthusiastically embraced.[58] Catholic social thought does not hesitate to make concrete, specific suggestions, aware that moral conversion issues forth in action. So, what does a globalization of solidarity look like?

- It begins with protecting weaker nations and groups of people from the harmful consequences of economic globalization.[59]
- It means including every nation into the globalized economy on terms that allow members of that nation to benefit. This requires the reduction of ruinous international debt for nations and access to credit for poor individuals.[60]
- It demands the reduction of inequality within nations. As Pope John Paul II wrote, "If the aim is globalization *without marginalization,* we can no longer tolerate a world in which there live side-by-side the immensely rich and the miserably poor, the have-nots deprived even of essentials and people who thoughtlessly waste what others so desperately need. Such contrasts insult the dignity of the human person."[61]
- It incorporates interreligious dialogue and a widespread awareness that religion means responsibility for human flourishing.[62]

---

58. Based on incomplete historical research, I believe this term originated with now-Cardinal Oscar Andrés Rodríguez Maradiaga. See "*Synodus Episcoporum* Bulletin of the Commission for Information of the Special Assembly for America of the Synod of Bishops," Vatican Website, December 16, 1997, http://www.vatican.va/news_services/press/sinodo/documents/bollettino_17_ speciale-america-1997/02_inglese/b06_02.html.

59. John Paul II, *Ecclesia in America* [Post-Synodal Apostolic Exhortation on the Encounter with the Living Jesus Christ: The Way to Conversion, Communion and Solidarity in America], January 22, 1999, §56.

60. John Paul II, John Paul II, *From the Justice of Each Comes Peace for All* [1998 World Day of Peace Message], January 1, 1998, §4, 6.

61. John Paul II, *From the Justice of Each Comes Peace for All,* §4.

62. John Paul II, "Meeting with the Representatives of Other Religions," November 7, 1999, http://w2.vatican.va/content/john-paul-ii/en/travels/1999/ documents/hf_jp-ii_spe_07111999_new-delhi_meeting-other-religions.html.

• It encourages nations and groups to promote their own legitimate rights as long as those rights are not enjoyed at the expense
of others. This translates into "the voluntary limitation of unilateral advantages so that other countries and peoples may share in
the same benefits."[63] If group bias tends to exclude information
that would encourage a group to lessen its own status, a globalization of solidarity resists its effects.

A globalization of solidarity will also include learning from societies where cultural values strongly inculcate solidarity, the option
for the poor, and other authentically Christian values that are less
welcomed in the individualistic, wealthy West. For theologians, this
means attending to voices from the Global South who have made
it quite clear what their cultures can teach wealthy societies in our
unequal age. For example, Tanzanian theologian Laurenti Magesa
finds that Catholic social thought resonates considerably with an
indigenous African communitarian ethic; both perspectives envi-
sion economies that put human relationships at the center.[64] Teresia
Hinga, born in Kenya and now teaching in the U.S., explains that
responding to global poverty in a globalized age demands Christians
become "better Samaritans." While "good Samaritans" provide aid in
response to immediate need, "better Samaritans" accompany those
in need to discover that the root causes of poverty often lie in the
exploitation of nations by global economic forces skewed toward the
wealthy West.[65] Similarly, Indian theologian Shaji George Kochuthara
confronts cozy notions of aid when he notes that the duty of wealthy
nations to help poorer ones is not a gift but a "justice of restitution,"

---

63. John Paul II, "To the Secretary General and the Administrative Committee on Coordination of the United Nations," April 7, 2000, http://w2.vatican.va/
content/john-paul-ii/en/speeches/2000/apr-jun/documents/hf_jp-ii_spe_
20000407_secretary-general-un.html, §3.

64. Laurenti Magesa, "African Indigenous Spirituality, Ecology, and the
Human Right to Integral Development," in *The World Market and Interreli-
gious Dialogue*, eds. Catherine Cornille and Glenn Willis (Eugene, OR: Cascade
Books, 2011), 170–71.

65. Teresia Hinga, "Becoming Better Samaritans: The Quest for New Models
of Doing Socio-Economic Justice in Africa," in *Applied Ethics in a World Church:
The Padua Conference*, ed. Linda Hogan (Maryknoll, NY: Orbis Books, 2008),
85–97.

given the international history of resource extraction along colonial patterns.[66] In a globalized age, the horizon of those from historically poorer nations is, by default, drawn to include the wealthy West. For those of us who benefit from global inequality, a globalization of solidarity means extending our horizons to incorporate insights that our biases and scotoses would rather exclude.

Conclusion

Lonergan explained how understanding proceeds from knowledge of facts to knowledge of value and then to action.[67] We have explored how economic inequality is bound up with our processes of understanding. It is historically shaped by understandings limited by bias. It continues today to shape the moral knowing of persons in societies, encouraging violence, cruelty, and the willed indifference that Lonergan calls scotosis. Nevertheless, structural change and moral conversion—meaningful efforts toward the globalization of solidarity—are always possible.

---

66. Shaji George Kochuthara, "Economic Inequality: An Ethical Response," *Religions* 8, no. 8 (August 2017): 141.

67. Ryoko Tamura, "Interiority Analysis as an Integrated 'Meta-Cognition': A Way of Self-Recovery from Poor Educational Achievement," in *Grace and Friendship: Theological Essays in Honor of Fred Lawrence*, eds. M. Shawn Copeland and Jeremy D. Wilkins (Milwaukee, WI: Marquette University Press, 2016), 280–81.

CHAPTER FOUR

Solidarity and the Possibility of Global Human Rights

Nicholas Olkovich (St. Mark's College)

G lobalization is a multifaceted reality whose meaning and effects are highly contested. Broadly, it refers to a set of inter-related processes—technological, economic, social, political and cultural—that "serve to break down traditional barriers that have separated peoples, nations and cultures from one another."[1] Increased interdependence and the recognition of cultural and religious diversity raise questions about the nature and scope of solidarity and the possibility of a global ethic. Standard affirmations of the latter typically focus on the universality of human rights, as expressed in statements such as *The Universal Declaration of Human Rights* of the United Nations.[2] The dominant neoliberal interpretation of human rights links development and political stability with the expansion of market capitalism and civil-political liberties. Inspired by post-modern, post-colonial, and communitarian critiques of Enlightenment rationalism and individualism, critics characterize neoliberal globalization as a form of cultural imperialism that denies the communal dimensions of human living. The deconstruction of Western universalism has encouraged an embrace of cultural particularity that, in its extreme form, sanctions the rejection of cosmopolitan ideals and the proliferation of cultural and religious exclusivisms.

The tension between distorted forms of universalism and particularism obscures the possibility of a third alternative. Forced to

---

1. Rebecca Todd Peters, *Solidarity Ethics: Transformation in a Globalized World* (Minneapolis: Fortress Press, 2014), 3.

2. UN General Assembly, *The Universal Declaration of Human Rights* (1948).

rethink the meaning of solidarity, authors such as Richard Rorty have developed post-metaphysical forms of cosmopolitanism that respond to the post-modern critique. Although Rorty's "postmodernist bourgeois liberalism" avoids many of neoliberalism's most glaring deficiencies, it is not without its own limitations. In my judgment, the relativization of cultures and religions need not force us to choose between tribalism's return to premodern absolutisms and Rorty's tension-riddled form of post-modernism. Drawing on the work of David Hollenbach and Bernard Lonergan, I will articulate an alternative ethic of solidarity that aims to avoid both extremes while integrating some of Rorty's strongest insights.

Neoliberal Globalization and its Discontents

I will first consider how and why the relativization of culture and religion has strengthened the need for solidarity. The backstory concerns neoliberal globalization and its discontents. The rise of neoliberal economic theory coincided with the rejection of the post-war welfare compromise between socialism and capitalism and found unique expression in the policies of Margaret Thatcher and Ronald Reagan.[3] Proponents of neoliberal globalization argue that respect for "market mechanisms" and the "logic of profitability" are essential for sustained human development.[4] These commitments encourage the establishment of a minimal state designed to maintain a "limited set" of civil-political rights that enable individuals to pursue their own distinctive conceptions of fulfillment.[5] Typically, the universal character of such rights is underwritten by appealing to what Alasdair MacIntyre calls "tradition-independent reason."[6] The rationalist's appeal to universal reason justifies a particular form of Western exceptionalism that correlates the global spread of capitalism and

---

3. Peters, *Solidarity Ethics*, 4. See also Paul O'Connell, "On Reconciling Irreconcilables: Neo-liberal Globalisation and Human Rights," *Human Rights Law Review* 7 (2007): 483–509, at 496.

4. See, e.g, Peters, *Solidarity Ethics*, 4; and O'Connell, "On Reconciling Irreconcilables," 489, 499.

5. O'Connell, "On Reconciling Irreconcilables," 497.

6. See, e.g., Alasdair MacIntyre, *After Virtue*, 3rd ed. (Notre Dame: University of Notre Dame Press, 2007).

human rights with the "end of history," the final stage in civilizational evolution.[7]

This prominent interpretation of economic and political globalization has been harshly criticized by authors wary of the Enlightenment.[8] Critics argue that the notion of a universal reason accessible to individuals qua individuals is a myth that masks how all human knowing and choosing is shaped by particular traditions of inquiry. Roughly synonymous with what Richard Falk calls globalization "from above,"[9] the exportation of neoliberal ideology is a form of cultural imperialism, a forced homogenization that imposes a partisan conception of the human good on non-Western traditions.[10] According to communitarian authors, neoliberal culture socializes individuals to conceive the human person as a self-interested monad who uses reason instrumentally to satisfy his or her insatiable desire for money and property.[11] This truncated account of the person as *homo economicus* informs free market ideology and Western liberalism's tendency to construe human rights through the "paradigm of the right to be left alone."[12] By conceiving the individual and her freedoms in abstraction from communal bonds and responsibilities, critics argue that Western individualism makes it impossible to speak

---

7. See Francis Fukuyama, *The End of History and the Last Man* (Toronto: Maxwell Macmillan Canada, 1992). See also Peters, *Solidarity Ethics*, 5.

8. See, e.g., Linda Hogan, *Keeping Faith with Human Rights* (Washington, DC: Georgetown University Press, 2015), chapter 1.

9. See Richard Falk, "The Making of Global Citizenship," in *Global Visions: Beyond the New World Order*, eds. Jeremy Brecher, John Brown Childs, and Jill Cutler (Boston: South End Press, 1993), 39–50.

10. Rhoda E. Howard, "Human Rights and the Culture Wars: Globalization and the Universality of Human Rights," *International Journal* (Winter 1997–8): 94–112, at 94, 97; and Rhoda E. Howard-Hassmann, "Culture, Human Rights, and the Politics of Resentment in the Era of Globalization," *Human Rights Review* 6 (2004): 5–26, at 7.

11. O'Connell, "On Reconciling Irreconcilables," 496; and Meghan Clark, "Anatomy of a Social Virtue: Solidarity and Corresponding Vices," *Political Theology* 15 (2014): 26–39, at 32.

12. David Hollenbach, *The Global Face of Public Faith: Politics, Human Rights and Christian Ethics* (Washington, DC: Georgetown University Press, 2003), 220. See also Clark, "Anatomy of a Social Virtue," 32.

of a genuine common good.[13] In practice, the spread of individualism has disproportionately benefited Western elites at the expense of developing nations.[14]

As a reaction to distorted forms of Westernization, the instinct for cultural preservation and the return to a tradition-dependent conception of rationality is both legitimate and understandable.[15] Yet, not all who benefit from the deconstruction of neoliberal neutrality welcome the relativization of cultures and religions. Many worry that the anger and resentment towards the West generated by neoliberalism's program of "cultural subversion" jeopardizes the project of universal human rights.[16] The fear is that returning to tradition without trying to articulate a common ethic will lead to various forms of cultural and religious tribalism, exclusivism, and fundamentalism that absolutize one set of meanings and values to the exclusion of all others.[17] The result is a two-sided battle between what Benjamin Barber calls "McWorld" and "Jihad,"[18] between a false form of individualism that destroys the integrity of communities and what Anthony Giddens calls "beleaguered" forms of tradition.[19] Contrary to a tribalist rejection of genuine diversity, Richard Rorty argues that cultural relativization challenges individuals to rethink the cosmopolitan project.

Richard Rorty's Post-Modern Liberalism

Central to Rorty's alternative is an antirepresentationalism that combines elements of historicism and pragmatism. The former leads him

---

13. See, e.g., Howard, "Human Rights and the Culture Wars," 98–102; and Clark, "Anatomy of a Social Virtue," 32.

14. See, e.g., Peters, *Solidarity Ethics*, 6.

15. Howard, "Human Rights and the Culture Wars," 100, 105.

16. Howard-Hassmann, "Culture, Human Rights, and the Politics of Resentment," 5, 6, 8; and Howard, "Human Rights and the Culture Wars," 94–95.

17. Neil J. Ormerod and Shane Clifton, *Globalization and the Mission of the Church* (London: T&T Clark, 2009), 155; and Howard-Hassman, "Culture, Human Rights, and the Politics of Resentment," 10.

18. Benjamin Barber, *Jihad vs. McWorld* (New York: Times Books, 1995).

19. Anthony Giddens, *Runaway World: How Globalization is Reshaping Our Lives* (New York: Routledge, 2000), 67.

to affirm a multiplicity of culture-specific "final vocabularies" or "established traditions" into which individuals are socialized.[20] Since vocabularies are human creations that cannot be tested for accuracy against an independent reality, Rorty replaces the classical metaphysician's concern for "objectivity" with "solidarity" or an "internalist" conception of truth as "intersubjective agreement."[21] Siding with Friedrich Nietzsche and Charles Darwin's conception of humans as "clever animals," Rorty regards language as a distinctively human tool that helps individuals cope with environmental pressures.[22] Beliefs are not pictures that represent reality but rather "habits of action" or "adaptations to the environment" designed to help humans "enjoy more pleasure and less pain."[23] These two themes establish a value pluralism or "romantic polytheism" that denies the possibility of ordering desires against an independent standard.[24]

This rejection of representational realism informs a distinctive critique of moral foundationalism and rationalism. According to Rorty, the notion of language-independent reality sanctions universal conceptions such as "essential humanity" shared in slightly different ways by Greek metaphysicians, Christian theologians, and Enlightenment rationalists.[25] Proponents of this approach correlate the ahistorical core of the subject with rationality, an "extra added

---

20. Richard Rorty, *Contingency, Irony, Solidarity* (Cambridge: Cambridge University Press, 1989), 73; and *An Ethics for Today: Finding Common Ground Between Philosophy and Religion* (New York: Columbia University Press, 2009), 24.

21. See, e.g., Richard Rorty, "Introduction: Antirepresentationalism, Ethnocentrism and Liberalism," in *Objectivity, Relativism and Truth: Philosophical Papers, Volume 1* (Cambridge: Cambridge University Press, 1991), 6, 13; and "Solidarity or Objectivity?," in *Volume 1*, 23, 24, 27.

22. See, e.g., Richard Rorty, "Human Rights, Rationality, and Sentimentality," in *Truth and Progress, Volume 3* (Cambridge: Cambridge University Press, 1998), 175; and "Introduction," 5.

23. Rorty, "Introduction," 11; and Richard Rorty, *Philosophy and Social Hope* (Toronto: Penguin, 1999), xxii–xxiii.

24. Richard Rorty, "Pragmatism as Romantic Polytheism," in *The Rorty Reader*, eds. Christopher J. Voparil and Richard J. Bernstein (Malden, MA: Wiley Blackwell, 2010), 445–447.

25. Rorty, "Introduction," 14; and Richard Rorty, "The Priority of Democracy to Philosophy," in *Volume 1*, 176.

ingredient" that distinguishes humans from other animals.[26] The result is a strongly dichotomized reading of the relationship between affect—the "empirical bundle of desires and passions"—and reason— the "transcendent, dominant controller" responsible for ordering and disciplining affect.[27] This picture of rationality, as the source of human dignity and "universal moral obligation created by membership in the species," provides philosophical foundations for Enlightenment liberalism's affirmation of universal human rights.[28] In contrast, Rorty conceives conscience as a product of socialization and characterizes moral norms as "we-intentions" that emerge out of "relation[s] of reciprocal trust among a closely knit group, such as a family or clan."[29] Citing the neo-Humean approach of Annette Baier, Rorty argues that these biologically-grounded, affectively-laden and socially cultivated bonds "naturally" or "spontaneously" motivate pro-social actions.[30]

This account of the emergence and character of ethical norms largely parallels the particularist critique of Western universalism. Unlike those communitarians who argue that the deconstruction of Enlightenment liberalism's traditional "philosophical" foundations invalidates the human rights project, Rorty commits himself to disengaging and retrieving liberalism's "political" dimensions.[31] The result is a post-modern form of "liberal ironism" that conceives liberalism as one among many contingently-grounded traditions. At the heart of Rorty's antifoundationalist "redescription" of liberalism is his modified distinction between public and private spheres.[32] In contrast to metaphysicians such as Plato and Immanuel Kant

---

26. Rorty, "The Priority of Democracy to Philosophy," 176; and Richard Rorty, "Rationality and Cultural Difference," in *Volume 3*, 186.

27. Rorty, *Contingency, Irony, Solidarity*, 10, 21. See also Rorty, *An Ethics for Today*, 13.

28. Richard Rorty, "Justice as a Larger Loyalty," in *Philosophy in Cultural Politics, Volume 4* (Cambridge: Cambridge University Press, 2007), 55. See also Rorty, *Contingency, Irony, Solidarity*, 57, 84, 94.

29. Rorty, "Justice as a Larger Loyalty," 45. See also Rorty, "Human Rights, Rationality, and Sentimentality," 181.

30. Rorty, "Justice as a Larger Loyalty," 45. See also Rorty, *Philosophy and Social Hope*, 76, 78.

31. Richard Rorty, *Truth, Politics, and 'Post-Modernism'* (Assen: Van Gorcum, 1997), 35–36; and Rorty, *Contingency, Irony, Solidarity*, 57, 62–63, 67.

32. Rorty, *Contingency, Irony, Solidarity*, 54–55.

who appeal to a common human nature capable of specifying public norms whose fulfillment are essential to self-perfection, Rorty
argues "there is no way to bring self-creation together with justice at
the level of theory."[33] He accordingly focuses on articulating the relationship between two "equally valid, yet forever incommensurable"
emphases, the public aims of justice and solidarity and the private
search for happiness.[34]

According to Rorty, dignity and human rights are "social con-
structions," a particular set of "we-intentions" that specify the conditions for private self-creation and the acceptable public limits
of polytheism.[35] These we-intentions include those civil-political
liberties that neoliberals tend to overemphasize as well as a "quasi-
communitarian" commitment to limiting "cruelty," "suffering," and
"humiliation."[36] Rorty expresses the latter in his hope for a "classless
society," a community in which "income and wealth are equitably
distributed and . . . which . . . ensures equality of opportunity as
well as individual liberty."[37] The result is a post-modern form of utilitarianism that associates concern for the common good with support
for the broadest collection of private perfections.[38]

Rorty's account of the development of liberal we-intentions
centers on the distinction between "thick" and "thin" morality, or
between small-scale local norms and the demands of justice that
arise when "loyalty to a smaller group conflicts with . . . loyalty
to a larger group."[39] The movement from different thick moralities
to a common thin standard proceeds along two interrelated tracks,
one rational and one affective. Rorty correlates rational progress
with a capacity to develop an agreement on "how to coexist without
violence."[40] This "free consensus" replaces the "quest for a ranking

---

33. Rorty, *Contingency, Irony, Solidarity*, xiii–iv.

34. Rorty, *Contingency, Irony, Solidarity*, xv.

35. Rorty, *Philosophy and Social Hope*, 85–86.

36. Rorty, *Contingency, Irony, Solidarity*, xv; and Rorty, *Philosophy and Social Hope*, 86.

37. Richard Rorty, *Achieving Our Country: Leftist Thought in Twentieth-Century America* (Cambridge, MA: Harvard University Press, 1998), 30–31, 8–9.

38. Rorty, *An Ethics for Today*, 8.

39. Rorty, "Justice as a Larger Loyalty," 45. See also 42, 46.

40. Rorty, "Justice as a Larger Loyalty," 52. See also 53–54.

of human needs that does not depend upon such consensus" with a commitment to tolerance and cooperation.[41] From this perspective, "the only test of a political proposal is its ability to gain assent from people who retain radically diverse ideas about the point and meaning of human life."[42] Since private religious perfection is irrelevant to public policy, religious believers are free to hold whatever commitments they like, as long as they do not impose their viewpoints on other citizens.[43]

At the same time, the expansion of trust and loyalty to those beyond family and clan is primarily a product of enlarging one's moral "sensitivity."[44] According to Rorty, the difference between loyalty to one's own community and the commitment to universal justice is not one between affectivity and rationality but rather merely a difference of degree.[45] Specifically, the enlargement of an individual's moral horizon—the movement from thick to thin morality or universalized justice—is facilitated by a "sentimental education" that fosters identification and cooperation with outsiders.[46] "Solidarity" is not a fact that is discovered by human reason's effort to isolate some metaphysical foundation, but is rather something created, a "goal to be achieved" by humankind's "imaginative ability to see strange people as fellow sufferers."[47] As a result, "novels and ethnographies which sensitize one to the pain of those who do not speak our language must do the job which demonstrations of a common human nature were supposed to do."[48]

---

41. Rorty, "Pragmatism as Romantic Polytheism," 448.

42. Rorty, *Philosophy and Social Hope*, 173.

43. Rorty, "Pragmatism as Romantic Polytheism," 450. See also Richard Rorty, "Anticlericalism and Atheism," in *The Future of Religion*, ed. Santiago Zabala (New York: Columbia University Press, 2005), 32.

44. Rorty, *Philosophy and Social Hope*, 78–79; and Rorty, "Human Rights, Rationality, and Sentimentality," 176, 181, 183–184.

45. Rorty, *Philosophy and Social Hope*, 73–75. See also Rorty, "Justice as a Larger Loyalty," 42, 44.

46. Rorty, *Philosophy and Social Hope*, 78–83; and Rorty, *Contingency, Irony, Solidarity*, 94.

47. Rorty, *Contingency, Irony, Solidarity*, xvi. See also Rorty, *An Ethics for Today*, 9.

48. Rorty, *Contingency, Irony, Solidarity*, 94. See also Rorty, "Human Rights, Rationality, and Sentimentality," 172, 185.

Typically, the norms that structure cooperative ventures remain implicit in social practice. Moral philosophy's primary task is not to discover and articulate timeless moral principles but rather to formulate reminders that objectify "our culturally influenced intuitions."[49] In *Achieving Our Country: Leftist Thought in Twentieth-Century America*, Rorty aims to objectify the meanings and values implicit in one particular strand of American democratic practice. Rorty's account of American democracy is heavily shaped by the progressive politics of the reformist Left or by "all those Americans who, between 1900 and 1964, struggled within the framework of constitutional democracy to protect the weak from the strong."[50] According to Rorty, pride in the reformist Left's efforts to create a "classless and casteless society" generates a distinctive brand of nationalism that conceives America as "a country to be achieved."[51] Rorty also applauds Walt Whitman and John Dewey's attempts to disconnect this progressive project of "self-improvement" from any metaphysical or divine authority that might ground it.[52] The result is a post-metaphysical form of exceptionalism that conceives America as "the vanguard of humanity," the "first nation-state to have the courage to renounce hope of justification from on high—from a source which is immovable and eternal."[53] This secularized form of eschatology replaces God as the "unconditional object of desire" with hope for a "utopian America" that combines respect for individual freedom with equality of opportunity.[54]

Rorty critiques the cultural Left's tendency to conceive America pejoratively as a project to be rejected outright rather than reformed. On the one hand, the cultural Left's fascination with the "politics of difference" has led its proponents to think "more about stigma than about money, more about deep and hidden psychosexual motivations than about shallow and evident greed."[55] Although this focus on otherness has helped those who are "humiliated for reasons other

---

49. Rorty, "Human Rights, Rationality, and Sentimentality," 171. See also Rorty, "Justice as a Larger Loyalty," 46–47.

50. Rorty, *Achieving Our Country*, 43.

51. Rorty, *Achieving Our Country*, 30, 13–15.

52. Rorty, *Achieving Our Country*, 15–20.

53. Rorty, *Achieving Our Country*, 22, 27.

54. Rorty, *Achieving Our Country*, 20, 17, 8.

55. Rorty, *Achieving Our Country*, 76–77.

than economic status," these gains have been offset by their unwillingness to address increasing economic inequality and insecurity.[56] On the other hand, the cultural Left's preoccupation with philosophical efforts to expose power (in the Foucauldian sense) has produced a "spectatorial" movement that is more concerned with naming and rejecting "the system" than with effecting real change.[57] Both tendencies leave the cultural Left ill-equipped to respond to the negative effects of neoliberal globalization and inadvertently encourage right-wing populist movements.[58] According to Rorty, the contemporary Left must make peace with its reformist past, commit to developing a "concrete political platform," and devote itself to cultivating a shared sense of national pride capable of motivating commitment to such a program.[59] Some complain that Rorty's patriotism stands in tension with his commitment to universal solidarity.[60] He is not convinced the two ideals are incompatible, however. Specifically, Rorty argues that a more humane form of globalization will likely require the establishment of a world government but also that American pride can be harnessed in support of global justice.[61] Global solidarity is in this sense always rooted in but goes beyond the liberal nation-state's respect for citizen's rights.

Rorty's antirepresentationalism prevents him from arguing that this account of liberalism—his particular rendering of the norms implicit in American political culture—can be justified by some form of universal reason. Ironism is, as Rorty was fond of saying, compatible with "wholehearted enthusiasm and whole-hearted contempt for democracy."[62] At the same time, Rorty carefully distinguishes his

---

56. Rorty, *Achieving Our Country*, 80, 84–86.

57. See, e.g., Rorty, *Achieving Our Country*, 77–79, 94–96.

58. Rorty, *Achieving Our Country*, 84–89. See also 91–92. The most (in) famous passage in *Achieving Our Country* describes the hypothetical rise of "fascism" and a "strong man" figure in American politics that many have since come to link in prophetic ways with the rise of Donald Trump.

59. Rorty, *Achieving Our Country*, 99–101.

60. See, e.g., Martha Nussbaum, "Patriotism and Cosmopolitanism," *Boston Review* 19, no. 5 (1994): 3–4.

61. Rorty, *Achieving Our Country*, 3, 105. See also Rorty, *Philosophy and Social Hope*, 233.

62. Rorty, "Pragmatism as Romantic Polytheism," 448. See also Rorty, *Philosophy and Social Hope*, xxxi.

"ethnocentrism" or tradition-dependent conception of rationality from the "self-refuting" claim that "every belief is as good as every other."[63] Although liberals may appeal to the concrete advantages of democracy, pragmatic polytheism dictates that dialogue within and between traditions will be primarily rhetorical and hence "inconclusive."[64] Nonetheless, Rorty remains convinced that liberalism is contagious, and that, if people have the opportunity to experience life in a democratic community, they will likely affirm its superiority.

Tensions in Rorty's Alternative

There is much to appreciate in Rorty's critical and constructive projects. The critiques of representational realism, essentialism, and moral rationalism highlight the practically-oriented, socially embedded, and affectively-grounded nature of human knowing and choosing. His embrace of ironism also avoids the false neutrality of Western universalism and the misguided communitarian return to absolutism. The result is an antifoundationalist account of solidarity and human rights that purports to be more hospitable to difference and more oriented toward justice. Although his alternative sidesteps many of neoliberalism's most glaring deficiencies, it is not without its own tensions. Two issues deserve particular attention.

The first concerns the rational and affective bases of liberal we-intentions. In the absence of a transcultural standard capable of grounding human rights, Rorty's ethnocentric liberal must persuade non-liberals to adopt her own particular final vocabulary by appealing to practical concerns. Rorty's tendency to conceive rationality in primarily instrumental terms may be interpreted in ways that reduce the basis for adherence to liberal norms to self- or group-interest. The result appears to be a *modus vivendi* form of consensus—a temporary and pragmatic rather than moral convergence—whose viability is a function of its capacity to protect individuals and groups from interference.[65] This approach to

---

63. Rorty, "Solidarity or Objectivity?," 23. See also Rorty, "Postmodernist Bourgeois Liberalism," 202.

64. Rorty, *Philosophy and Social Hope*, xxxi. See also Rorty, "Solidarity or Objectivity?," 29.

65. Hollenbach discusses the limitations of this type of approach to democracy in *The Global Face of Public Faith*, 241–242.

democracy may provide a basis for adopting civil-political rights that guarantee freedom from coercion, but it may also be construed in ways that subvert Rorty's hope for a classless society. A *modus vivendi* arrangement certainly commends tolerance, but it is unclear how tolerance can avoid being understood in ways that encourage indifference to alternative projects of self-creation rather than genuine solidarity. Although Rorty explicitly rejects this sort of "live-and-let live" attitude, his unwillingness to affirm an intrinsic, even if limited, connection between the liberal's commitment to social justice and her quest for private self-perfection appears to imply it. His appeal to patriotism may mitigate this tendency at the level of the nation-state, but the public-private split appears ill-equipped to motivate, for example, the global economic redistribution that he regards as essential to a liberal utopia.

In both instances, Rorty would likely argue that an expansion of sentimentality is essential for motivating genuine solidarity, but it is unclear how *feeling* divorced from principled reasons that commend respect and concern for others can overcome these other tendencies. Part of the problem concerns Rorty's self-identification as a "freeloading atheist," a label that highlights his efforts to disengage Christianity's focus on neighborly love from its motivating source in the reality of the transcendent.[66] Charles Taylor poses two challenges to Rorty's brand of exclusive humanism. On the one hand, Nietzsche's deconstruction of the Enlightenment's emphasis on equality has generated an anti-humanist backlash against democracy and universal human rights that shares much with certain violent fundamentalist visions.[67] On the other hand, Taylor worries that exclusive humanism provides a rather fragile motivation for universal solidarity and that its high-minded ideals can, ironically, generate anger and resentment in the face of persistent failure.[68] Both challenge the adequacy of exclusive humanism's moral horizon.

The second concern focuses on the status of Rorty's antirepresentationalism. According to Rorty, the movement beyond the "correspondence theory of truth" is not the product of an insight

---

66. Rorty, "Postmodernist Bourgeois Liberalism," 201–202.

67. Charles Taylor, *A Catholic Modernity?*, ed. James L. Heft (New York: Oxford University Press, 1999), 27–29.

68. Taylor, *A Catholic Modernity?*, 30–34.

into the "nature of a pre-existent entity" called "truth" but rather the result of "changing the way we talk."[69] Rorty gauges the utility of this redescription by its capacity to dissolve or transcend "traditional philosophical problems," thereby helping humans "come to terms with Darwin."[70] Despite Rorty's best efforts to evade this charge, the pragmatic pole of Rorty's position appears to conceive humans distinctively as spontaneously intersubjective, "clever animals" driven to satisfy their irreducibly distinct desires. Even if one grants Rorty's claim that antirepresentationalism is not metaphysically correct but simply more useful, this response presupposes pragmatic utilitarianism's picture of the subject. Antirepresentationalism is useful for inculcating his partisan account of human nature. There is a claim to uniqueness here such that Rortyian liberals understand the nature of reality in a way that those who remain committed to the truth of comprehensive doctrines do not. This position prejudges discourse in ways that inhibit voices having access to the public realm on their own terms. Rorty's "tolerance" not only might be construed in ways that encourage "indifference" rather than solidarity, it might also be intolerant of the differences that the liberal ironist professes to celebrate. Is this laudable but tension-riddled retrieval of cosmopolitanism all we can hope for? Drawing on the work of Bernard Lonergan and David Hollenbach in this paper's final section, I intend to sketch a middle-ground approach that retrieves Rorty's emphasis on irony without sacrificing the possibility of identifying some commonality amid difference.

Lonergan and Hollenbach on Human Rights and Solidarity

Lonergan develops a "general invariant structure" of the human good that distinguishes between three interrelated levels. The first level of the human good is constituted by the subject's sensitive and vital spontaneity, those instinctual drives and tendencies that propel individuals to procure particular goods that satisfy fundamental

---

69. Rorty, *Contingency, Irony, Solidarity*, 20.

70. Rorty, *Philosophy and Social Hope*, 65–66.

biological needs.[71] Such predispositions include the individual's appetite for self-preservation as well as her "spontaneous intersubjectivity," the collection of pro-social emotions that ground primitive forms of cooperation.[72] Roughly correlative with what Catholic social thought regards as the human person's natural sociality, these spontaneous feelings of "belonging together" supply the groundwork for primitive and all subsequent variations of community. These sensitive and vital spontaneities supply a "coincidental manifold" that is subject to a higher integration through the individual's distinctively human capacities for understanding, reflection, deliberation, and choice.[73]

At the second level of the human good, the focus shifts from the isolated satisfaction of particular needs to the "good of order," the variety of social practices and institutions that set the conditions of possibility for the recurring realization and distribution of particular goods.[74] According to Lonergan, the ongoing development of technological innovations, economic schemes, legal systems, and political institutions constitutive of civil community or society are paradigmatic examples of the good of order.[75]

The key to the third level of the human good lies in grasping the distinction between the social and cultural dimensions of living. Society is equivalent to a community's "way of life" or those frameworks that condition the possibility of orderly and predictable cooperation at the second level of the human good.[76] By contrast, culture

71. Bernard Lonergan, *Insight: A Study of Human Understanding*, Collected Works of Bernard Lonergan (CWL) 3, eds. Frederick E. Crowe and Robert M. Doran (Toronto: University of Toronto Press, 2005), 233, 632; and "The Role of the Catholic University in the Modern World," in *Collection*, CWL 4, eds. Frederick E. Crowe and Robert M. Doran (Toronto: University of Toronto Press, 1993), 108–109.

72. Lonergan, *Insight*, 233, 238, 240; and Lonergan, *Method in Theology* (Toronto: University of Toronto Press, 1972), 58–59.

73. Lonergan, *Insight*, 620, 622, 631–632, 640–641, 643, 648; and "Theology and Man's Future," in *A Second Collection*, CWL 13, eds. William F. Ryan and Bernard J. Tyrell (Toronto: University of Toronto Press, 1996), 144.

74. Lonergan, *Insight*, 238–240, 619–620; and *Method in Theology*, 49–50.

75. Lonergan, "The Role of the Catholic University," 109. Lonergan traces the development of technology-economy-polity in *Insight*, 232–247.

76. Bernard Lonergan, "Belief: Today's Issue," in *A Second Collection*, 91; and Bernard Lonergan, "The Absence of God in Modern Culture," in *A Second Collection*, 102.

arises as humans aim to "discover and express the appropriateness, the meaning, the significance, the value and the use of their way of life as a whole and in its parts."[77] This "complex web of meanings and values which make a way of life worth living, and a society worth belonging to" supply the criteria for assessing the relative value of any particular good and the institutional frameworks that serve their recurrent satisfaction.[78] Lonergan distinguishes between pre-reflexive forms of culture constituted by an implicit or non-objectified set of meanings and values and superstructural forms whose emergence he ties to the birth of classical culture around 500 BCE.[79]

He further distinguishes between classical and empirical notions of the cultural superstructure. Classicists maintain that there is only one set of meanings and values normative for all human beings.[80] The rise of an empirical notion of culture is roughly correlative with the post-modern affirmation of cultural and religious diversity. The emergence of historical consciousness precipitates what Lonergan calls the "contemporary crisis of meaning."[81] Diverse forms of cultural and religious exclusivism typically welcome the deconstruction of Western universalism but evade the challenges associated with an empirical notion of culture by returning to pre-modern classicism. Although Rorty's ironism takes seriously the relativization that marks the starting-point of the contemporary crisis, he tends to equate the search for transcultural norms with their classicist expression. From this perspective, the search for cross-cultural norms is fundamentally incompatible with historical consciousness. Rorty's effort to build a consensus by appealing to pragmatic grounds is commendable but, in my judgment, his ironism represents an inadequately critical negotiation of the contemporary crisis.

---

77. Lonergan, "The Absence of God," 102. See also Lonergan, *Insight*, 261–262.

78. Lonergan, "Belief," 90–91; and "The Role of the Catholic University," 108–109.

79. See e.g., Bernard Lonergan, *Topics in Education*, CWL 10, eds. Robert M. Doran and Frederick E. Crowe (Toronto: University of Toronto Press, 2000), 73–76, 55–57, 87; and "Dimensions of Meaning," in *Collection*, 235–237.

80. See, e.g., Bernard Lonergan, "The Transition from a Classicist Worldview to Historical Mindedness," in *A Second Collection*, 1–10.

81. See, e.g., Lonergan, "Dimensions of Meaning."

In contrast to both fundamentalism and ironism, Lonergan argues that the contemporary crisis of meaning challenges individuals to identify transcultural norms compatible with a tradition-dependent conception of rationality. Lonergan's effort to avoid both absolutism and relativism closely resembles what David Hollenbach terms "dialogic universalism,"[82] a form of "rooted cosmopolitanism"[83] that seeks some limited account of unity-amidst-diversity. Dialogic universalism combines an "embedded" conception of rationality with the recognition that human beings "share certain very general characteristics" that make dialogue and cooperation between members of distinctive traditions possible.[84] At the heart of Hollenbach's dialogic universalism is an attitude of "intellectual solidarity," a stance that transcends tolerance conceived as "peaceful coexistence" to a "positive engagement with others."[85] Intellectual solidarity refers to a set of "dispositions" that enable individuals to approach members of other traditions in a "spirit of hospitality" or with "epistemological humility" rather than with suspicion, fear, or a desire to dominate.[86] Grounded in the recognition of our shared humanity, this "receptive orientation" to otherness finds expression in the give-and-take process of mutual teaching and learning whereby "people who see the world differently" work towards a shared conception of the common good.[87]

Lonergan's approach complements Hollenbach's account of dialogic universalism and intellectual solidarity by further specifying those elements that underlie and motivate dialogical exchange. His resolution of the contemporary crisis of meaning focuses on identifying the transcendental conditions of particular "traditions" and their ongoing interaction. Lonergan correlates these presuppositions with

---

82. Hollenbach, *The Global Face of Public Faith*, 10–12; and David Hollenbach, *The Common Good and Christian Ethics* (Cambridge: Cambridge University Press, 2002), 152–153.

83. See Kwame Anthony Appiah, *The Ethics of Identity* (Princeton, NJ: Princeton University Press, 2005).

84. Hollenbach, *The Common Good and Christian Ethics*, 153.

85. Hollenbach, *The Common Good and Christian Ethics*, 138, 154. See also Hollenbach, *The Global Face of Public Faith*, 12–13, 47–48.

86. Hollenbach, *The Common Good and Christian Ethics*, 138; and *The Global Face of Public Faith*, 45, 46–49.

87. Hollenbach, *The Common Good and Christian Ethics*, 138. See also Hollenbach, *The Global Face of Public Faith*, 46–47.

the subject's threefold desire for intelligibility, reality, and value, an orientation to self-transcendence that is the source of and norm for all social, cultural and personal development.[88] The distinction between *a posteriori* tradition-dependent norms and the subject's *a priori* basic horizon provides the basis for reinterpreting Rorty's distinction between thick and thin forms of morality. Whereas Rorty draws the thick-thin distinction along metaphysical versus post-metaphysical lines, Lonergan distinguishes between a thin, heuristic form of metaphysics and comprehensive doctrines that represent answers to the question that is the human spirit. According to Lonergan, the shift in the control of meaning from thick to thin is at least partly a function of self-appropriation, a process whereby individuals objectify, verify, and take open-eyed control of their desire for knowledge and value.[89] Self-appropriation does not yield a tradition-independent standpoint but rather a set of tradition-transcendental norms that modify the way in which individuals relate to their heritage and to others situated differently. The result is a historically conscious account of natural law that is capable of forming the focus of an "overlapping consensus" in contexts marked by cultural and religious diversity.[90]

Hollenbach and Lonergan's resolution of the contemporary crisis of meaning illuminates the connection between human dignity and human rights that is central to modern Catholic social thought. Elsewhere, I have developed a two-level account of democratic norms that distinguishes between remote and proximate elements.[91] The former refers to the subject's orientation to knowledge and value that is the transcendental source of human dignity. It also refers to the way in which the subject's capacities for self-transcendence generate moral claims that resonate with others' transcendental intending.[92] If the identification of these remote democratic norms constitutes what Hollenbach calls the "Kantian moment" in the quest for a global ethic,

---

88. See, e.g., Lonergan, *Method in Theology*, 1–25.

89. See, e.g., Lonergan, *Method in Theology*, 14.

90. I have taken the term "overlapping consensus" from John Rawls' *Political Liberalism* (New York: Columbia University Press, 2005).

91. See Nicholas Olkovich, "Rethinking the Politics-Religion Distinction," *Political Theology* 19 (2018): 227–246.

92. Hollenbach makes this argument in *The Global Face of Public Faith*, 245–247. John Haughey also makes this argument in "Responsibility for Human Rights: Contributions from Bernard Lonergan," *Theological Studies* 63 (2002): 764–785.

the subsequent effort to objectify the concrete demands of human dignity constitutes what he calls the "Aristotelian moment."[93] The articulation of human rights further thematizes Lonergan's thin or heuristic conception of the good by specifying proximate norms whose fulfillment safeguards human dignity. Human rights specify the minimum required for human development, those conditions—embodied in social practices and institutional frameworks—that support and sustain the shared search for meaning, truth, and value in freedom and dialogue. These conditions include those civil-political rights that guarantee personal and associational liberties like the right to religious freedom as well as those socio-economic rights that secure citizens' basic needs. According to Hollenbach, since this natural law account of human rights rests on "minimal metaphysical presuppositions," it remains, in principle, compatible with alternative thick conceptions of human dignity and fulfillment.[94]

Reference to the remote foundation of proximate norms in human consciousness provides a critical basis for differentiating between authentic and inauthentic forms of democratic practices and institutions. Institutions function authentically when the subject's orientation to self-transcendence guides the formation, revision, and implementation of proximate standards. When human rights theory and practice are disengaged from their source and norm in the natural law, the results are precisely those aberrations that communitarians and fundamentalists rightly reject. The proper response is not to abandon liberal democracy but to transform it by fostering self-appropriation as a foundation for democratic health.

The tension between authentic and inauthentic forms of democratic practice finds expression in contemporary debates concerning the meaning and value of the right to religious freedom. Neoliberals and Rortyian ironists tend to conceive religious liberty in primarily negative terms as an immunity that guarantees individuals' freedom from interference in matters that pertain to private perfection. Although Hollenbach affirms the importance of this negative conception of rights, he argues that it must also be understood as a "social empowerment" that enables citizens to participate in "a community of discourse that seeks to discover the truth about

---

93. Hollenbach, *The Global Face of Public Faith*, 245–248.

94. Hollenbach, *The Global Face of Public Faith*, 248–249.

how they should live together."[95] Religious freedom, in this broader sense, is not synonymous with the privatization of religion but is rather an institutional expression of a community's commitment to intellectual solidarity. Those institutional frameworks that protect civil-political rights set important conditions of possibility for what Hollenbach calls "deliberative democracy." In a deliberative democracy, all individuals—religious or non-religious—can freely influence the shape of the society in which they live, but they must also be prepared to argue in ways that respect the free and equal status of their fellow citizens.[96] This account of civil-political rights is more open to diversity and hence more consistent than neoliberal and Rortyian accounts that tend to restrict discourse *a priori.*

This position also has implications for the nature of international political discourse. Since domestic policy decisions often have international consequences in today's increasingly interdependent world, citizens must also consider the way in which their commitments can enhance or limit the dignity of members in the global community. The "globalization of citizenship" also requires efforts to construct and sustain those transnational political institutions that support the establishment of a robust global civil society.[97] The latter is essential to rectify what has been called "globalization's democratic deficit"[98] and to cultivate what Falk terms "globalization from below," a bottom-up process that encourages the participation of the marginalized in global decision-making.[99]

A similar tension marks discussion concerning the status of socio-economic rights. According to Lonergan, the neoliberal tendency to restrict the scope of rights to civil-political liberties that protect individuals from coercion truncates the human good in a manner characteristic of the "general bias of common sense." General bias arises when self-interested distortions of practical intelligence threaten culture's capacity to pass critical judgment on the character of institutional frameworks and the particular goods whose

---

95. Hollenbach, *The Common Good and Christian Ethics*, 162.

96. Hollenbach, *The Common Good and Christian Ethics*, 142–146.

97. Hollenbach, *The Common Good and Christian Ethics*, 219, 224–225.

98. See Joseph S. Nye, Jr., "Globalization's Democratic Deficit: How to Make International Institutions More Accountable," *Foreign Affairs* 80, no. 4 (2001): 2–6.

99. See Falk, "The Making of Global Citizenship," 39–50.

satisfaction they serve.[100] In contrast, Lonergan argues that economic and cultural orders are subject to a higher integration by the subject's desire for knowledge and value. "Contributive justice" requires that all individuals work to create social and economic structures that result in the equitable distribution of what John Rawls calls "all-purpose means," those "primary goods" that ensure citizens' basic needs are met.[101] Respect for human dignity thus includes the fulfillment of certain "material conditions"—the minimum requirements of "social solidarity"—that enable genuine participation in economic, political, and cultural life.[102] Since the scope of human rights is universal, the cultivation of positive forms of interdependence demands the transformation of those practices and institutions that benefit Western elites at the expense of developing nations.

This two-level account of democratic norms also agrees with Rorty that human rights discourse is a social construction whose historical emergence is linked with certain distinctively Western developments. The commitment to intellectual solidarity dictates that the cultivation of a common ethic will proceed in and through a global dialogue that attends to the particularities of other cultural and religious traditions. Although Lonergan and Hollenbach can accept the tradition-dependent and dialogical dimensions of human rights discourse, neither is willing to deny the possibility of grounding such norms through historically conscious conceptions of human nature and dignity. This posture is consistent with Rorty's claim that rhetorical persuasion, rather than force, is the most appropriate means to the global spread of human rights, although it does not preclude humanitarian intervention in cases of particularly grievous violations.[103] Although reference to the common horizon that makes cross-cultural dialogue possible does not guarantee agreement, it does provide a criterion to which conversational partners can appeal. Human rights discourse includes a rhetorical element, but it need not be limited to that.

---

100. For a discussion of general bias, the longer cycle of decline, and its reversal, see Lonergan, *Insight*, 250–268.

101. See Hollenbach's discussion of "contributive" and "distributive" justice in *The Common Good and Christian Ethics*, 194–197. See also Rawls, *Political Liberalism*, 178–181.

102. Hollenbach, *The Common Good and Christian Ethics*, 248.

103. For Hollenbach's discussion of the relationship between persuasion and humanitarian intervention, see *The Common Good and Christian Ethics*, 250–254.

Finally, by tracing the source of responsibility for human rights to the subject's inborn desire for self-transcendence, this two-level account of democratic norms can ease the tension between public justice and private perfection in Rorty's liberalism. Since fulfillment is a by-product of fidelity to one's inborn orientation, commitment to the public norms of justice is not an optional add-on to but rather a constitutive dimension of personal and communal self-realization. Education for self-appropriation is thus an essential component in efforts to foster the global common good. Nonetheless, it is clear that the commitment to intellectual and social solidarity that human nature at its best commends is one thing and fidelity to that vision is another. Like Rorty, Lonergan argues that humans are spontaneously intersubjective and that this biologically-grounded pro-sociality is typically limited to kin and other in-group members and weakened by spontaneous forms of self-regard. Both group and individual egoism occlude the individual's natural desire for knowledge and goodness and, by extension, contribute to distortions in the practice and theory of human rights.[104] Intellectual and social solidarity are therefore not solely the product of self-appropriation. Sustained authenticity requires the expansion of spontaneous intersubjectivity, the broadening of fellow-feeling and sentimentality that finds its source in love. According to Lonergan, this broadening is a function not merely of what Rorty calls sentimental education but also of what Lonergan calls religious experience.

The experience of unrestricted being-in-love is a free gift that incipiently fulfills our natural desire for knowledge and value.[105] This gift heals the distortions of human consciousness and simultaneously strengthens our capacity for authentic living.[106] Religious conversion dissolves the tension between public norms and private perfection by connecting human flourishing with horizontal communion and by grounding the latter in the subject's experience of vertical communion with the transcendent. Vertical communion relativizes and orders our terrestrial commitments and motivates the cultivation of practices and institutions that embody commitments to intellectual and social solidarity. The latter are the social expression of what Christians call social grace, the alternative to

---

104. See, e.g., Lonergan, *Insight*, 244–250.

105. Lonergan, *Method in Theology*, 105–107.

106. See, e.g., Lonergan, *Method in Theology*, 105, 106–107, 115–116, 240–242, 283–284, 289.

what the tradition has termed "social sin."[107] Just as the subject's orientation to self-transcendence is methodologically prior to all particular traditions, so too the experience of unrestricted being-in-love is methodologically prior to its interpretation.[108] This claim allows Lonergan to argue that grace may be present and operative even in the lives of those who, like Rorty, explicitly deny God's existence. Religious believers can uniquely situate the gift of that love vis-à-vis the subject's natural orientation and commend its essential role in the humanization of globalization.

Conclusion

I have argued that neither neoliberal forms of globalization nor reactionary forms of tribalism that reject globalization and the possibility of universal human rights *tout court* adequately negotiate what Lonergan calls the contemporary crisis of meaning. In his efforts to avoid both extremes, Rorty develops a post-modern form of cosmopolitanism that aims to be both more hospitable to difference and more responsive to economic injustice. Although his alternative avoids many of neoliberalism's more objectionable dimensions, it is not without its own tensions. Not only does Rorty's historicism prevent him from commending the very connection between public and private concerns essential to his liberal utopia, his pragmatic conception of the subject undermines his efforts to avoid metaphysical controversy. Drawing on the work of Hollenbach and Lonergan, I developed an alternative account of democracy and human rights that aimed to sublate many of Rorty's best insights. At the core of my alternative sits the distinction between remote and proximate democratic norms and the role that the gift of God's love plays in the authentic development of both. Lonergan's thin conception of the good and his heuristic account of redemption can supply a framework for guiding the articulation and implementation of a global common good. The development of the latter is essential to the ongoing humanization of globalization.

---

107. On the notion of "social grace," see, e.g., Robert M. Doran, *The Trinity in History: A Theology of the Divine Missions, Volume 1* (Toronto: University of Toronto Press, 2012), chapter 5.

108. Lonergan, *Method in Theology*, 11, 107, 119–120, 240–241, 278, 283.

The Dynamics of Grace in the Humanization of Globalization

Joseph Ogbonnaya (Marquette University)

"Grace is . . . the ultimate condition of possibility of the integrity of the three dialectics constitutive of historical process, and the articulation of the experience of grace thus constitutes the first set of special categories in a theology that would mediate between a cultural matrix and the significance and role of Christian faith in that matrix. It is in this way that the objectification of the dialectics constitutive of history allows for the construction of a systematic theology that would understand Christian doctrine in the light of an understanding of human history."

—ROBERT M. DORAN[1]

G lobalization cuts across disciplines and national boundaries with equally lasting impacts on the human person and societies. It makes possible the integration of economic, political, technological, cultural, social, ecological factors responsible for progress and development. Powered by advances in science and communication technology, globalization affects all aspects of human life, including making the state subservient to capitalism through the activities of the transnational corporations. Not only does commercial entrepreneurship hold the key to society, the logic of capitalism seems determined to tie human happiness as well as political, social, and cultural changes to the accumulation of capital. Yet, globalization is multifaceted and is beyond merely economic growth. As a complex process that has recorded tremendous success in its stated aims of improving living conditions by creating opportunities for

---

1. Robert M. Doran, *Theology and the Dialectics of History* (Toronto: University of Toronto Press, 1990), 90.

the exercise of human freedom (albeit limited to mere materiality) through the production of goods and services in a free-market economy, globalization raises serious moral questions of social justice that concern the human and social sciences.[2]

Theology's interest in globalization arises in response to these and other related issues: global inequality expressed in the widening gap between the rich and the poor, the preference of material goods over human beings manifest in the exploitation of migrant workers and depersonalization of migrants, the degradation of the environment through an unsustainable quest for economic growth, and the increase of global insecurity engendered both by geopolitical inequality and worldwide materialism. These and many more issues affect the dignity of the human person created in the image and likeness of God. Human beings are stewards of God's creation and ought to benefit from as well as protect the environment. Since globalization is inevitable, this paper, using the emphasis that Christian theological anthropology places on the dignity of the human person, dialogues with contemporary development discourse as it impacts the historical dynamics of progress. The aim is for theology not only to humanize globalization but to function as a liberating and revealing force. It will do so by critically assessing how the dynamics of globalization might achieve an integral development that caters to the full dimensions of human value: vital, social, cultural, personal, and religious.

The healthy interrelationship between these values allows for progress and development. Since the integral scale of values is Robert Doran's appropriation and advancement of Bernard Lonergan's scale of values, I intend to do three things: (1) present Doran's integral scale of values; (2) relate it to his notion of social grace; and (3) appraise the integral scale of values in light of an economics for a humane globalization.

Doran's Appropriation of Lonergan's Scale of Values

For Bernard Lonergan, societal development depends on the order of values that human beings choose to recognize, live by, act upon, prioritize, include, or exclude in their lives and actions. He distinguishes

---

2. Joseph Ogbonnaya, "Globalization and African Catholicism: Towards A New Era of Evangelization," *Australian eJournal of Theology* 22, no. 1 (April, 2015): 19–32, at 21.

values in a preferential order, or scale: vital, social, cultural, personal, and religious values in an ascending order.[3] However, Lonergan does not specify how the levels within the scale relate to each other. He recognizes how scales of value preference can shift through a conversion experience. In light of this possibility, in the functional specialty "Dialectic," Lonergan urges his readers to continually scrutinize their intentional responses to values and their implicit scales of preference.[4] He recognizes how the scale of values can collapse in societies headed for decline, especially for what he calls the "longer cycle of decline." However, it is still unclear how these values might unify human life and action and how they might promote societal development and transformation. In a response to this exigency, Robert Doran develops a deeper understanding of the relationship of these levels in the scale of values.

Doran appropriates Lonergan's analysis of progress and decline, as discussed in the seventh chapter of *Insight*. He calls this appropriation "the integral scale of values."[5] By this, he means the functioning of the scale of values in view of the integral dialectics of the subject, community, and culture. For him, society is composed of five basic constituents which interrelate dialectically: "intersubjective spontaneity, technological institutions, the economic system, the political order, and culture."[6] He relates the scale of values to each of the levels of consciousness, arguing that "the scale is based on the increasing degrees of self-transcendence to which one is carried or to which a community is carried in response to values at the different levels."[7] Thus, vital values are correlated to experience, social values to understanding, cultural values to judgment, personal values to deliberation, and religious values to God's gift of his love. Concretely, exercising the ministry of the suffering servant of God in history is "to work for the establishment of the integral scale of values or, what comes to the

---

3. Bernard J.F. Lonergan, *Method in Theology* (Toronto: University of Toronto Press, 1971), 31.

4. Lonergan, *Method in Theology*, 240.

5. Doran, *Theology and the Dialectics of History*, 93.

6. Doran, *Theological Foundations II: Theology and Culture* (Milwaukee, WI: Marquette University Press, 1995), 234.

7. Robert M. Doran, *What is Systematic Theology?* (Toronto: University of Toronto Press, 2005), 181.

same thing, the establishment of the appropriate relation between the social infrastructure and the cultural superstructure of society."[8]

Doran views the scale of values from "above downwards" and from "below upwards" in the concrete life of human subjects. In this relationship of mutual conditioning, Doran argues, "the higher levels condition the schemes of recurrence of the more basic levels, while problems in the effective recurrence of the more basic levels offer an occasion for, and establish the proportions to be met by, the questions that prompt the needed developments at the higher levels."[9] For example, from below upwards, vital values (e.g., health, housing, and balanced nutrition) are conditioned by social values (the requisite economic, technological, political, and judicial order). At the same time, social values equally require vital values to function properly, as it will be impossible for a social order to function without the provision of the basic necessities of life that vital values provide. Cultural values give meaning to the social order, while cultural values depend on the effective functioning of the institutions of society. Each order established in a society is the creation of meaning, a meaning that is accepted as a guide for and is unique to the community. At the same time, there cannot be cultural values without a society. While the person of integrity generates the meaning that informs the culture, the common meaning of a culture forms the human person. The human person will not form authentic meaning without the religious value of God's grace. Conversely, from above downwards, religious values create the conditions for personal value, and personal integrity creates the conditions for authentic cultural values. The integrity of a culture at both levels determines whether a social order is just or not, and a just social order determines how to distribute vital values equitably.[10]

Doran is convinced that "the scale of values determines the relations among the dialectics of the subject, culture, and community."[11] This means that the scale of values includes the constituents of the human subject, culture in both its infrastructural and superstructural elements, and the makeup of the communal relations within which human existence thrives. Accordingly, their integrity "is the

---

8. Doran, *Theological Foundations II*, 219.

9. Doran, *Theological Foundations II*, 515.

10. Doran, *Theology and the Dialectics of History*, 95–96, 178.

11. Doran, *Theology and the Dialectics of History*, 96.

key to the structure of society."[12] Vital, social, and everyday cultural values are the infrastructure of society, while the reflexive, objectifying dimension of culture is the superstructure of society. An integral scale of values establishes a new law on earth, reversing various factors that distort the constituents of community, such as when a given element of a society assumes the role of another constituent of society and comes to dominate or control that society. The infrastructure of society is constituted by the tension between spontaneous intersubjectivity ("the primordial base of human community")[13] and the technological, economic, and political institutions of society.[14] The superstructure of society is the reflexive level of culture that includes scientific, scholarly, philosophical, and theological reflections on society. Both levels of culture attend to the integrity of the community. At the everyday infrastructural level, culture integrates social values. At the superstructural level, culture reflects critically on the everyday function of culture, that is, on "the pursuit of the beautiful, the intelligible, and the true."[15] The infrastructural and the superstructural levels of culture are coordinated to recurrently guarantee progress. Culture is thus indispensable for historical process, as the endurance of its integrity determines the progress or the decline of a given society. "The transformation of culture on a global scale is the condition of the possibility of a humane infrastructural order of society," Doran writes.[16] The reverse is the case when culture ceases to play its critical role vis-à-vis the infrastructural constituents of societal values for a culture can become distorted when an element of practical intelligence, especially the economic, assumes its function. Decline sets in, and eventually, it can deteriorate to become not just "the shorter" but "the longer cycle of decline."[17] Doran paints the picture clearly:

---

12. Doran, *Theology and the Dialectics of History*, 93.

13. Doran, *Theological Foundations II*, 233.

14. Doran, *Theological Foundations II*, 248.

15. Doran, *Theological Foundations II*, 248–9.

16. Doran, *Theology and the Dialectics of History*, 502.

17. Bernard Lonergan, *Insight: A Study of Human Understanding*, Collected Works of Bernard Lonergan 3, eds. Frederick E. Crowe and Robert M. Doran (Toronto: University of Toronto Press, 2005), 251–61.

[Cultural values] retreat into the margins of society, or become the tools of economic interests. Legal and political institutions take the place of culture as the sources of the public meanings and values governing the society's way of life. And these institutions are themselves now determined by economic interests, so that the meanings and values that govern the way of the society become ultimately economic. Legal and political institutions . . . become the instruments of economic interests and distort the process of society in accord with those interests. The function of politics is twisted into an ideological defense mechanism for the interests of social groups . . . the political slips out of the infrastructure and begins to usurp more and more the functions of culture, becoming a mendacious but quite public determinant of the meanings and values informing the way of life of the society. Then the social order becomes less and less the product of people who have been educated in the pursuit of beauty, intelligibility, and truth; it is the product of a distorted aesthetic consciousness, a perverted intelligence, and an uncritical rationality. Morality and religion follow suit, retreating into the margins of society and becoming merely private concerns. As personal values are thus amputated, the good is rendered inefficacious in the structuring of the cultural and social order. And religious values are either explicitly denied and even forbidden in the public cultural domain, or they are twisted into perverse supports for the distorted culture and society, as in American civil religion.[18]

In the current, neoliberal form of globalization, the economy seems to have captured the state, and the rest of the constituents of society seemingly obey only the laws of economics to the detriment of both the infrastructure and the superstructure of society. Humanizing globalization has the potential of reversing this trend, as understood precisely in terms of the integral dialectics of the subject, culture, and community.[19]

Because of the importance of culture in the historical process, Doran deems it necessary to discern the relation between the three

---

18. Doran, *Theological Foundations II*, 249–50.

19. Doran, *Theology and the Dialectics of History*, 504.

dialectics (of community, culture, and subject) with three of the levels of value (social, cultural, and personal), both from below and from above. The relation of these three dialectics to one another he calls generally the "analogy of dialectic."[20] Specifically, the dialectic of the subject is constituted by what Doran calls "neural demands for conscious integration and psychic representation, on the one hand, and, on the other hand, the concern of dramatically patterned intentionality and imagination for dramatic artistry in world constitution and concomitant self-constitution."[21] This refers to the process of making one's life a piece of art, of one becoming an independent self, capable of originating value, affirming oneself and freeing oneself from one's mother's apron strings. The dialectic of community is constituted by a tension between spontaneous intersubjectivity and the demands of practical intelligence. Spontaneous intersubjectivity refers to the relations of family members, friends, and other forms of harmonious relationship between members of a community. Practical intelligence refers to the social order, that is, the various institutions of society designed rationally by members of a community to organize a politics, economics, and technology that ensure the recurrent provision of vital values.

The dialectic of community can be distorted if practical intelligence presumes to control spontaneous intersubjectivity. A prime example is the economic imperialism manifest in the capitalistic control of human desire, a distortion worsened when the state's political economy becomes subservient to capitalistic, multinational corporations. The dialectic can also break down when politics becomes a totalitarian control of power seeking to dominate all aspects of the societal order. Another example is the technological control of desire in postmodern societies.

The dialectic of culture—Doran's construction from his analysis of the search for direction in the movement of life (influenced by Eric Voegelin)—is constituted by cosmological and anthropological constitutive meanings.[22] The dialectic of culture can be understood from the perspective of personal value, of the interior differentiation of consciousness, to refer to how the dialectic of community influences

20. Doran, *Theological Foundations II*, 338.

21. Doran, *Theology and the Dialectics of History*, 72.

22. Doran, *Theology and the Dialectics of History*, 506.

the human subject. Cosmological insight explains order in history through the rhythms of non-human nature while anthropological meaning interprets order as world-transcendent, based often on reason and thus societal order articulated theoretically through philosophy. Cosmological constitutive meaning is often communitarian as the movement of life derives from the divine order, to society, and then to the individual. For instance, according to Eric Voegelin:

> All the early empires, Near Eastern as well as Far Eastern, understood themselves as representatives of a transcendent order, of the order of the cosmos; and some of them even understood this order as a "truth." Whether one turns to the earliest Chinese sources in the *Shû King* or to the inscriptions of Egypt, Babylonia, Assyria, or Persia, one uniformly finds the order of the empire interpreted as a representation of cosmic order in the medium of human society. The empire is a cosmic analogue, a little world reflecting the order of the great, comprehensive world. Rulership becomes the task of securing the order of society in harmony with cosmic order; the territory of the empire is an analogical representation of the world with its four quarters; the great ceremonies of the empire represent the rhythm of the cosmos; festivals and sacrifices are a cosmic liturgy, a symbolic participation of the cosmion in the cosmos; and the ruler himself represents the society, because on earth he represents the transcendent power which maintains cosmic order. . . . Not only does cosmological representation survive in the imperial symbols of the Western Middle Ages or in continuity into the China of the twentieth century; its principle is also recognizable where the truth to be represented is symbolized in an entirely different manner.[23]

Meanwhile, anthropological constitutive meaning insists on humans finding their true nature in God.[24] God is therefore the measure of all things. First appearing in the political culture of Athens,[25] the

---

23. Eric Voegelin, *The New Science of Politics: An Introduction* (Chicago: University of Chicago Press, 1952), 54, 59.

24. Voegelin, *The New Science of Politics*, 68.

25. Voegelin, *The New Science of Politics*, 77.

movement of order of anthropological truth is from the world-transcendent divine measure, to the individual, and then to the society.[26] Hence, anthropological meanings are often individualistic. Cosmological constitutive meaning correlates to psychic sensitivity while anthropological constitutive meaning correlates to intentional consciousness. For this reason, cosmological constitutive meaning or cultural symbolization emphasize experience while anthropological cultural symbolizations underscore reason. An integral constitutive cultural symbolization or meaning must combine both cosmological and anthropological constitutive meanings. As we will see, this integration is the function of grace. As Doran writes:

> Exclusively cosmological constitutive meaning betrays the fact that the distinctly intentional dimensions of human consciousness have either not yet been discovered or, having been discovered, have subsequently been forgotten. Exclusively anthropological constitutive meaning betrays the fact that the sensitive psychic dimensions of human consciousness have been relegated to oblivion as the disengagement of spirit from psyche succumbs to the hubris that instrumentalizes the capacities of cognition and decision in the service of power. Both cosmological and anthropological constitutive meaning stand in need of the soteriological higher synthesis that would integrate one with the other; and this is so because the psyche without direction from the spirit and the spirit without a base in the psyche are the two features of the constant and permanent structure of the human that stand in need of redemption.[27]

The Dynamics of Grace

The dialectics of history that Doran highlights, of which globalization is a part, is a dialectic "not of contradictories, but of contraries."[28] This means its integrity lies in preserving the tension of opposites, an integrity made possible not by either of its constituents but by a third principle. Voegelin writes, "a society must exist as an ordered

---

26. Doran, *Theology and the Dialectics of History*, 508.

27. Doran, *Theology and the Dialectics of History*, 510.

28. Doran, *Theology and the Dialectics of History*, 442.

cosmion, as a representative of cosmic order, before it can indulge in the luxury of also representing a truth of the soul."[29] In other words, the cosmological truth values of traditional societies must remain in tension with the theoretical structure of society articulated philosophically in the anthropological principle. Integrity, which can be regarded as development from above, is generated by the soteriological truth of the religious value of God's love, or grace. Thus, the integrity of the dialectic of the subject is made possible by the grace of universal willingness. The integrity of the dialectic of the community is the grace of critical culture brought about by cosmopolis. The integrity of the dialectic of culture is the soteriological principle of the "Law of the Cross."

In the dialectic of the subject, grace is the communication of the antecedent willingness to do the good that one knows is morally worthwhile.[30] Willingness here refers specifically to one's value orientation.[31] The gift of willingness is the gift of persuasion to persevere in the unrestricted, detached desire to know. The gift of willingness in its mature form is the love for God and the living of one's life as guided by this love for God.[32] This gift of universal willingness equally demands the gift of grace in the community because the relations of the components of the dialectics of community determine how well one can make one's life a work of art. The reversal of social decline also depends on the relations of these elements of society. Such a reversal depends on persons of integrity, creative minorities characterized by "the self-appropriation of intelligent, rational, and deliberative consciousness, and the consequent self-appropriation of the sensitive spontaneities of the psyche."[33] This self-appropriation is

---

29. Voegelin, *The New Science of Politics*, 162.

30. Doran, *Theology and the Dialectics of History*, 198.

31. Doran, *Theology and the Dialectics of History*, 196. Doran explains further: "The experience of grace is the experience of the gift of willingness. . . . What we are suggesting is that the communication of a willingness that is universal specifies the goal of such development. Such universal willingness is also the ground of the mentality and commitment that Lonergan calls cosmopolis. The intellectual ministry of cosmopolis is thus a function of the religious development of those engaged in it" (*Theology and the Dialectics of History*, 199).

32. Doran, *Theology and the Dialectics of History*, 201.

33. Doran, *Theology and the Dialectics of History*, 364.

the task of a cosmopolis committed to implementing the integral dialectics of community.

Again, by the integral dialectics of community, Doran means the taut balance of spontaneous intersubjectivity and practical intelligence enabled by critical culture, which itself is the work of a creative minority whose life is characterized by moral integrity under the assistance of the grace of God. As Doran writes, "the source of this integrity is supernatural. It is grace as healing a distortion, and grace as elevating a person to habitual schemes of recurrence in one's inclinations and actions, schemes beyond the capacity of unaided nature. More precisely, it is grace that heals precisely because it elevates."[34] The integrity of the dialectic is the function of culture, in both its infrastructural and superstructural forms. Cosmopolis assumes responsibility for this cultural integrity. It is a set of intellectual habits that has the responsibility of constituting and promoting the cultural values that can inform a social order alternative to totalitarian structures that dominate societies in the contemporary situation.[35] Such intellectual habits generate the cultural values "capable of promoting an integral dialectic of community on a global scale."[36] By adhering to the detached, unrestricted desire to know, the culture in question can thus overcome the omnicompetent claims of instrumental rationality that cut off questions of ultimate values and long-term theoretical solutions in preference for short-term practicality.

The transition from the anthropological principle to the soteriological principle fulfils the human yearning for the divine through the communication of God's love manifest in the Incarnation. It invites humans to imitate the self-sacrificing love of Jesus Christ on the Cross (the "Law of the Cross") in their own lives and dealings in society. The soteriological differentiation of consciousness integrates the dialectic of culture constituted by cosmological and anthropological differentiations of consciousness. A soteriological differentiation of consciousness requires a cooperation with God under the Law of the Cross in the constitution of humanity within any cultural framework.

---

34. Doran, *Theology and the Dialectics of History*, 350.

35. Doran, *Theology and the Dialectics of History*, 365.

36. Doran, *Theology and the Dialectics of History*, 366.

Social Grace

Doran's appropriation of the scale of values and its complexification as the integral scale of values suggests that social transformation is ultimately the work of God's grace in human subjects. Grace-filled individuals (the creative minority) can catalyze changes through their converted lives and affect the rest of the levels of value. The grace of God catalyzes a new world as charity imbues human societies with love, helping people to be reconciled, to forgive, and to live selflessly according to the Law of the Cross. Doran affirms:

> Briefly, the gift of God's love, that is, the gift of the Holy Spirit (religious values) is the condition of the possibility of sustained personal integrity (personal value); persons of integrity represent the condition of possibility of genuine meanings and values informing ways of living (cultural values); the pursuit of genuine cultural values is the constitutive dimension in the establishment of social structures and intersubjective habits (social values) that would render probable something approaching an equitable distribution of vital values to the human community (vital values).[37]

As opposed to social sin, which refers to the biases that obstruct the functioning of the scale of values, the integral functioning of the full scale of values is what Doran means by "social grace." Social grace is the grace that transforms the social order, primarily at the level of cultural value, as well as the communal recognition of originating value, beyond mere satisfactions to values as such. It moves grace beyond the life of the individual, to the "actual development of common meanings, in the functioning of the good of order, and in the delivery of vital goods to the entire community."[38] Social grace fills cultural value with divine love (religious value) such that it transforms social structures and makes it not only easier to distribute vital values but "make[s] it possible that human beings live in harmony and peace with one another."[39] Social grace is "in biblical terms the reign of God in human history."[40]

---

37. Doran, *Theology and the Dialectics of History*, 86.

38. Doran, *Theology and the Dialectics of History*, 89.

39. Doran, *Theology and the Dialectics of History*, 97.

40. Doran, *Theology and the Dialectics of History*, 99.

Because the integral scale of values promotes the reign of God in human history, its anthropology demands internal and spiritual healing brought about by the grace of God as well as external and physical healing that goes deep down to the psyche. So too does it demand healing for the whole community of humankind and the promotion of human integrity and virtue, itself responsible for a critical culture and a harmonious social order that secures human vital needs. The church's sacraments and worship imbue the people of God with grace for virtuous living to achieve a world-cultural community, an inclusive community characterized by love, as opposed to a post-historic imperialistic community that excludes people of other cultures. Furthermore, in light of the reign of God for which we pray to be realized on earth, Doran's notion of social grace emphasizes holistic healing and conversion to overcome the sinful biases that impede the complete liberation of the human person: individually, socially, economically, politically, morally, psychically, and religiously.

Critical Appraisal

The integral scale of values has as its goal in social grace the establishment of the Kingdom of God, a salvation that covers the entire range of human needs and overcomes those forces of evil undermining God's action in the world. It is "a call to conversion, *a challenge to change*, an invitation to realize the Reign of God, an urge to enter into the creative dynamism of God's action in the world, making all things new."[41] It presupposes Lonergan's position on the goodness of being[42] and transcendent being as the ground of all our values.[43] It appropriates and extends Lonergan's scale of values. While Lonergan's scale can be considered as merely heuristic, Doran establishes the structure of society, history, social transformation, and the possibility of a world-cultural community around the scale. The absence or distortion of the scale introduces evils that harm social, cultural, personal, and religious value. Patrick Byrne describes this deterioration:

---

41. Michael Amalados, "Mission as Prophecy," cited in Stephen B. Bevans and Roger P. Schroeder, *Constants in Context: A Theology of Mission for Today* (Maryknoll, New York: Orbis Books, 2004), 316.

42. Lonergan, *Insight*, 663.

43. Lonergan, *Method in Theology*, 103.

As with natural disasters, human evil does involve the destruction of intelligibilities. Property and human fabrications are stolen or destroyed. Intricate networks of trust and cooperation are ruined. Cultural and religious institutions once devoted to cultivating higher values are corrupted. Human beings are killed, and loving patterns of personal relations are shattered.[44]

The question remains, however: does Doran's appropriation serve as a probable structure for societal progress and development? Since Doran's position is based on Lonergan's scale of values, we might begin by asking whether Lonergan's scale is normative. Byrne understands Lonergan's scale of values by applying the *Insight* criteria for the natural hierarchy of values (physical, chemical, biological, sensitive and human) to the scale of values found in *Method in Theology* through Lonergan's "explanatory genera."[45] This explains progress through a higher viewpoint which relates lower and the higher orders in a hierarchy of values that are "scientifically, logically autonomous, serially related, hierarchically ranked, and emergent."[46] Byrne discovers the relationship of the scale of values within the natural hierarchy of values. He also understands the scale of values in an integral manner akin to Doran's analysis:

Not only does the gift of grace (unrestricted being-in-love) heal and reverse biases, it also makes it possible to incorporate the free operations of human historical citizenship into the operations of realizing the infinite goodness of God's valuation of human history. . . . Religiously converted persons recognize at least implicitly that God's love sets the conditions under which human history is to be realized. They recognize that God's meanings and symbols—as, for example, when *hesed* or *agape* become the criteria for the daily decisions of individuals about how to realize vital, social, cultural, and personal values. It involves embracing the personal values of freedom and dignity completely and without subjugation, but with the even more profound valuation as of them as gifts of unconditioned love.[47]

---

44. Patrick H. Byrne, *The Ethics of Discernment: Lonergan's Foundations for Ethics* (Toronto: University of Toronto Press, 2016), 379–380.

45. Lonergan, *Insight*, 280–283.

46. Byrne, *The Ethics of Discernment*, 392.

47. Byrne, *The Ethics of Discernment*, 399.

Even though Byrne disagrees with Doran's correlation of the scale of values to the levels of consciousness, he lauds Doran's recognition of the reciprocal form of conditioning from above and from below. Byrne's position here is clearly an advance from his earlier works on the scale of values when he appeared to have paid insufficient attention to Doran's appropriation of the scale of values and concentrated on Max Scheler and Dietrich von Hildebrand's possible influences on the development of Lonergan's scale of values instead.[48] Byrne acknowledges and agrees with his anonymous reviewer's reference to Lonergan's metaphysical structure of the scale of values in *De Redemptione* where Lonergan correlates the scale to potency, form, act, and agent.[49] This recognition seems to justify Doran's correlation of the scale of values to the five levels of human consciousness even though Lonergan had not acknowledged the fifth level by the time he wrote *Method in Theology*. Thus, I agree with Byrne that "Doran may well have hit upon the proper explanation for Lonergan's scale. His approach might even be what Lonergan had in mind."[50] With the integral scale of values confirmed, it can now be applied to the contemporary situation.

The Imperative of the Integral Scale of Values

Thomas Piketty's massively rigorous work shows that the tendency of returns on capital to exceed the rate of economic growth drives income inequality.[51] The maldistribution of wealth and the attendant extreme income inequality that benefits very few and marginalizes many others stirs discontent and undermines democratic values. Other developmental economists share Piketty's view. For instance, according to Joseph E. Stiglitz, "there is mounting concern about the increase in inequality and about the lack of opportunity, and how these twin trends are changing our economies, our democratic

---

48. See, e.g., Patrick H. Byrne, "Which Scale of Value Preference? Lonergan, Scheler, Von Hildebrand, and Doran," in *Meaning and History in Systematic Theology: Essays in Honor of Robert M. Doran, SJ*, ed. John Dadosky (Milwaukee, WI: Marquette University Press, 2009), 19–49.

49. Byrne, *The Ethics of Discernment*, 407.

50. Byrne, *The Ethics of Discernment*, 404.

51. See Thomas Piketty, *Capital in the Twenty-First Century*, trans. Arthur Goldhammer (Cambridge, MA: Harvard University Press, 2014).

politics, and our societies."[52] The ensuing poverty results squarely from globalization and, with little regard for the welfare of actual people, the imposition of the policies of the Washington Consensus on nations.

Globalization links peoples and nations together. It increases the flow of knowledge through greater communication networks and educates ordinary people in a way never before imaginable. Economically, it enhances the export of goods and services, lifting those countries with export-dependent economies out of poverty and improving the standards of living. It provides employment opportunities as well as gives people increased autonomy and a better sense of purpose. It fosters human dignity in enhancing people's capabilities. More capital means better infrastructure and other amenities, including efforts towards peaceful coexistence and greater security.

However, globalization's success is also its failure. It has thrown more people into poverty because its promised free trade is one-sided and hardly free. Developed countries apply protectionist policies for their products. Exports from developed countries are blocked by some bureaucratic policies, while the markets of developing countries are unnecessarily flooded with foreign goods. It also has not ensured stability as economies are linked, meaning that problems in one country invariably affect others. Collapsed economies harm the social order as crimes increase and insecurity abounds. It equally hurts the political system, often corrupting it. When we defend self-interest, it is important to consider not only the individual level but also the institutional level of corporations, not only the wealthy but also developed nations whose altruism does not trump their self-interest. The policy- and decision-makers of the world economy orchestrate the poverty and marginalization of many.

Attitudes to globalization are often influenced by one's attitude to inequality. On the one hand, those concerned with economic efficiency think less of social justice and instead tout market efficiency as the panacea to social progress. They advocate for an economic theory whereby the wealth of the rich trickles down unintentionally. Such economists consistently promote the limited role of governments and the belief that income redistribution devalues meaningful

---

52. Joseph E. Stiglitz, *The Price of Inequality* (New York: W.W. Norton & Company, 2013), ix.

labor. On the other hand, economists who think that markets often fail in their efficiency are concerned more with income inequalities, elevated levels of poverty, and the social consequences that these trends portend. They advocate for a larger role of the government in the economy to stem the tide of inequality. There is, therefore, an intrinsic connection between economics and politics. Economic policies depend on those making the political decisions. Another world is possible beyond globalization, especially in its economic form.

Stiglitz identified six areas for the reform of globalization: the pervasiveness of poverty, the need for foreign assistance and debt relief, the aspiration to make trade fair, the limitation to liberalization, the protection of the environment, and the transformation of the flawed system of global governance.[53] These areas symptomatic of globalization show the interdependence of not only economics and politics but the full range of values in a society that enable the recurrence of schemes for the human good. In other words, the transformation of society and the eradication of poverty require the full range of Lonergan's scale of values, as interpreted by Doran: vital, social, cultural, personal, and religious values interacting from below and from above. When the integral scale of values is neglected, the infrastructure of society—spontaneous intersubjectivity and practical intelligence—becomes distorted. When that happens, instead of mutually conditioning each other, the values that constitute the scale can foster the neglect of some values. Instead of progress, there is decline. For instance, the schemes of recurrence of events in the social order for the provision of vital values break down. Goods and services are maldistributed. The meanings and values that inform a social order do not inform and motivate it, and inefficient institutions collapse. Culture either retreats to the margins of society or becomes a tool for economic interests. Legal and political institutions become a part of the superstructure of society, support a distorted economic infrastructure, and usurp the function of culture. Individuals can lose their personal integrity and twist cultural values through dramatic, individual, group, and general biases.

The distortion of the integral scale of values is responsible for global poverty. Globalization's prioritization of economics over other

---

53. Joseph E. Stiglitz, *Making Globalization Work* (New York: W.W. Norton and Company, 2007), 13–24.

constituents of practical intelligence (like politics and technology) and its neglect of spontaneous intersubjectivity demeans the human person. It reduces the person to *homo economicus*, human goals to materiality, and human happiness to pleasure—all to be calculated by Jeremy Bentham's mathematical calculus regarding economic efficiency. Humans become rationally-construed automatons who choose goods only for pleasure. Unsurprisingly, the emphasis on the invisible hand of the market seeks to surpass public institutions and the state, becoming a law unto itself to protect self-interest. With profit as the primary motive, humans become mere statistical units fit only as consumers of goods and serve as measures of economic efficiency. As Robert Davies explains, the consequence is reflected in the "inherent dangers in the potential for inhumane application of market principles in countries and communities without the developed institutions and checks and balances needed to protect people and whole communities from the harsh and untoward effects of unfettered market capitalism."[54] Against these dangers, contemporary Protestant thought and Catholic social teaching recognize the potential positives of market productivity, such as the new possibilities for investment and employment. At the same time, while not condemning competitiveness per se, both do warn against how excessive competitiveness can erode human relationships, undermine a life of faith, and permit the poor treatment of workers.

While countries enact various policies to bridge income gaps and inequality, ameliorating global poverty arising from global inequality must be the major focus. We urgently must reform markets to ensure greater participation and implement truly fair trade with laws not skewed to benefit rich and industrialized countries. We need a market that recognizes integral human development in a way that goes beyond profit. We need a world more conscious of social justice. We need a global reform of globalizing institutions. We need a politics, economics, and technology that serve the common good, promote quality human relationships, and empower personhood and, hence, we need the assiduous implementation of the integral scale of values.

---

54. Robert Davies, "Foreword," in *Making Globalization Good*, ed. John H. Dunning (New York: Oxford University Press, 2003), vii.

CHAPTER SIX

Communitarian Solutions to the Ecological Crisis

MICHAEL NORTHCOTT, BERNARD LONERGAN, AND ROBERT DORAN IN DIALOGUE

Gerard Whelan, S.J. (Pontifical Gregorian University)

One aim of this book is to explore the interrelatedness of globalization and ecology using the analytical tools provided by both Bernard Lonergan and Robert Doran. This article contributes to this project by turning to the thought of the theologian and ecological ethicist, Michael Northcott. Northcott is widely recognized as an authority in this field. He also has the gift of synthesizing the work of a wide range of other authors before presenting his own opinion. He serves as a helpful guide for students of Lonergan's thought who wish to find a point of entry into debates on issues of globalization and ecology. Northcott specifically proposes a form of communitarian ethics and communitarian approaches to economic and political systems, to redress the ecological crisis. This article analyzes Northcott's thought and identifies both strengths and weaknesses in his argument. In a concluding section, it explores lines of possible future reflection that result from such a critical engagement with Northcott.

Part 1: Michael Northcott and the Ecological Crisis

Northcott is an English Anglican priest who was a professor of Christian Ethics and Practical Theology at the University of Edinburgh from 1989 to 2017. In 1996, he published *The Environment and Christian Ethics*, which established him as an authority figure in his field.[1] Since then, he has been a prolific publisher, expanding on themes introduced in his seminal work. Northcott is alert to how one must treat ecology in an interdisciplinary manner and does so to an impressive degree. However, he writes in a non-systematic manner. It becomes the responsibility of his interpreters to offer a systematic presentation of the main lines of his thought.

The Ecological Crisis and Its Misdiagnosis

Northcott acknowledges that any Christian theological reflection on ecology today must contend with an article published in 1967 by a professor of history at Princeton University: "The Historical Roots of Our Ecologic Crisis."[2] In this article, Lynn White locates the roots of the ecological crisis in what he describes as the "anthropocentrism" of Western culture, which assumes that "we are superior to nature, contemptuous of it, willing to use it for our slightest whim." White then suggests this anthropocentrism has its origins in Christianity, which he describes as "the most anthropocentric religion the world has seen," adding, "Christianity bears a huge burden of guilt" for the crisis.

Northcott by no means refutes all aspects of White's argument. He agrees that any adequate analysis of the ecological crisis must locate the historical roots of a cultural attitude of disrespect for the natural environment. However, he conducts his own study of these historical roots and does not find Christianity the main culprit. Rather, he identifies rationalistic and individualistic tendencies in the Enlightenment to have played this role. He agrees with a feminist author, Val Plumwood, who criticizes those who pursue a "quest for a logical, abstract and universal moral discourse of contracts and absolute forms of norms and responsibilities" which, "eschews the normal human discourses of love and care, reciprocity, emotional attachment and familial concern."[3]

Northcott next follows the same structure of argument as White. Having studied philosophical questions, he examines their economic

---

1. Michael S. Northcott, *The Environment and Christian Ethics* (Cambridge: Cambridge University Press, 1996).

2. Lynn White, "The Historical Roots of Our Ecologic Crisis," *Science* 155 (1967): 1203–1207.

3. Northcott, *The Environment and Christian Ethics*, 117. See, e.g., Val Plumwood, *Feminism and the Mastery of Nature* (New York: Routledge, 1993).

and political consequences. He notes how Enlightenment thinking interacted with the industrial revolution and helped legitimate behavior destructive of the environment. He asserts, "the rise of individualism is closely associated with the quest for material fulfilment through ecologically damaging consumerism."[4] He studies how multi-national corporations played a central role in establishing a globalized economic system. He states that the behavior of these corporations "is an important but largely unacknowledged root cause of the ecological crisis."[5] He suggests that the structure of these organizations involves the "disembedding of social systems of production and exchange from cultural, moral or ecological limits or moorings."[6]

Next, Northcott notes an irony. He acknowledges that the reality of the ecological crisis has prompted an increasing number of philosophers, social scientists, and politicians to seek to redress it. However, he suggests that most actors remain trapped within the straitjacket of Enlightenment thinking. At a philosophical level, he presents an extensive and respectful overview of debates in ecological ethics.[7] However, he concludes that most participants in these debates fall into one of the categories of Enlightenment thinking identified by Alasdair MacIntyre: utilitarian (Hume), consequentialist (Mill), and deontological approaches (Kant). Next, he studies the work of many eco-theologians and arrives at similar conclusions. He suggests that, in each case, reflection is at best inadequate and at worst self-defeating.[8]

---

4. Northcott, *The Environment and Christian Ethics*, 41.

5. Northcott, *A Moral Climate: The Ethics of Global Warming* (London: Darton, Longman, and Todd, 2007), 6. See also, 7, 15. See also Northcott, *Place, Ecology, and the Sacred* (London: Bloomsbury Publishing, 2015 (Kindle Edition)), location 1635 (references for this book are offered according to location information included in Kindle books).

6. Northcott, *The Environment and Christian Ethics*, 41–2.

7. Northcott, *The Environment and Christian Ethics*, 86–123.

8. Northcott, *The Environment and Christian Ethics*, Chapter 3 ("The Turn to Nature") and Chapter 4 ("The Flowering of Ecotheology"). In the realm of eco-theology, Northcott identifies one group of thinkers who are less reliant on Enlightenment reasoning and attempt instead to develop a "biocentric" spirituality, specifically the "Gaia hypothesis" of James Lovelock. He concludes that "this approach undermined the real differences that there are between human selves and the non-human world" (*The Environment and Christian Ethics*, 115).

Having brought his analysis of culture up to the present, North-cott attempts to provide a similar study of current issues of economics and politics as they appertain to ecology. He conducts a detailed study of debates on issues of both global warming and the reduction of biodiversity. Regarding the former, he acknowledges that in recent years "the political tide has begun to turn on global warming."[9] However, he notes that governments who accept the reality of global warming have focused exclusively on questions of limiting human-generated greenhouse gasses, without addressing broader cultural questions such as the consumerist society that produces these gases. He states, "this is a serious misreading of the nature of the ecological crisis. Global warming is the earth's judgment on the global market empire, and on the heedless consumption it fosters."[10]

When Northcott studies questions of biodiversity, he finds that governments have mobilized less on this issue than on global warming. Also, he finds that the economic exploitation of multinational corporations is pronounced, operating as they do in sectors such as forestry, the oceans, and, above all, the agro-food industry. As on other ecological issues, he finds that the ethical voices being raised against the destruction of biodiversity tend to be unduly influenced by Enlightenment thinking. Here he discusses the work of the conservation movement, as represented by organizations such as the Sierra Club in the U.S. and a multiplicity of similar organizations in Europe. He notes that these organizations call for the establishment of nature reserves from which human economic activity is excluded. He recognizes the influence of Enlightenment romantic philosophy in such policies and suggests that this retains an Enlightenment-influenced dualism between humans and nature. He points out, "a potential implication of their critique is that it is the presence of humanity that is the heart of the problem."[11] He suggests that humanity can be at the heart of a solution.

---

9. Northcott, *A Moral Climate*, 6.

10. Northcott, *A Moral Climate*, 6. See also, 7, 15.

11. Northcott, *Place, Ecology and the Sacred*, location 1273.

Communitarian Solutions to the Ecological Crisis

Northcott next proposes a set of philosophical and theological ideas he describes as "communitarian."[12] He offers no precise definition of this term, but claims that all his work can be understood as proposing a communitarian outlook. He states that a key characteristic of communitarianism is that it stresses relationality:

> The reversal of the environmental crisis . . . will only come about when we recover a deeper sense for the relationality of human life to particular ecosystems and parts of the biosphere, and where communities of a place foster those virtues of justice and compassion, of care and respect for life, human and non-human, of temperance and prudence in our appetites and desire, which characterize to this day many of those surviving indigenous communities on the frontiers of the juggernaut of modernity.[13]

Northcott identifies several authors who promote a communitarian vision, but, above all, seeks to weave together his own description. In *The Environment and Christian Ethics*, much of his reflection on this issue combines philosophical reasoning referring to biblical metaphors. Turning to the Old Testament, he notes how the covenant between God and the Chosen People included a just stewardship of the land by Israel. He notes in the letters of St. Paul a tendency to relate Christian revelation to philosophies of natural law.[14] From this basis, Northcott outlines the notion of natural law of Thomas Aquinas.[15] He also comments on an authority within his own Anglican

---

12. Northcott, *A Political Theology of Climate Change* (London: SPCK, 2013), 200, 255.

13. Northcott, *The Environment and Christian Ethics*, 123.

14. Regarding the natural-law thinking of St. Paul, Northcott states: "Through this account of divine purposiveness in created order, and of the embodied relationality which characterizes that order, we can critique the modern scientific evacuation of meaning and purposiveness, and hence of moral significance in the natural order" (Northcott, *The Environment and Christian Ethics*, 223).

15. One Thomist reviewer of *The Environment and Christian Ethics* praises Northcott's outline of the theory of natural law of Aquinas, stating "it would be difficult, again, in the space, to provide a better account" (Fergus Kerr O.P., review of *The Environment and Christian Ethics*, in *New Blackfriars* 79 (1998): 5–7).

tradition. He notes that the Anglican divine of the sixteenth century, Richard Hooker, stated, "from true religion flow all the other virtues."[16] Finally, Northcott recognizes that natural law thinking from the medieval and early modern eras must be rearticulated to speak to modern audiences. In a statement that serves as a conclusion of his work, he speaks of a central challenge for philosophers and theologians today: to conduct an "ecological repristination of natural law ethics."[17]

In *A Moral Climate: The Ethics of Global Warming*, Northcott explores one aspect of what a repristination of natural law ethics might involve. He identifies how Enlightenment ethics presupposes a "disembodied subject" and notes there is a growing group of phenomenologists, anthropologists, and even natural scientists who challenge these presuppositions by stressing a notion of "embodied cognition." He accepts that such voices are not yet mainstream in philosophy, but he expresses the hope that "It may be that climate change offers not only a decisive moment in the earth's history, but a post-industrial way of conceiving earth-human relations where the biological energy and nutrient flows of the earth and the bodies, both individual and collective, of humans are brought into a new alignment."[18]

In *A Political Theology of Climate Change*, Northcott turns to questions of legal and political philosophy. On this issue, his ideas become controversial as he engages with a German thinker with Nazi links, Carl Schmidt.[19] Schmidt draws on the German romantic tradition to describe how individuals must experience a sense of national community and shared ethnic identity—often associated with a religion—in order to participate in social institutions.[20] Schmidt urges governments

---

16. Northcott, *The Environment and Christian Ethics*, 234–235.

17. Northcott, *The Environment and Christian Ethics*, 309.

18. Northcott, *A Moral Climate: The Ethics of Global Warming*, 181.

19. Carl Schmidt, *The Concept of the Political*, trans. George D. Schwab (Chicago: University of Chicago Press, 1996 (original publication 1932)); *The Nomos of the Earth in the International Law of Jus Publicum Europaeum*, trans. G. L. Ulman (N.Y.: Telos Press, 2003 (original publication 1950)).

20. Schmidt had a strange relationship with the Nazi party. He had been a devout Catholic up until the 1920s, when he was refused an annulment for his marriage and broke with the church. He joined the Nazi party in 1933 and was quickly appointed editor of a Nazi magazine for lawyers. Soon, however, senior Nazis began to notice the stress on spiritual and religious themes in his writing

to wrest control of economic production from faceless international elites, suggesting that the common good is best served when a tensive balance between nation-states is established in the international arena with populist governments seeking the best interests of their own populations.[21] Northcott acknowledges there are differences between the thought of Schmidt and that of more left-wing political philosophers, such as Alasdair MacIntyre. However, he suggests that elements of these diverse thinkers converge in offering communitarian insights:

> MacIntyre's critique of the democratized, emotivist, liberal self is the analogy in philosophical liberalism to Schmidt's account of the dehistoricized, despatialized, and despiritualized nation in political liberalism and international relations. Both discern a conflict between the liberal account of the autonomous individual, and the familial, geographical, historical, national, and religious contexts of individuals gathered into political collectives.[22]

Finally, Northcott relates the thought of Schmidt to ecological ethics. He submits, "Climate change is the definitive border-infringing crisis; it represents a critical threat to the borders of states."[23] On this issue, he suggests that even nationalistic thinking such as that

and he was dismissed from his editorial job in 1936 and ejected from the Nazi party. He was accused of being a crypto-Catholic and placed under investigation. Only the intervention of some senior saved him from being sent to a concentration camp. After the War, Schmidt spent a year in an American internment camp. Afterwards, he refused to attend a program of de-Nazification, which effectively barred him from receiving any academic appointment in subsequent years.

21. There is a superficial resemblance between the nationalism of Schmidt and the "America first" doctrine of President Donald Trump. However, in his studies in the 1950s, Schmidt expressed admiration for the way that the USA was acting as a "moral policeman" in international affairs. He suggested that it was a practical necessity that some power exercise such a role. He drew parallels between the role that the U.S. was playing in the Cold War and the role played by the Holy See in medieval Europe. On a different point, unfortunately, the criticism Schmidt offered of financial elites included no small amount of anti-Semitism.

22. Northcott, *A Political Theology of Climate Change*, 250–251.

23. Northcott, *A Political Theology of Climate Change*, 212.

of Schmidt should accept that joint action by states is necessary to address this shared problem.

Northcott's book, *Place, Ecology, and the Sacred: The Moral Geography of Sustainable Communities*, is devoted, as its title suggests, to reflecting on the importance of a sense of place. Here, Northcott advances beyond the nationalistic reflections of Schmidt, who paid scant attention to civil society or the value of indigenous cultures. By contrast, Northcott notes how, before the invention of the nation-state, humans lived for millennia in communities "highlighting the importance of face to face relationships of education and nurture, and of small-scale communities of place, in the formation of moral agents."[24] He suggests that, today, creating small-scale communities of place will imply conducting a campaign of resistance against corporate power. He adds, "religious tradition is a potentially powerful source of such resistance."[25] He notes the broad religiosity of indigenous cultures and highlights how they often associated geographic features with heroic myths, and locations of beauty with a sense of the sacred and often with direct hierophanies of God.[26] He proposes that features of such a vision must be retrieved in culture today.

Besides such extensive philosophical and theological reflection, Northcott bravely tries to demonstrate the economic and political consequences of communitarian thinking. He refers to authors who have worked in this area, such as E. F. Schumacher, author of *Small is Beautiful*, and Jane Jacobs, author of *The Economy of Cities*.[27] He also conducts his own analysis, paying detailed attention to debates on questions of carbon emissions and biodiversity. However, most of Northcott's commentary on economic and political issues avoids technical detail.[28] Ultimately, he remains skeptical about the possibility of technological solutions and generalizes that those working in areas such as Green economics, or

---

24. Northcott, *Place, Ecology and the Sacred*, location 2045–2047.

25. Northcott, *Place, Ecology and the Sacred*, location 378–379.

26. Northcott, *Place, Ecology and the Sacred*, see location 497–501, and 986–991.

27. On E. F. Schumacher, see Northcott, *Place, Ecology and the Sacred*, locations, 1141, 2065. On Jane Jacobs, see *A Moral Climate*, 402.

28. See, Northcott, *Place, Ecology and the Sacred*, location, 2094–2098.

those employing advanced technology to address environmental problems, fall prey to technocratic thinking. Northcott offers the most technical detail in *A Moral Climate*. In a chapter entitled "Ethical Emissions," he analyzes global policies on the reduction of carbon emissions. However, he arrives at a conclusion that dismisses these efforts. He suggests that until politicians propose policies that seek to redress the underlying materialistic consumerism of culture, they will remain trapped in liberal patterns of thinking that represent "the original sin of capitalism."[29]

Northcott's economic reflections primarily concentrate on offering anecdotal examples of small-scale initiatives that provide models for a wider response to the environmental crisis in economic and political systems. He describes the positive implications for biodiversity when the government of Scotland passed laws that allowed communities of crofters in the Western Isles to buy their islands back from powerful landlords and to establish economic cooperatives. Continuing his praise of the cooperative movement, he describes a movement of small farmers in Central America called "*La Vía Campesina*," which has also achieved impressive results in fostering economic progress for the poor as well as increasing biodiversity. Elsewhere, he discusses many concrete questions of social organization, employing religious principles as sources of evaluative commentary. He addresses issues of architecture and urban planning referring to the Gothic cathedral, transport systems with reference to a notion of pilgrimage, and food production systems referring to the Eucharist.[30]

Strengths and Weaknesses of Northcott

There is little in the thought of Northcott that is so clearly based on erroneous presuppositions about knowing or being as to be called a counterposition. However, two weaknesses come close to this. First, in many places, his appeal for a communitarian and natural law ethic is based on biblical metaphors and not on philosophical warrants. Pushed to an extreme, this tendency could represent a fideism that implies a lack of confidence in what Lonergan understands as the

---

29. Northcott, *A Moral Climate*, 165.

30. Northcott, *A Moral Climate*, 153, 155.

pure desire to know that is oriented to knowing being and value.[31] A second weakness is that Northcott is so critical of modernity that his appeal for a society based on ecological virtues risks being nostalgic, incapable of being brought into dialogue with modern science, and, consequently, impractical.[32]

Many strengths are also evident in the writings of Northcott. First, he is loyal to maintaining a distinction between cultural superstructure and the infrastructure of economics, politics, and intersubjective bonds. He also recognizes the important ways changes in the former lead to changes in the latter. Second, his desire to mediate theological insights to philosophical problems anticipates Lonergan's notion of special theological categories and general theological categories. Third, Northcott is acute in his analysis of bias in Enlightenment philosophy and decline in modern culture. His observation that many ecological ethicists fail to break with Enlightenment bias is especially valuable. This can highlight the group bias at the heart of decision-making in our globalizing culture. Similarly, his comments imply a resistance to what Doran explains as the coopting of the superstructure by the infrastructure and the exaggeration of anthropological principles within culture at the expense of cosmological principles. Fourthly, Northcott's intuition about the value of communitarian and natural law ethics is a position of such importance it deserves to be advanced. He calls for an "ecological repristination of natural law philosophy." While he himself makes little progress in conducting such a task, his desire to do so anticipates the notion of

---

31. One reviewer of Northcott suggests that non-Christian readers are unlikely to find this method of argument persuasive, stating, "his argument poses the perennial question of how Christian ethics can be part of a wider public moral debate outside the Christian community, a collaboration that is needed, but for which a common ground must be found" (Anthony Egan S.J., review of *A Moral Climate: The Ethics of Global Warming*, in *Theological Studies*, 70 (2009): 491–493). Egan continues his criticism, asserting that Northcott's "method of appealing to scripture is non-scientific." He suggests that Northcott's "basically allegorical reading of Scripture offers paradigms of social criticism and moral outrage" (Egan, 492).

32. A number of Lonergan scholars have pointed to similar problems with the thought of Alasdair MacIntyre to whom Northcott often refers. See Michael P. Maxwell, "A Dialectical Encounter Between MacIntyre and Lonergan on the Thomistic Understanding of Rationality," *International Philosophical Quarterly* 33 (1993): 385–400; and Neil Ormerod, "Faith and Reason: Perspectives from MacIntyre and Lonergan," *The Heythrop Journal* 46 (2005): 11–21.

transposition found in Lonergan and Doran. Similarly, the attention paid by Northcott to questions of "embodied cognition" and the value of the symbols of place employed by indigenous cultures anticipates what Doran discusses in respecting a cosmological pole in culture, alongside an anthropological pole.

Part 2: Further Reflections on Globalization and Ecology

Based on this dialectical encounter with Northcott, I now offer general reflections on how to address issues of globalization and ecology today. These reflections can broadly be understood as an attempt to advance the position in Northcott's thought. I relate his considerations to Doran's explanation that decline today is characterized by a cultural attitude that conceives of a "post-historic man," and that, conversely, progress is represented by a "world-cultural humanity." Doran states:

> Post-historical humanity would . . . lock our psyches and imaginations and questioning spirit into ever more rigid straitjackets. . . . World-cultural humanity would entail the building of a crosscultural communitarian alternative . . . so that "one world" would be constituted . . . as a process of intercultural dialogue and mutual enrichment that enjoys the diversities and frees us to grow.[33]

Discerning Progress in Populism

In reading the communitarian reflections of Northcott, one is struck by how his work of recent years can sometimes echo the rhetoric of populist leaders. When Northcott quotes Carl Schmidt, one can hear echoes of Prime Minister Theresa May promising to "take back control" and President Donald Trump promising to "put America first."[34]

---

33. Robert M. Doran, *Theology and the Dialectics of History* (Toronto: University of Toronto Press, 1990), 37.

34. When Northcott stresses the importance of religiosity in forming communities of resistance to transnational corporate power he echoes President Erdogan of Turkey, Prime Minister Modi of India, and various countries of Eastern Europe. See Pankaj Mishra, in *The Age of Anger: A History of the Present* (London: Penguin Books (Kindle Edition), 2017).

Christopher Lasch notes that "populist and communitarian traditions are distinguishable but historically intertwined." He explains that "populism is rooted in the defense of small proprietorship, which was widely regarded, in the 18th and early 19th centuries, as the necessary basis of civic virtue." He explains that communitarianism emerged simultaneously with a conservative sociological tradition "that found the sources of social cohesion in shared assumptions so deeply ingrained in everyday life that they don't have to be articulated—in folkways, customs, prejudices, habits of the heart." He points out that "both traditions shared certain common reservations about the Enlightenment," and concludes, "if terms like populism and community figure prominently in political discourse today, it is because the ideology of the Enlightenment is visibly crumbling."[35] Another commentator, Pankaj Mishra, makes a similar point. He notes that, since the beginning of the Enlightenment, exaggerated rationalism created a kind of alter-ego in rationalism. He traces how populist movements, employing romantic reasoning and symbols, regularly emerged in industrializing Europe during the nineteenth century. Finally, Mishra suggests that the surprise of academic and media figures today at the outbreak of a wave of populism results from "a crippling historical amnesia."[36]

What conclusions might be drawn from these links for a critical realist analysis of globalization and ecology? One is that it might be profitable to identify dimensions of progress in the new populism (even though evidence of decline is more obvious). I suggest there are at least two such aspects.

A first progressive aspect of populism is a readiness to accept a radical critique of the cultural and economic consensus that has been directing globalization to date. The analysis of Northcott underlines how group bias characterizes the direction of globalization, which has contributed to the ecological crisis. Here we can recall the description of Lonergan in *Insight* about how situations characterized by group bias can be corrected: "the sentiments of the unsuccessful can be crystalized into militant force by the crusading either of a

---

35. Christopher Lasch, "Communitarianism or Populism? The Ethic of Compassion and the Ethic of Respect," *New Oxford Review* (May 1992): 5–12.

36. Pankaj Mishra, *The Age of Anger*, location 702 (quotations from this book employ location information provided by Kindle books). See also, Mishra, *The Age of Anger*, Chapter 1, "Prologue: Forgotten Conjunctures."

reformer or a revolutionary."[37] While Lonergan criticizes revolutionary approaches to correcting group bias, such as Marxism, he supports non-violent class conflict whose aim is to correct group bias.

A second dimension of progress in populism is an openness to cosmological dimensions of culture. This is especially evident in the way populists use symbolism to evoke an alternative socio-economic system in the present. One can recognize a romantic aesthetic at work when President Donald Trump has himself photographed with muscular coal miners as he passes laws to favor their industry. Similarly, one can recognize a traditionalist aesthetic at work in movies emerging from England about World War II and the heroism of figures like Winston Churchill. Mishra, a commentator from India, detects a similar use of symbolism—often stressing robust Hindu masculinity—in the political rhetoric of Prime Minister Narendra Modi.[38]

Without a doubt, critical realist thinking should proceed with caution here as some of the most biased aspects of populism—including xenophobia and racism—are associated with its use of symbolism. But when Doran calls for a world-cultural humanity, his vision includes restoring a cosmological notion of culture that exists in tension with an anthropological notion. This includes a respect for the role of symbol in culture, an issue to which rationalistic liberalism pays scant attention. Might there exist in populism the capacity for a greater use of "positional" symbols?

Transcending Dichotomies of Communitarianism and Liberal Rationalism

A second general reflection counterbalances the positive evaluation of communitarianism and populism in the previous section. Kenneth Melchin is a social-ethicist who bases his approach on Lonergan. He worries that some members of the Lonergan community in North America associate themselves too easily with certain communitarian thinkers. He suggests that Lonergan has more in common with

---

37. Bernard J.F. Lonergan, *Insight: A Study of Human Understanding*, Collected Works of Bernard Lonergan, vol. 3, eds. Frederick E. Crowe and Robert M. Doran (Toronto: University of Toronto Press, 2005), 250.

38. Mishra, *The Age of Anger*, Chapter 5, "Regaining My Religion."

liberalism than with communitarianism, as he writes in his "What Is a Democracy, Anyway? A Discussion Between Lonergan and Rawls."[39] However, a closer reading of his article implies a less provocative point: Lonergan's thought represents a "higher viewpoint" transcending the dichotomy of communitarianism and liberalism.

Melchin recalls that John Rawls is a prominent proponent of liberal ethics and identifies four main principles upon which Lonergan and Rawls can agree and upon which communitarians can be weak: pluralism, democracy, social contract, and the separation of church and state. He offers a Lonergan-based explanation of what each of these four principles should mean. He adds that debates between communitarians and liberals occur mostly in the English-speaking world but adds that they are mirrored by debates in Continental European philosophy. He suggests that the real dichotomy is between "contextualists" and "proceduralists." He explains that the former hold that "ethical values are irreducibly tradition-bound" and that the latter appeal to "reasonable procedures grounded in universal rationality whereby citizens from diverse traditions can engage in meaningful discourse about conflicting values." He acknowledges that Lonergan's thought has much in common with contextualism: "Lonergan's work contains lots of insights on the historicity and constitutive functions of meaning that resonate with the communitarians and the hermeneutic philosophers." However, he then claims that Lonergan is primarily a proceduralist: "The basic architecture of his work in *Insight* and *Method in Theology* places him squarely on the side of those who argue for universal features of human rationality that are shared by all human traditions."[40]

Melchin's study serves as a helpful warning to us in our present study. We have noted how Northcott proposes a somewhat nostalgic notion of communities of virtue and not to advance far in his project of "an ecological repristination of natural law ethics." Melchin would say this is a serious weakness not to be underestimated. Melchin

---

39. Kenneth R. Melchin, "What Is a Democracy, Anyway? A Discussion Between Lonergan and Rawls," *Lonergan Workshop* 15 (1999): 99–116.

40. Melchin, "What Is a Democracy, Anyway?," 99–100. When speaking of tensions within continental philosophy, Melchin refers to debates between hermeneutical philosophers, such as Hans-Georg Gadamer, and neo-Marxists, such as Jürgen Habermas.

insists that it is only by employing an ethics grounded in intellectual conversion that social ethics today can be successfully negotiated. He adds that intellectual conversion alerts one to the constants of authentic interiority that are held in common by all cultures.[41] He might add that when Northcott offers apparently endless examples of ecological misbehavior in some quarters and ecological best practices in other quarters, Northcott is evading an appeal to interiority as a basis for communitarian philosophy.

At one level, Melchin seems to suggest that liberal thinkers such as Rawls may be more open to the call to intellectual conversion than communitarians. However, a closer read of Melchin's article reveals that he is not, in fact, asserting this. He explains that the proceduralism of Lonergan advocates that citizens follow the transcendental precepts: be attentive, be intelligent, be reasonable, be responsible. He criticizes the proceduralism of Rawls for being conceptualist.[42] Similarly, he finds that Rawls, at least occasionally, adopts a relativist approach to truth, what Melchin describes as a "practical agnosticism."[43] In the end, the social ethics being proposed by Melchin echoes communitarianism as much as liberalism, while transcending each. He writes, "A democratic political society, dedicated to the task of facilitating collective learning on the public good, will be most fully served when citizens are collectively committed to these transcendentals, since the transcendentals are the root of the learning process itself."[44]

Communitarian Economics

My final general point emerges from the previous two. Whether one describes Lonergan as closer to communitarianism or liberalism, his economic theory—and the metaphysics of emergent probability

---

41. Melchin explains that critical realist ethics should be grounded in the metaphysics developed by Lonergan in *Insight*. The doctoral dissertation of Melchin is entitled *History, Ethics, and Emergent Probability: Bernard Lonergan's Emergent Probability and its Import for his Philosophy of History and his Ethical Foundations* (Montreal: Concordia University, 1983).

42. Melchin, "What Is a Democracy, Anyway?," 106.

43. Melchin, "What Is a Democracy, Anyway?," 109.

44. Melchin, "What Is a Democracy, Anyway?," 112.

upon which it is based—shows how the superstructure of constitutive ideas and values interact with the infrastructure of economic and political activity to produce either progress or decline. This is a "missing link" in the ecological ethics of Northcott. Relating Lonergan's economics to questions of ecology is a valuable task that warrants serious further study. For the moment, I indicate the potential of this line of inquiry through the work of two authors who relate Lonergan's economic thought to current issues.

The first is Paul St. Amour in his article, "Lonergan and Piketty on Income Inequality."[45] This article shows how a Lonergan-based analysis can help populists engage in intelligent reform in confronting a globalizing situation marred by group bias. St. Amour notes that a recently published work by Thomas Piketty has caused a stir amongst academic economists. Piketty conducts a long-term study of income inequality in capitalist economies and observes that tendencies toward extreme inequality have always been strong. He notes that a reduction of inequality occurred in the decades following World War II but suggests this may have been an anomaly and that patterns of inequality now seem to return to a long-term mean. He then recommends radical government intervention to rectify this deep-seated tendency in the capitalist system. St. Amour praises the work of Piketty, but adds that "his immense and statistically incisive work begs to be situated in a deeper theoretic context."[46] He then briefly explains the theoretical context that Lonergan provides.

Lonergan's theory of macroeconomics concentrates on how the financial sector of an economy interacts with the so-called "real economy" to produce economic growth. Lonergan then notes that the discovery of new technology can produce a wave of new economic growth. However, for this wave to occur, money must be withdrawn from other uses in the economy to provide funds for capital investment in machines and the like that employ the new technology and provide new products to consumers. Lonergan calls this a phase of "surplus expansion" in an economy. It requires that a capitalist class

---

45. Paul St. Amour, "Lonergan and Piketty on Income Inequality," Marquette University Lonergan Colloquium (Annual Meeting of the International Institute for Method in Theology), March 22, 2018, available at https://www.lonerganresource.com/pdf/lectures/Amour_-_Lonergan_and_Piketty_on_Income_Inequality.pdf.

46. St. Amour, "Lonergan and Piketty on Income Inequality," 41, 47.

of citizens exist who will inevitably gain personal profit as they accumulate and redirect funds within an economy. Lonergan adds that the government must request of the broader population a period of "belt tightening" as the economy enters such a period. Next, however, Lonergan insists that when an economy returns to a period of "basic expansion," it is important that governments increase taxes on the rich and redistribute wealth within the economy.[47]

Having outlined this theoretical background, St. Amour suggests that the analysis of Piketty reveals that governments throughout history have tended to act as if there is an almost permanent need for surplus expansion in economies. St. Amour deduces that Piketty reveals that deep-seated tendencies to group bias have persisted in capitalist economies. He concludes that populations should pressure their governments to begin a reforming process of class confrontation against such an unjust situation. However, in the end, St. Amour proposes less extreme tax-increases than Piketty. He suggests that the needed economic reform must respect that periods of surplus expansion occur in economies and that these continue to require the existence of a class of capitalists who can direct flows of finance that can assist new waves of economic growth.

The second is Paul Hoyt O'Connor in his article, "Lonergan's Economics and its Relevance to the Basque Country."[48] This author reports on a major study he is conducting on the recent economic performance of the Basque Country. He notes that, because of policies of decentralization in the Spanish constitution, the Basque government has considerable autonomy in the economic management of its region. He also notes that the Basque economy fared better than the rest of Spain during economic disruptions like the oil-crisis of the 1970s and the financial crisis of 2008. He notes the wide acknowledgement that a cause of the relative success of the Basque Country is that the government intelligently intervened to support a high-technology sector. This sector was based on small start-up firms that received

---

47. For a more comprehensive explanation of Lonergan's economic theory, see Michael Shute, *Lonergan's Discovery of the Science of Economics* (Toronto: University of Toronto Press, 2010).

48. Paul Hoyt O'Connor, "Lonergan's Economics and its Relevance to the Basque Country," *Lonergan's Anthropology Revisited: The Next Fifty Years of Vatican II*, ed. Gerard Whelan S.J. (Rome: G&B Press, 2015), 321–334.

government support in many forms. Hoyt-O'Connor hypothesizes that, unbeknownst to itself, the Basque government was implementing the kind of macroeconomic policies that Lonergan would propose. He hopes that if he can affirm this hypothesis, it may lead to an acceptance of Lonergan's theory of macroeconomics among mainstream economists.

Hoyt-O'Connor studies an opposite situation to the one studied by Piketty and St. Amour. It is one where progress has been unfolding in an economy. He does not directly study the ecological impact of economic growth in the Basque Country, but I hazard to say it has not destroyed the environment, as it is based on small-scale companies in the service industry. The analysis of Hoyt-O'Connor highlights a point we have noted as important for Northcott: that a just ordering of society requires the smooth functioning between authentic culture and authentic economic decision-making, between superstructure and infrastructure. It is worth noting that the nationalist political philosophy of the Basque Country is a communitarian one. It preserves the autonomy of a region's population that is relatively uniform both culturally and ethnically.

If Hoyt-O'Connor succeeds in establishing that the government of the Basque Country made economic decisions as Lonergan would have prescribed, might his study also shed light on the presuppositions in political culture that such decisions require? This echoes some of the insights about the ecological importance of a "sense of place" articulated by Northcott.

Conclusion

In this chapter, I considered questions of globalization and ecology by conducting a dialectical analysis of the thought of Michael Northcott that employs the heuristic categories of both Bernard Lonergan and Robert Doran. I have suggested there is much value in the thought of Northcott and his communitarian proposals, both at the levels of culture and concrete social structures, for redressing the ecological crisis. At the same time, I have suggested that Northcott's non-systematic style of interdisciplinary thinking can benefit much from being grounded in Lonergan's epistemology, metaphysics, and writing on method. I then identified three themes that warrant exploration in the light of such a dialectical reading of Northcott.

One was that there might be more progress present in current populism than most intellectuals acknowledge. This progress includes an ability to recognize the depth of decline in mainstream, liberal, culture. Might this imply that critical realists could seek to form alliances with certain thinkers of a populist tendency?[49]

The second theme follows a different direction than the first. It employs an article by Kenneth Melchin which suggests that there is a bias at work in communitarianism (and presumably populism) that may inhibit the further step toward intellectual conversion. He turns to rationalist ethicists like John Rawls as interlocutors with whom Lonergan-based social-ethicists should have greater success. He admires a "proceduralism" in liberal thought which, he believes, makes it potentially open to intellectual conversion. He suggests that such ethicists are likelier than communitarians to appreciate the value of intellectual conversion for the formation of a cultural "cosmopolis" that could mediate redemption to history. However, a closer examination of Melchin's argument reveals that he is critical also of a tendency toward conceptualism and relativism in Rawls. This leaves students of the thought of Lonergan with a perhaps familiar dilemma: a feeling of disconnection from debates—in ecology as with other themes. How then can one advance from such a splendid Lonerganian isolation?

The third theme I investigate involves exploring the relevance of Lonergan's work on economics to questions of globalization and ecology. I pursue this question out of a sense that the economic reflections of Northcott struggle to relate the "ought" of ecological ethics to the "is" of technological and economic change. Here I comment briefly on how there is a communitarian dimension to the economics of Lonergan and how he bravely tries to produce ethical precepts grounded in the objective dynamics of economic systems. I suggest that more research deserves to be done relating Lonergan's economics to the ecological issue.

In conclusion, writing to an audience friendly to Lonergan, I return to a theme Melchin raised. How can one bring a critical realist voice to bear on debates on globalization and ecology and hope

---

49. For an argument from a representative of the so-called "green conservative movement," see John Grey, *Beyond the New Right: Markets, Government, and the Common Environment* (London: Routledge, 1993.)

to win a hearing? There is a challenge here that, I suspect, many of us have to bear with often. As Richard Liddy points out, there is a "startling strangeness" to Lonergan's thought, and this can make it difficult to find a point of entry in many current debates in the humanities today.[50] However, for both Lonergan and Doran, a resistance by academics to interiorly differentiated consciousness can be an expression of the habitual moral impotence of individuals and of decline in culture. This problem introduces the question of the presence of a supernatural solution to the problem of evil and the manner in which theology involves a "praxis of meaning" where a model of authentic intellectual activity is presented. This, in turn, can help mediate God's grace to secular realms of human intellectual endeavor, catalyzing a greater willingness to employ an interiorly differentiated consciousness. I have not explored this question in this article, but look to other contributions in this book to answer it.

---

50. Richard M. Liddy, *Startling Strangeness: Reading Lonergan's* Insight (Lanham, MD: University Press of America, 2007).

Towards an Integral Ecology

CHAPTER SEVEN

Hearing and Answering
the One Cry of Earth and Poor

An Integral Ecology, Eucharistic Healing,
and the Scale of Values

Lucas Briola (Saint Vincent College)

T he intrinsic connection between the present ecological crisis
and global poverty is well-documented. Rising water levels
are gradually swallowing low-lying islands in the Pacific and
Indian oceans and swamping farmlands in places like Bangladesh and
Burma, devastating the homes and livelihoods of some of the world's
poorest populations.[1] Rapidly shifting weather patterns caused by climate change, such as the increasing occurrence of droughts, acutely
affect impoverished subsistence farmers in places like Madagascar.[2]
Mountaintop removal mining continues to poison water sources and
pollute the air in sections of Appalachia, one of the poorest regions of
the United States.[3] The list could continue; suffice it to say, the poor
most palpably experience the consequences of environmental harm.

Indeed, this volume focuses on the connections between the
redemptive responses required by the current ecological crisis and
the dark, dehumanizing underbelly of globalization. Catholic social
teaching confirms that bond, most recently in the "integral ecology"

---

1. Jeff Goodell, *The Water Will Come: Rising Seas, Sinking Cities, and the
Remaking of the Civilized World* (New York: Little, Brown and Company, 2017).

2. Celia A. Harvey et al., "Extreme Vulnerability of Smallholder Farmers to
Agricultural Risks and Climate Change in Madagascar," *Philosophical Transactions of the Royal Society B* 369, no. 1639 (2014): 20130089.

3. Erik Reece, *Lost Mountain: A Year in the Vanishing Wilderness, Radical Strip
Mining and the Devastation of Appalachia* (New York: Riverhead Books, 2006).

Pope Francis outlines in *Laudato si'*. As this volume demonstrates, however, making these connections is enormously complex. We need sustained reflection to implement the aims of *Laudato si'* in the church's life. Many essays in this collection argue that the thought of Bernard Lonergan offers considerable assistance for the task. This essay concurs, focusing on the close link between the cries of the earth and the poor in the encyclical and its consequences for enlisting ecclesial mission to serve an integral ecology. Such a link illustrates the close association Catholic social teaching makes between a humane globalization and an integral ecology.

I will proceed in four parts. First, I will briefly rehearse the history of the comprehensive approach papal teaching takes to the ecological crisis and the tensions that arise within that approach. Second, given this tension, I will present Pope Francis's emphasis on the linked cries of the earth and the poor in *Laudato si'* and the opportunities it affords. Third, I will read this feature of the encyclical through Robert Doran's development of Bernard Lonergan's "scale of values," both to systematize Pope Francis's assertion and to expand Lonergan's heuristic to incorporate a cry of the earth. Fourth, from this dialogue, I will sketch the Eucharistic dynamic of healing as a response to that interconnected cry.

Lingering Tensions within a Comprehensive Approach to the Ecological Crisis

Catholic social teaching has always taken a comprehensive approach to the ecological crisis. Celia Deane-Drummond submits, "Ecology perceived as an aspect of other social injustices perhaps marks out the distinctive contribution of CST to ecotheology."[4] The precise way popes fashioned such valuable connections in this body of reflection, however, carries tension.

Pope John Paul II considerably deepened this inclusive approach.[5] In his programmatic *Redemptor hominis*, for instance, he asserted that

---

4. Celia Deane-Drummond, "Joining in the Dance: Catholic Social Teaching and Ecology," *New Blackfriars* 93, no. 1044 (2012): 193–212, at 197. See also Donal Dorr, *Option for the Poor and for the Earth: From Leo XIII to Pope Francis*, rev. ed. (Maryknoll, NY: Orbis Books, 2016), 468.

5. See Marjorie Keenan, *From Stockholm to Johannesburg: An Historical Overview of the Concern of the Holy See for the Environment: 1972–2002* (Vatican City: Vatican Press, 2002).

environmental degradation cannot be addressed apart from other social issues, whether industrialization, war, weapons, or abortion.[6] As he came to enshrine ecological concern into his famously humanistic agenda, this comprehensive approach to the environment came under the heading, "human ecology." He wrote in *Centesimus annus*:

> In addition to the irrational destruction of the natural environment, we must also mention the more serious destruction of the *human environment*, something which is by no means receiving the attention it deserves. Although people are rightly worried—though much less than they should be—about preserving the natural habitats of the various animal species threatened with extinction, because they realize that each of these species makes its particular contribution to the balance of nature in general, too little effort is made to *safeguard the moral conditions for an authentic 'human ecology'*. Not only has God given the earth to man, who must use it with respect for the original good purpose for which it was given to him, but man too is God's gift to man. He must therefore respect the natural and moral structure with which he has been endowed.[7]

According to John Paul, those moral conditions for an authentic human ecology include a protection of family structures—"the heart of the culture of life"—and a denunciation of abortive practices and mentalities, the "culture of death" (*CA* 39). Perceiving ties between environmental concerns and threats against human life was a natural outgrowth of the pope's social approach to the ecological crisis. "Human ecology" came to express this development.[8] That shift in vocabulary proved to be an important one for evaluating John Paul II's actual execution of the comprehensive approach he sought.

A closer examination of the passage quoted above reveals a significant tension. Although the pope rues the paltry attention environmental

---

6. John Paul II, *Redemptor Hominis* [Encyclical at the Beginning of the Papal Ministry of John Paul II], March 4, 1979, §8.

7. John Paul II, *Centesimus Annus* [Encyclical on the Hundredth Anniversary of *Rerum Novarum*], May 1, 1991, §38. Emphasis original.

8. See, e.g., John Paul II, *Evangelium Vitae* [Encyclical on the Value and Inviolability of Human Life], March 25, 1991, §42; and *Pastores Gregis* [Post-Synodal Apostolic Exhortation on the Bishop, Servant of the Gospel of Jesus Christ for the Hope of the World], October 16, 2003, §70.

harm receives and insightfully continues to connect environmental concern to other social issues, this passage—particularly in John Paul's use of a phrase like "the *more serious* destruction"—implies a contrastive, if not competitive, relationship between human and natural ecologies.[9] The overriding humanistic concern in his writings suggest that this contrastive relationship justifies placing a greater importance on matters of human ecology than on matters of natural ecology in ecclesial discourse. Published two years after *Centesimus annus,* the omission of any mention of the environment in *Veritatis splendor*—despite deeming it *"necessary to reflect on the whole of the Church's moral teaching"*—only confirms this worry.[10] This contrast risks undermining the valuably integrated, catholic approach to the environment John Paul II's use of "human ecology" originally expresses.

Pope Benedict XVI adhered to this comprehensive approach, likewise employing "human ecology" to articulate it. He was considerably more circumspect in attaching any contrastive connotations to the term, however. For instance, in his only social encyclical, *Caritas in veritate,* the pope declared that *"The way humanity treats the environment influences the way it treats itself, and vice-versa"* (*CV* 51). Accordingly, Benedict continued, the church's responsibility towards creation must preserve both a human and a natural ecology: "The deterioration of nature is in fact closely connected to the culture that shapes human coexistence: *when 'human ecology' is respected within society, environmental ecology also benefits"* (*CV* 51). This tie means that the environmental crisis is deeper than mere economics; it is a moral crisis that requires a holistic conversion:

> If there is a lack of respect for the right to life and to a natural death, if human conception, gestation and birth are made artificial, if human embryos are sacrificed to research, the conscience of society ends up losing the concept of human ecology and, along with it, that of environmental ecology. . . . The book of nature is one and indivisible: it takes in not only the environment but also life, sexuality, marriage, the family, social

---

9. Dorr, *Option for the Poor and for the Earth,* 375, 474.

10. John Paul II, *Veritatis Splendor* [Encyclical on Some Fundamental Questions of the Church's Moral Teaching], August 6, 1993, §4. Emphasis original. See Sean McDonagh, *Passion for the Earth: The Christian Vocation to Promote Justice, Peace, and the Integrity of Creation* (Maryknoll, NY: Orbis Books, 1994), 135.

relations: in a word, integral human development. Our duties towards the environment are linked to our duties towards the human person, considered in himself and in relation to others. It would be wrong to uphold one set of duties while trampling on the other. Herein lies a grave contradiction in our mentality and practice today: one which demeans the person, disrupts the environment and damages society (*CV* 51).

Benedict clarified the profound, seamless interdependence between matters of human ecology and natural ecology.[11] He was consequently set to recover the valuably comprehensive approach offered in Catholic social teaching.

Nevertheless, criticisms persisted. As with John Paul II, commentators bemoaned Benedict XVI's failure to appropriately broaden Catholic social concern to the environment.[12] Some proposed that the pope never stated clearly how the two ecologies linked.[13] More problematic, however, was the continued use of the term, "human ecology," which had become freighted with contrastive connotations under John Paul II. This convention continued to allow competitive interpretations of the relationship between human and natural ecology.[14] Such interpretations subsume matters of natural

---

11. See David Cloutier, "Working with the Grammar of Creation: Benedict XVI, Wendell Berry, and the Unity of the Catholic Moral Vision," *Communio* 37 (Winter 2010): 606–633.

12. John O'Keefe, "Pope Benedict's Anthropocentrism: Is it a Deal Breaker?", *Journal of Religion & Society Supplement* 9 (2013): 85–93, at 88–89; Daniel P. Scheid, *The Cosmic Common Good: Religious Grounds for Ecological Ethics* (New York: Oxford University Press, 2016), 23–25; Jame Schaefer, "Solidarity, Subsidiarity, and Preference for the Poor: Extending Catholic Social Teaching in Response to the Climate Crisis," in *Confronting the Climate Crisis: Catholic Theological Perspectives*, ed. Jame Schaefer (Milwaukee: Marquette University Press, 2012), 409–410; and Dorr, *Option for the Poor and for the Earth*, 377, 384.

13. See, e.g., Maura A. Ryan, "A New Shade of Green? Nature, Freedom, and Sexual Difference in *Caritas in Veritate*," *Theological Studies* 71, no. 2 (June 2010): 335–349, at 345.

14. See, e.g., Liju Porathur, "Ecology Vis-à-vis Human Ecology after Pope Benedict XVI," *Journal of Dharma* 39, no. 2 (April–June 2014): 405–422, at 411, 422; and Jay W. Richards, "What Exactly Is Human Ecology?", *The Spotlight—A Monthly Digest from The Institute for Human Ecology at The Catholic University of America* (September 2017), https://ihe.catholic.edu/exactly-human-ecology/.

ecology into matters of human ecology, despite Benedict's recurrent insistence on their interdependent integrity. This possibility, too, diminishes the valuable integral approach to the environment that furnishes Catholic social teaching with its distinctive value. Only the next papacy would fully secure the seamlessness of this desired approach.

An Integral Ecology as a Response to the One Cry of the Poor and the Earth

Despite early speculation that Pope Francis would concentrate his soon-to-be-released encyclical on human ecology, in the official presentation of *Laudato si'*, Cardinal Peter Turkson explained, "Pope Francis *puts the concept of integral ecology at the center of the Encyclical* as a paradigm able to articulate the fundamental relationships of the person with God, with him/herself, with other human beings, with creation."[15] Indeed, "human ecology" plays a relatively minor role in the encyclical, appearing only five times. Four of those references are found in Chapter Four, "Integral Ecology." There, human ecology appears as simply one ecology alongside many ecologies, including environmental ecology. Kevin Irwin rightly concludes, "any separation between 'natural' ecology and 'human' ecology . . . is transcended. This approach also reflects the best of the 'both . . . and' rhetoric that marks much of the Catholic theological tradition."[16] "Integral ecology" reflects that catholic approach, a term aptly summarized by the encyclical's refrain, "everything is interconnected."[17] As a more inclusive term than either human or natural ecology, integral ecology sublates the two ecologies, precluding the privileging

---

15. Peter Turkson, "Conferenza Stampa per la presentazione della Lettera Enciclica «*Laudato si'*» del Santo Padre Francesco sulla cura della casa commune: Intervento del Card. Peter Kodwo Appiah Turkson," *Bollettino: Sala Stampa della Santa Sede*, June 18, 2015, https://press.vatican.va/content/salastampa/it/bollettino/pubblico/2015/06/18/0480/01050.html#eng. Emphasis added.

16. Kevin W. Irwin, *A Commentary on* Laudato Si': *Examining the Background, Contributions, Implementation, and Future of Pope Francis's Encyclical* (New York: Paulist Press, 2016), 117, 119.

17. Francis, *Laudato Si'* [Encyclical on Care for Our Common Home], May 24, 2015, §70, 91, 92, 117, 120, 137, 138, 142, 240.

of one over the other while still preserving the aims of both.[18] This vocabulary shift better conveys the comprehensive approach taken by Catholic social teaching than human ecology could. This advance is heavily indebted to the distinct focus Pope Francis places on the poor in *Laudato si'*. References to "poverty," "the poor," "excluded," and "vulnerable" permeate the encyclical, occurring no less than 97 times (meanwhile, "earth" appears 65 times, "creation" 66 times, and "nature" 81 times). The pope hails St. Francis of Assisi—both the papal namesake and encyclical's inspiration—as "the example par excellence" of a figure who grasps the interrelatedness of care for the earth and care for the poor (*LS* 10). Popes John Paul II and Benedict XVI unquestionably associated concern for the poor with environmental concern. What distinguishes Pope Francis's approach, however, is the hermeneutical privilege he grants the poor in scrutinizing the harm done to our common home.[19] As the encyclical's first chapter makes plain, the path towards "becoming painfully aware," the seeing that leads to truthful judging and responsible acting, courses through the perspective of the poor.[20]

---

18. As Lonergan defines sublation: "[W]hat sublates goes beyond what is sublated, introduces something new and distinct, puts everything on a new basis, yet so far from interfering with the sublated or destroying it, on the contrary needs it, includes it, preserves all its proper features and properties, and carries them forward to a fuller realization within a richer context" (*Method in Theology* (New York: Herder and Herder, 1972), 241).

19. See Rohan M. Curnow, "Which Preferential Option for the Poor? A History of the Doctrine's Bifurcation," *Modern Theology* 31, no. 1 (January 2015): 27–59. Curnow insightfully shows how the papacies of John Paul II and Benedict XVI differed in their interpretation of the "option for the poor" from the more hermeneutical interpretation liberation theologians afford it. While Curnow does not cover the papacy of Francis, Francis quite clearly falls in the latter category (see, e.g., Gerard Whelan, "*Evangelii Gaudium* as 'Contextual Theology': Helping the Church 'Mount to the Level of its Times,'" *Australian eJournal of Theology* 22, no. 1 (2015): 1–10.)

20. Pollution often leads to health hazards "especially for the poor," "the worst impact" of climate change is felt by the poor in developing countries, the poor are those who most often lack access to clean water and so "*are denied the right to a life consistent with their inalienable dignity*," and green spaces in urban settings are rarely found "in the more hidden areas where the disposable of society live" (*LS*, §20, 25, 29–30, 45, emphasis original).

For Pope Francis, as Bruno Latour rightly detects, social concern and environmental concern intersect at the *one* cry of the poor and the earth *Laudato si'* channels.[21] Exhibiting the strong influence of Leonardo Boff, who pioneered this link, Pope Francis urges that in a truly integral ecology, "we have to realize that a true ecological approach *always* becomes a social approach; it must integrate questions of justice in debates on the environment, so as to hear *both the cry of the earth and the cry of the poor*" (*LS* 49, emphasis original).[22] "Sister [earth] *cries* out to us" and "*groans* in travail" (Rom 8:22), indicating that "the earth herself, burdened and laid waste, is among the most abandoned and maltreated of our poor" (*LS* 2, emphasis added). Rapid social and environmental decline "have caused sister earth, along with all the abandoned of our world, to *cry out, pleading* that we take another course" (*LS* 53, emphasis added). The response this cry summons confirms the hermeneutical privilege it enjoys.

Pope Francis insists that this cry and the failure to answer it expose a deeper cultural malaise of disconnection and domination instantiated by the technocratic paradigm (see *LS* 101–114). "The human environment and the natural environment deteriorate together," he notes (*LS* 48). Broadening this listening to the cry of *all* who are vulnerable—including the unborn, a central preoccupation of human ecology—Pope Francis writes·

> Neglecting to monitor the harm done to nature and the environmental impact of our decisions is only the most striking sign of a disregard for the message contained in the structures of nature itself. When we fail to acknowledge as part of reality the worth of a poor person, a human embryo, a person with disabilities—to offer just a few examples—it becomes difficult to hear the cry of nature itself; everything is connected (*LS* 117, see also 120).[23]

---

21. Bruno Latour, "La grande clameur relayée par le pape François," in Laudato si': *Encyclique, édition commentée: Texte intégral, réactions et commentaires,* eds. F. Louzeau and B. Toger (Paris: Parole et silence, 2015), 222–223.

22. Francis likewise speaks of the "intimate relationship between the poor and the fragility of the planet" (§16). See also, e.g., §53, 91, 93 and the final stanza of the "Christian Prayer in Union with Creation" which Francis includes at the end of the encyclical.

23. See also Francis's 2018 homily for the World Day of the Poor, where he asserts, "The *cry of the poor*: it is the stifled cry of the unborn, of starving

To become deaf to the cries bellowing from one of these structures of nature is to become deaf to others. To dominate or exploit any of them out of a *libido dominandi* reveals a fundamental disregard for their intrinsic worth. Pope Francis extends this same logic to another dimension of human ecology, respect for human bodies, as indicative of a more general respect for the giftedness of creation (*LS* 155).[24] He also expands this cohesive vision to animals, explaining how care for, indifference to, or domination of animals indicates care for, indifference to, or domination of fellow human persons:

> Moreover, when our hearts are authentically open to universal communion, this sense of fraternity excludes nothing and no one. It follows that our indifference or cruelty towards fellow creatures of this world sooner or later affects the treatment we mete out to other human beings. We have only one heart, and the same wretchedness which leads us to mistreat an animal will not be long in showing itself in our relationships with other people. . . . Everything is related, and we human beings are united as brothers and sisters on a wonderful pilgrimage, woven together by the love God has for each of his creatures and which also unites us in fond affection with brother sun, sister moon, brother river and mother earth (*LS* 92).

Since "everything is related," the cry emerging from any of these structures determines the shape of comprehensive care outlined in *Laudato si'*. An integral ecology seamlessly concerns all the vulnerable, fragile entities that populate both human and natural ecologies, from the unborn, human bodies, the economically downtrodden, non-human animals, and the earth itself. Through this privileging of the poor and vulnerable broadly construed, Pope Francis surmounts the obstacles that frustrated the comprehensive approach to the ecological crisis Popes John Paul II and Benedict XVI both sought.[25] Francis hence unleashes the full contribution of this catholic, integral approach.

---

children, of young people more used to the explosion of bombs than happy shouts of the playground. . . ." (November 18, 2018, http://w2.vatican.va/content/francesco/en/homilies/2018/documents/papa-francesco_20181118_omelia-giornatamondiale-poveri.html).

24. See also Robert Ryan, "Pope Francis, Theology of the Body, Ecology, and Encounter," *Journal of Moral Theology* 6, Special Issue 1 (2017): 56–73.

25. Dorr, *Option for the Poor and for the Earth*, 422–423, 458, 468–469.

The pope's integral call to care is spurred by the single desperate cry of earth and poor. Without a doubt, this accent is an innovative feature of the encyclical. Despite its centrality, however, using a word like "cry" is a rhetorical, descriptive device. Since the publication of *Laudato si'*, Cardinal Turkson has coined the phrase, "preferential option for the poor and for the earth," hoping to capture the meaning of this expanded horizon.[26] This theme warrants further systematic explanation if it is to be more than sentimental exhortation. Exactly what does Pope Francis mean when he speaks of the joined cries of the earth and the poor? How does this preferential option play an integrating function for the ecology in the encyclical? Without further systematic explanation, one risks impoverishing the theme's meaning.

An Explanatory Framework—An Option for the Poor within the Integral Scale of Values

Throughout his career, Bernard Lonergan exhibited a profound, if subtle, concern for the church's redemptive efficacy in the world. Touched by two world wars, the Great Depression, the rise of Communism and Fascism, and animated by the burgeoning body of Catholic social teaching, as William Loewe writes, Lonergan "began to search for an understanding of the church's redemptive mission in the context of historical reality."[27] Lonergan hoped to develop what he called a "*summa sociologica*," "a Thomistic metaphysic of history that will throw Hegel and Marx . . . into the shade," a theology of history that could provide the requisite explanatory framework for the church's self-understanding of its mission. While Lonergan's contemporaries contented themselves with general assertions *that* the church "saved," Lonergan concerned himself with specifically *how*, in theory, the church "saved."[28] He believed this theoretical reflection

---

26. See, e.g., Peter Turkson, "*Laudato si'* from Silicon Valley to Paris," Address to Santa Clara University, November 3, 2015, https://zenit.org/articles/cardinal-turkson-addresses-santa-clara-university-on-laudato-si/.

27. William P. Loewe, Lex Crucis: *Soteriology and the Stages of Meaning* (Minneapolis, MN: Fortress Press, 2016), 313.

28. Joseph A. Komonchak, "Lonergan's Early Essays on the Redemption of History," *Lonergan Workshop* 10 (1994): 159–77, at 177.

could aid a fuller realization of Catholic social teaching.[29] Despite how highly he esteemed such a theory, however, Lonergan never actually penned a full-length *summa* on the topic. Extant only are his early unpublished manuscripts on history and scattered references to the dynamics of history in his various philosophical and theological works, mainly centered on other questions.

The work of Robert Doran largely resolves the lacuna Lonergan bequeathed, as Gerard Whelan correctly argues.[30] In his *Theology and the Dialectics of History*, Doran develops Lonergan's positions on dialectic, the scale of values, and healing and creating to sketch a theory of the "immanent intelligibility of the process of world history" and the church's role in serving what he labels the *integral* scale of values.[31] As Doran presents it, *creating* works up the scale of values.[32] Each lower level conditions the problems to be met by the emergence of higher levels, some of which are constituted by an ever-tensive yet creative dialectic between "limitation" and "transcendence." The recurring distribution of *vital values* (food, water, shelter) is secured on the level of *social values* (economies, polities, and technologies). A tension between spontaneous intersubjectivity (limitation) and practical intelligence (transcendence) characterizes social values. The need to maintain this dialectic is met through the emergence of *cultural values*, the level of meanings and values. Borrowing from Eric Voegelin, Doran proposes that this level contains a cosmological

---

29. See, e.g., Bernard J.F. Lonergan, "Lonergan's *Pantôn Anakephalaiôsis* [The Restoration of All Things]," *Method: Journal of Lonergan Studies* 9 (1991): 134–172, at 157; and "Questionnaire on Philosophy: Response," in *Philosophical and Theological Papers 1965–1980*, CWL 17, eds. Robert C. Croken and Robert M. Doran (Toronto: University of Toronto Press, 2004), 370. See also Patrick Brown, "'Aiming Excessively High and Far': The Early Lonergan and the Challenge of Theory in Catholic Social Thought," *Theological Studies* 72 (September 2011): 620–44.

30. Gerard Whelan, *Redeeming History: Social Concern in Bernard Lonergan and Robert Doran* (Rome: Gregorian & Biblical Press, 2013); and "Transformations, Personal and Social, in Bernard Lonergan and Robert Doran," *The Lonergan Review* 5, no. 1 (2014): 22–38.

31. Robert M. Doran, *Theology and the Dialectics of History* (Toronto: University of Toronto Press, 1990), 144.

32. For Lonergan's exposition of the scale of values, see *Method in Theology*, 31–32.

(limitation) and an anthropological (transcendence) pole. *Personal values* respond to the need for those cultural values to be personally appropriated or critically judged. As Doran's notion of "psychic conversion" clarifies, subjects too are constituted by a dialectic between one's unconscious neural functions (limitation) and yearnings for meaning and direction (transcendence). Finally, as the beginning of the fourth chapter of Lonergan's *Method in Theology* illustrates most powerfully, personal questions about the intelligibility, truthfulness, and good of the universe expand onto the realm of *religious values*.[33] An integral scale of values incorporates the full range of these values and safeguards the dialectical relationships that constitute it.

Nevertheless, biases, disvalue, misuses of human freedom and intelligence, and breakdowns of dialectics mar this fragile ecology. As Doran describes it, globally imperialistic market forces dominate the contemporary situation, one teetering towards a post-historic humanity.[34] The presence of decline foregrounds the dynamics of *healing* in history. According to Doran, the integrity of the scale is recovered as healing moves down the scale, from religious values downwards, since a given level cannot resolve its particular breakdowns on its own. This claim contextualizes the entrance of divine revelation into history that catalyzes the religious, moral, intellectual, and psychic conversion of the subject and so introduces a soteriological culture restorative of a balanced social dialectic.[35] As developed in Neil Ormerod's recent "experiment," the church serves this integral scale, understood descriptively as the "Kingdom of God," with a fidelity that will inevitably take the shape of the Cross, its carrier the Suffering Servant.[36] Doran's work possesses immense explanatory power for understanding the church's mission.

His transposition of the preferential option for the poor into this framework is one of his greatest achievements.[37] The scale of values,

---

33. Lonergan, *Method in Theology*, 101–104.

34. Doran, *Theology and the Dialectics of History*, 37.

35. Doran has discussed the implications of Trinitarian theology for this level in his *The Trinity in History: A Theology of the Divine Missions, Volume 1: Missions and Processions* (Toronto: University of Toronto Press, 2012).

36. Neil Ormerod, *Re-Visioning the Church: An Experiment in Systematic-Historical Ecclesiology* (Minneapolis, MN: Fortress Press, 2014), 97.

37. See Rohan Michael Curnow, *The Preferential Option for the Poor: A Short History and a Reading Based on the Thought of Bernard Lonergan* (Milwaukee, WI: Marquette University Press, 2012), 188–190, 196.

Doran submits, secures the hermeneutical privilege and inductive approach that the preferential option for the poor enjoins. The relationship of more basic levels to higher levels in the scale stands as the key insight behind this claim. Lower levels, it was noted, set the questions to be resolved by higher levels. Thus, it is the maldistribution of vital values that signals the depth of decline—whether it be corrupt social institutions, technocratic cultural assumptions, short-sighted personal decisions, and even privatized religious practices—and so determines the character of the requisite healing.[38] This framework makes the "cry" of the poor systematically intelligible. As Doran writes, concluding his treatment of the doctrine, "The voices of those who have been silenced must be released into speech."[39] His systematic undertaking amplifies the cry of the vulnerable to allow it to become all the more piercing.

Doran's allusion to "anthropological" and especially "cosmological" poles of the cultural dialectic undoubtedly offers much potential enrichment to the aims that Pope Francis outlines in *Laudato si'*.[40] One must wonder, however, if following Pope Francis in hearing the cry of the earth alongside that of the poor can grant an even more central place to caring for creation within the integral scale of values. Pope Francis's distinct hermeneutical privileging of these cries, when coupled with Doran, crystalizes the comprehensive, integral approach the encyclical outlines. I propose that the cry of the earth functions similarly to the cry of the poor in the scale of values. Stated otherwise, the "cry of the earth" indicates distortions on a level even more basic than that of vital values, distortions themselves that disrupt the equitable distribution of those basic needs.[41] Both cries condition the shape of healing needed within our common home. For the objectives of *Laudato si'*, Doran's work can convey the systematic meaning of what hearing and responding to the cries of the earth and the poor actually entail.

---

38. Doran, *Theology and the Dialectics of History*, 422–4.

39. Doran, *Theology and the Dialectics of History*, 423.

40. See Neil Ormerod and Cristina Vanin, "Ecological Conversion: What Does it Mean?," *Theological Studies* 77, no. 2: 328–352.

41. Neil Ormerod, Paul Oslington, and Robin Koning, "The Development of Catholic Social Teaching on Economics: Bernard Lonergan and Benedict XVI," *Theological Studies* 73 (2012): 391–421, at 415–416; and Patrick H. Byrne, *The Ethics of Discernment: Lonergan's Foundations for Ethics* (Toronto: University of Toronto Press, 2016), 393–400.

Responding to these Twin Cries: Redemptive Healing in an Ecological Key

Aided by the integral scale, Doran also adroitly corrects a few distortions that Marxist strains of liberation theology can feature.[42] He contends that, in hoping to respond to the maldistribution of vital values, Karl Marx collapses the scale by reducing historical process to economics, politics, and technology—social values—and so ignores the constitutive role culture plays in it.[43] Marxist theory, Doran continues, overlooks those cultural questions about human living irreducible to economics, technology, or politics and so perpetuates the very problems it hopes to resolve, namely the technocratic assumptions of general bias. In other words, Marxist thought fails to account for how healing comes "from above," how distortions on vital and social levels can only be rectified through cultural, personal, and, above all, religious transformation.

Pope Francis echoes this point in *Laudato si'*.[44] After lamenting various failed policy proposals, he confesses, "The problem is that we still lack the culture needed to confront this crisis" (*LS* 53) and so urges "a bold cultural revolution" (*LS* 114). As Mary Taylor rightly recommends, one can discern the dynamic of "healing" in our common home by starting from the final chapter of *Laudato si'*, especially if one is to avoid ideological reductions that would truncate the comprehensiveness of a truly integral ecology.[45] Within the encyclical, this final chapter offers the most extensive treatment of the religious values that generate the personal and cultural transformations that might assuage the distortions that the cries of earth and the poor portend.

Pope Francis's account of the Eucharist in the chapter is particularly noteworthy, given the redemptive dynamism it can introduce

---

42. Doran, *Theology and the Dialectics of History*, 424–39. In particular, Doran engages the thought of theologian Juan Luis Segundo here.

43. Doran, *Theology and the Dialectics of History*, 34–35, 94, 101, 105, 208–209, 359, 388–95, 410, 434, 553.

44. See Lucas Briola, "The Integral Ecology of *Laudato Si'* and a Seamless Garment: The Sartorial Usefulness of Lonergan and Doran's Turn to Culture," *The Lonergan Review* 9 (2018): 31–48.

45. Mary Taylor, "Ecology on One's Knees: Reading *Laudato Si'*," *Communio* 42, no. 4 (Winter 2015): 618–651, at 639.

in history through what Francis highlights as its educative, formative character.[46] To focus on the centrality of the Eucharist in the encyclical need not devolve into an abstract theological reductionism. Instead, since it is the cries of the earth and the poor that conditions the contours of healing in history, the healing dynamism of the Eucharist only becomes intelligible as a response to those overlapping cries. As Pope Benedict XVI once memorably exhorted, "A Eucharist which does not pass over into the concrete practice of love is intrinsically fragmented."[47] "No use," John Chrysostom preached, "if the temple is full of golden vessels but Christ himself is starving."[48] This pastoral insight likewise guides caring for our common home.

The reader will recall that, to yoke together the cries of earth and poor, Francis decried cultural malaises common to both. A gnostic disconnection from the earth below us reflected a parallel indifferent disconnection to those around us.[49] Undue exploitation of the earth (e.g., mountaintop removal) and violence against other humans and bodies uncovered a blanketing cultural logic of domination both represent. Unsurprisingly, Pope Francis highlights meanings and values alternative to these in describing the position of the Eucharist within an integral ecology. In response to a culture of disconnection, the Eucharist celebrates a profoundly relational read of reality, so "the whole cosmos gives thanks to God" (*LS* 236). As opposed to a culture of domination, the Eucharist ritualizes a sacramental worldview characterized by wonder and receptive thanksgiving, so "we are invited to embrace the world on a different plane" (*LS* 235). This

---

46. Francis discusses the Eucharist in the encyclical's concluding chapter, "Ecological *Education* and Spirituality," after a discussion of how environmental education must "instill good habits" and how certain resources might "*motivate* us to a more passionate concern for the protection of our world." He goes on to write how "the Eucharist is . . . a *source of light and motivation* for our concerns for the environment, *directing* us to be stewards of all creation" (see *LS*, §211, 216, 236).

47. Benedict XVI, *Deus Caritas Est* [Encyclical on Christian Love], December 25, 2005, §14.

48. John Chrysostom, *Commentary on Matthew*, Homily 50.3–4.

49. See Vincent Miller, "Integral Ecology Francis's Spiritual and Moral Vision of Interconnectedness," in *The Theological and Ecological Vision of Laudato Si': Everything is Connected*, ed. Vincent J. Miller (New York: Bloomsbury T&T Clark, 2017), 21–26.

vision enlivens all creation, sanctioning the irreducible "mystical meaning to be found in a leaf, in a mountain trail, in a dewdrop, in a poor person's face" (*LS* 233). Both worldviews, Francis continues, join in a sabbatical vision intent on healing fractured relationships within our common home and restoring the creatureliness of human vision (*LS* 237). These soteriological meanings and values counter those that endanger the poor and the earth.

The paradoxical disparity between these liturgically-celebrated claims and the cries that echo across our common home stimulates redemptive praxis, the healing dynamism in history.[50] Just as it can reveal its presence, the Eucharist can signal the *absence* of God's reign.[51] Proclaiming the sacramentality of creation defies the many ways humans unashamedly devastate so much of it. As Kevin Irwin adds, "The very liturgical use of what has been regarded as central bearers of divine revelation—water and food—may in fact bear the bad news that the goods of this good earth are no longer 'very good.' It is hard to sing the praises of 'brother sun and sister moon' when one's vision is clouded (literally) by urban pollution and smog."[52] In a similar manner, the profoundly relational vision instantiated by the Eucharist exposes the myriad divisions people erect among themselves and God, among each other, and among all of creation (see *LS* 66). Through such contrasts, the Eucharist supplies an alternative scheme of meaning and value able to break through and dispel the technocratic myth of "the way things are."[53]

---

50. For a case-study of this claim, see Lucas Briola, "Sustainable Communities and Eucharistic Communities: *Laudato si'*, Northern Appalachia, and Redemptive Recovery," *Journal of Moral Theology* 6, Special Issue 1 (March 2017): 22–33.

51. Mary Catherine Hilkert similarly notes how preaching can name, along with grace, "dis-grace" in the world (in *Naming Grace: Preaching and the Sacramental Imagination* (New York: Continuum, 1997), 111–12. On the liturgical interplay between absence and presence, see Louis-Marie Chauvet, *Symbol and Sacrament: A Sacramental Reinterpretation of Christian Existence* (Collegeville, MN: Liturgical Press, 1995), 159–89.

52. See Kevin W. Irwin, "Sacramentality and the Theology of Creation: A Recovered Paradigm for Sacramental Theology," *Louvain Studies* 23 (1998): 159–79, at 167–68.

53. Joseph Komonchak, "The Social Mediation of the Self," in *Foundations in Ecclesiology*, Supplementary Issue of the *Lonergan Workshop*, vol. 10 (Boston: Boston College, 1995), 118–19.

This anticipatory memory of God's will for the cosmos impels faithful service towards its realization, an obedience that inevitably takes a cruciform shape.[54]

Conclusion

Bernard Lonergan and Robert Doran hope to enrich ecclesial mission, particularly the form it takes in Catholic social teaching, through theoretical reflection. This essay confirms the worth of their endeavors. The scale of values—the fruit of this collective effort—can ground the truly catholic, integral vision promoted in *Laudato si'* and ascertain the shape of the church's care within an integral ecology. This dialogue can highlight more poignantly one of the central assertions Pope Francis makes in delineating this program, namely the intimate juncture between the cry of the earth and the cry of the poor. By amplifying these inseparable cries, the church is better suited to fulfill its single task of fostering both a *more human* globalization and an *integral* ecology.[55]

---

54. See William P. Loewe, "Towards a Responsible Contemporary Soteriology," in *Creativity and Method: Essays in Honor of Bernard Lonergan*, ed. Matthew Lamb (Milwaukee: Marquette University, 1981), 213–28.

55. I would like to thank Gerard Whelan, S.J., for first raising the question of the place of the preferential option for the poor in an integral ecology to me as well as Justin Petrovich and Catherine Petrany, for their most helpful editorial suggestions.

CHAPTER EIGHT

The Original Green Campaign

DR. HILDEGARD OF BINGEN'S *VIRIDITAS* AS COMPLEMENT TO *LAUDATO SI'*[1]

John D. Dadosky (Regis College)

"When you see aridity, make it green."

—HILDEGARD OF BINGEN[2]

"There is a mystical meaning to be found in a leaf, in a mountain trail, in a dewdrop, in a poor person's face."

—POPE FRANCIS[3]

Introduction

The recent encyclical by Pope Francis, *Laudato si'*, is a landmark in making the concerns of climate change and ecological responsibility part of the social doctrine of the Catholic Church. In a sense, it embodies the best of Franciscan and Ignatian spiritualities, both of which are part of the pope's intellectual and spiritual formation. Contemporaneous to the promulgation of the encyclical was the installation of a new art piece in a prominent setting at Loyola University of Chicago's Lakeshore campus on September 10, 2015. The title of the piece by the iconographer William Hart McNichols is *Viriditas:*

1. Reprinted with some minor editorial revisions by permission of the University of Toronto Press (https://utpjournals.press). DOI: 10.3138/tjt.2017-0226. The author is grateful to the UTP for granting permission to reprint.

2. Hildegard of Bingen, *The Letters of Hildegard of Bingen*, vol. III, trans. J.L. Baird and R.K. Ehrman (New York: Oxford University Press, 2004), 107.

3. Francis, *Laudato Si'* [Encyclical on Care for Our Common Home], May 24, 2015, §233. Subsequent references to his text in this paper will parenthetically cite the paragraph number in the document.

Finding God in All Things (see fig. 1).[4] Therein he sought to join three potential resources for a theology of creation that can address the exigencies of climate change and the ecological crises. The icon depicts St. Francis of Assisi, St. Ignatius of Loyola, and Hildegard of Bingen, along with the Christ child. The Holy Spirit hovers above the earth, and twelve green flames surround the planet, symbolizing the renewal of creation—*viriditas* (greenness), a theme close to the heart of Hildegard. McNichols's contemporary image provides the inspiration for this article—namely, to highlight an important resource for a spirituality and theology of the environment. In *Laudato si'*, the pope missed an opportunity to incorporate the thought of Hildegard of Bingen (1098–1170), the towering medieval figure, and her emphasis on the spirituality of *viriditas*, or "the greening" life force of God, which permeated her writings and music.

Of course, this was not the only missed opportunity in the encyclical. Notably absent is any reference from more recent times to *the* theological pioneer of ecological concerns, Thomas Berry.[5]

---

4. *Viriditas: Finding God in All Things* by William H. McNichols (2015). The image and description appear in John D. Dadosky, *Image to Insight: The Art of William Hart McNichols* (Albuquerque, NM: University of New Mexico Press, 2018), 150–152. Some of that description appears here, except abbreviated and with editorial changes. The image appears by permission of the artist.

5. See Thomas Berry, *The Dream of the Earth* (San Francisco: Sierra Club, 1988); *The Great Work: Our Way into the Future* (New York: Random House/Bell Towers, 1999); and Thomas Berry and Thomas Clarke, *Befriending the Earth: A Theology of Reconciliation between Humans and the Earth*, eds. Stephen Dunn and Anne Lonergan (New London, CT: Twenty-Third Publications, 1991).

The spirituality of his religious community, the Passionists, traditionally focused more narrowly on the contemplation of the death and resurrection of Christ. Berry has transposed that charism analogously to the death and resurrection of the planet.[6] But I will leave it to others more familiar with Berry's work to comment on his contributions and will focus this article on the theology of Hildegard of Bingen as complement to *Laudato si'*.

One of the most prominent women of her time, Hildegard's influence is only beginning. She *is* the original green campaign. The relevance of Hildegard is clearly discernible in her ominous warning: *"If we abuse our position to commit evil deeds, God's judgment will permit other creatures to punish us."*[7] In the face of recent unpredictable weather patterns alone, this warning should give even the most ardent climate change deniers pause—not that we are being punished by God, of course, but rather that we are beginning to experience the consequences of our short-sightedness concerning the environment.

The purpose of this article is to expound Hildegard's theology of *viriditas* with a particular emphasis on her use of it as a symbol of resurrection in the context of the divine plan of salvation. In a final section, I will highlight how these themes can address those of *Laudato si'*—both corroborating Pope Francis's call and also pointing a way forward in theology that complements and fills out his endeavor.

The Theology of *Viriditas*

Viriditas, or the theology of the "greening," is not Hildegard's invention. It emerges in isolated references in some of the church ancestors and was most likely introduced to her through the writings of Gregory the Great (540–604).[8] *Viriditas* addresses the newness and

---

6. John D. Dadosky, "The Transformation of Suffering in Paul of the Cross, Lonergan, and Buddhism," *New Blackfriars* 96, no. 1065 (September 2015): 542–563, at 562.

7. Hildegard of Bingen, *Book of Divine Works*, ed. M. Fox, trans. Robert Cunningham (Santa Fe, NM: Bear & Company, 1988), 63–64. Emphasis added.

8. Jeannette DiBernardo Jones, "A Theological Interpretation of *Viriditas* in Hildegard of Bingen and Gregory the Great," *Portfolio of the Department of Musicology and Ethnomusicology*, Boston University (January 2012): 2. References are to the .pdf version available on the author's Academia page, https://bu.academia.edu/JeannetteJones.

fecundity of creation as God's gift and also as intimately related to the theology of redemption in history. However, Hildegard integrates it, although not systematically, into her complex worldview as expressed in her theological reflections, letters, poetry, visions, and music.

Gregory's reflections on *viriditas* focus on his reading of the Book of Job, particularly when it invokes *greenness* in contrast to the desolate land: "to satisfy the waste and desolate land, and to make the ground put forth grass?" (Jb 38:27). We see the image invoked as a symbol of the renewing action of God's grace. This occurs in the context of redemptive history, where God's mercy extends through the incarnation of Jesus's promise to bring forth new life. This extends further for Gregory to the mission of the Church to bring forth fruits and to bring about the greening action of God's love within the created order.[9]

Gregory's first use of the "greening" pertains to the mission of Christ expanding the covenant to the Gentiles. The action of God principally works on inward hearts; the Lord "added to outward preaching inward inspiration; that the parched hearts of the Gentiles might become green, the closed might be opened, the empty filled, the unfruitful germinate" (§51).[10]

Next, Gregory identifies the various symbols of "green" or "green grass." Green grass can sometimes refer to the "verdure of temple glory" (§52).[11] By this, Gregory means that the grass is a symbol of the impermanence of this world, implying in an eschatological manner that a more beautiful or permanent beauty lies in the future.

Next, Gregory states that grass can be food for the devil, influenced by Job 40:20, which refers to God providing food for wild animals. Presumably, Gregory takes this to mean beasts or the lower nature and likewise associates it with the devil. I presume that today, ecotheologians would have a quite different reading of this passage.

Grass also refers to the "support for preachers" (Ps 147:8; Ps 104:14), by which he means that those devoted to God's will get what they need to sustain them in their work. Grass is also the fruit of good works and is analogous to the creation account (Gen 1:11), where the

---

9. Jones, "A Theological Interpretation of *Viriditas*," 2–3.

10. Gregory the Great, *Morals on the Book of Job*, trans. J.H. Parker (London: Oxford, 1844), 923.

11. Gregory the Great, *Morals on the Book of Job*, 924.

earth brings forth grass. This is especially pertinent for the ecological imagination. As Gregory states, "we suppose, without impropriety, the earth to have been a type of the Church, which brought forth the green grass, in that it produced, at the command of God, fruitful works of mercy" (§52).[12] Hence, the mission of the Church is to bring forth greenness in acts of mercy and God's love.

Finally, the green grass represents knowledge of the doctrine of the "eternal verdure" (greenness) (Is 35:7). The lack of this knowledge is analogous to a desert, while the message of the preachers contains the green grass, and the "bull rush" represents the receptivity in the hearts of those who listen and respond. *"Because there was no grass*: that is, because the knowledge of eternity was wanting in their hearts, and did not refresh them with the food of the verdure of inward doctrine. In this place then what else do we understand by green herbs, but the knowledge of heavenly doctrine, or works in accordance?" (§52).[13] For Gregory, the knowledge of the gospel is fertile and plants the seeds of growth amid perils, evil, and malevolent forces.

Gregory's comments then turn to the moral interpretation of greenness. By this, Gregory is now turning his attention to the Church *ad intra*, rather than to the Church *ad extra*, as he was when focusing on the "Gentiles" above. He has in mind those who have heard the Word and are members of the Church but who have not let it penetrate their hearts: "being stung with grace within, they open the ears of their heart to the words of life" (§53).[14] Therefore, their hearts are barren until the grace of God enters deeply into their hearts, and greenness sprouts forth:

> For while it grants a hearing to the word, it is overwhelmed with mystery. And it brings forth green herbs: because when watered by the grace of compunction, it not only willingly receives the words of preaching, but returns them back with abundant increase; so that it is now eager to speak what it could not hear, and that that which had become dry, even within, through not listening, feeds with its verdure as many as are hungry. Whence it is well said by the Prophet, *Send forth Thy Spirit, and they*

---

12. Gregory the Great, *Morals on the Book of Job*, 924.

13. Gregory the Great, *Morals on the Book of Job*, 924.

14. Gregory the Great, *Morals on the Book of Job*, 925.

shall be created, and Thou shall renew the face of the earth
[Ps 104:30]. For thus, thus [*sic*], the face of the earth is changed
by the virtue of renewal, when the mind which before was dry,
is watered by the coming of grace, and is, after its former barrenness, arrayed with the verdure of knowledge, as though by
grass which it had brought forth (§53).[15]

The greening refers here to the heart in one's personal transformation, which is born anew and symbolized by the fresh greenness—
an apt analogy for Pope Francis's notion of "ecological conversion"
(*LS* 217). In this article, however, I will focus on Hildegard's *viriditas*, since the theme occurs throughout her entire corpus rather than
one biblical commentary. If Gregory, adverting to biblical passages,
sowed the seeds for a theology of the *viriditas*, so to speak, then Hildegard nurtured the theology into a fecund field. For, what Gregory
teases out in one biblical commentary, Hildegard creatively develops
and integrates throughout her work. Still, Hildegard was not a systematic thinker, so we will look at some of the key passages from her
opus to illustrate what she meant by it. It will be up to contemporary
theologians to systematize her work further to meet the exigencies of
our time for an ecological theology, one that can support Pope Francis's call for an integral ecology and ecological conversion.

Hildegard and *Viriditas*

Let us look at some of the ways in which Hildegard invokes the notion
of *viriditas*. In Jeannette Jones's synopsis of Hildegard's notion of *viriditas*, she states that "*viriditas* is a complex term that encompasses
this redemptive background and a continued growing and prosper-
ing through a relationship with God."[16] *Viriditas* is the principal of
life. God imbues creation with it; people consume *viriditas* as they
consume plants for sustenance. People in turn can mediate the viridity back to the created order through the practice of the virtues.[17]
Theologically, the blessings of the Holy Spirit surround those who

---

15. Gregory the Great, *Morals on the Book of Job*, 925.

16. Jones "A Theological Interpretation of *Viriditas*," 13.

17. Hildegard of Bingen, *The Book of the Rewards of Life* (*Liber Vitae Merito-
rum*), trans. B.W. Hozeski (New York: Garland Publishing, 1994), xiii–xiv.

have faithfully carried out good works. The aroma (holiness) of their good virtues radiates: "It contained all the greenness of the herbs and flowers of both paradise and the earth, and its aroma was also full of all the greenness, just as the summer has the sweetest aroma of herbs and flowers."[18]

In contrast to Gregory, for Hildegard, *viriditas* becomes the central defining feature of God:

> Whereas it was conventional in theology to identify God through the order inherent in creation, Hildegard focuses on fruitfulness, vitality, and above all *viriditas* as attributes of the divine nature (II.1.2–3). Translators sometimes supply a range of terms to capture its meaning, which relates much more than the color green: freshness, vitality, fertility, fecundity, fruitfulness, verdure, growth. She uses the word as a metaphor of health, both physical and spiritual. Thus she understands the Word of God as a flame within the divine fire which became incarnate through the viridity of the Holy Spirit. The Word gives life to humanity by pouring into it "warmth in viridity," "just as a mother gives milk to her children" (II.1.7). Through the incarnate Word, divine viridity is seen (II.i.11). Indeed, Creation itself would not have been possible without this viridity (II.2.1).[19]

Barbara Newman summarizes succinctly: "*Viriditas*, literally 'verdure,' evokes all the resilience and vitality of nature and its source, the Holy Spirit."[20] *Viriditate*, according to the translators of Hildegard's letters, is "a totally untranslatable term." It literally means "'greenness' or 'greening' (as it is sometimes rendered)." Although this does not "render the immensity of the term for Hildegard," it refers to "the

---

18. Hildegard, *Book of the Rewards of Life*, 282.

19. Constant Mews, "Religious Thinker: 'A Frail Human Being' on Fiery Life," in *Voice of the Living Light: Hildegard of Bingen and Her World*, ed. Barbara Newman (Berkeley: University of California Press, 2008), 57–58. References are to Hildegard's *Scivias*.

20. Hildegard of Bingen, *Symphonia: A Critical Edition of the Symphonia armonie celestium revelationum* [Symphony of the Harmony of Celestial Revelations], trans. Barbara Newman (Ithaca, NY: Cornell University Press, 1988), 38–39.

very essence of life. . . . It might perhaps be best rendered as 'life-force,' for it, assuredly, has that sense in her imposing cosmological scheme of things."[21] They continue:

> This *viriditas*, this despair of translators, this "greenness" enters into the very fabric of the universe in Hildegard's cosmic scheme of things. In Hildegard's usage it is a profound, immense, dynamically energized term. The world in the height of the spring season is filled with *viriditas*, God breathed the breath of *viriditas* into the inhabitants of the garden of Eden, even the smallest twig on the most insignificant tree is animated with *viriditas*, the sun brings the life of *viriditas* into the world; and (in the spiritual realm) the prelate who is filled with *taedium* (weariness) is lacking in *viriditas*, the garden where the virtues grow is imbued with *viriditas*, the neophyte must strive for *viriditas*, and the holy Virgin is the *viridissima virga*. Hildegard can even speak with aplomb of a saint as the *viriditas digiti Dei*, "the *viriditas* of the finger of God," as she does of St. Disibod (Letter 74r).[22]

The theme of viridity is demonstrated in three principal songs of Hildegard, two of which are mentioned in the previous quote. The first song ascribes *viriditas* to the Blessed Mother. The title "O Greenest Branch" (*O viridissima virga*) expresses the hyperdulia toward Mary, as virgin and Mother of God, who is connected to the Tree of Jesse. The incarnation stems from her: "For the beautiful flower sprang from you." The fragrance of that flower renews the dried-out spices so that "they all appeared in their strength and greenness."[23] The "wheat" that comes forth from Mary (a eucharistic image) grows into a tree in which birds build their nests (the Church's birth) so that a "harvest is made ready for humans," an eschatological anticipation. In this song, we see that *viriditas* permeates the Blessed Mother, as

---

21. Hildegard of Bingen, *The Letters of Hildegard of Bingen*, vol. I, trans. J.L. Baird and R.K. Ehrman (New York: Oxford University Press, 1998), 30.

22. Hildegard of Bingen, *The Letters of Hildegard of Bingen*, I:30. The poem of Disibod is discussed further below.

23. Hildegard of Bingen, *Essential Writings and Chants of a Christian Mystic— Annotated and Explained*, trans. S.A. Kujawa-Holbrook (Woodstock, VT: Skylight Paths, 2016), 83.

full of grace, from whom emerges Christ, the transformation of the dead into life, and the emergence of the Church from the wheat of the Eucharist, anticipating the eschatological harvest. This song can be placed in the larger context of medieval Christianity that tended to emphasize the Davidic line stemming from the Jesse Tree (Is II:1–2). For Christians, this image from Isaiah predicts a lineage from David's father to Jesus, hence fulfilling the messianic prophecy. The imagination used to depict this tree in medieval artwork and Hildegard's fascination with this image fit harmoniously within her broader theology of *viriditas*.[24] Psychologically, it conditions Christians perhaps more readily to associate Christ with the created order—an association more difficult for some contemporary Christian imaginations to make. Hence, while not a systematic thinker, it is clear that *viriditas* permeates the traditional areas of systematic theology for Hildegard.

The second song is titled "O greenness of God's finger" (*O viriditas digiti Dei*). This is an unusual image but suggests that God's finger, perhaps as pointing, connotes the mission of renewal brought about in the redemptive plan.[25] The song was written in honour of St. Disibod (619–670), an Irish Benedictine monk and early evangelist in Ireland. The song begins as follows: "Greenness of God's finger, through you [Disibod] God has planted a vineyard." The song suggests that the greenness of God's creative actions through Disibod is successful in planting a vineyard (a church) in Ireland.[26] Here, *viriditas* is expressed in the faithful mission of a holy man, having been sanctified or made holy by God's finger, who is productive (full of viridity) in successfully planting the Church as a vineyard.

The third song, "O Noblest Greenness" (*O nobilissima viriditas*), a responsorial song, reflects Hildegard's belief that virginity is the highest form of human living. Such a state is "rooted in the sun" that "no earthly eminence comprehends." The virgins reflect God's

---

24. Margot Fassler, "Composer and Dramatist," in *Voice of the Living Light: Hildegard of Bingen and Her World*, ed. Barbara Newman (Berkeley: University of California Press, 2008), 156–159.

25. As far as I am aware, there is no direct connection between the saying "green thumb" and the title of this poem. However, it does offer an interesting analogy of God as having a green thumb and creation being Her garden. Analogously, human beings, as created in God's image, would have green thumbs when it comes to cooperating in the redemptive plan for the created order.

26. Hildegard of Bingen, *Essential Writings and Chants*, 80.

radiance and serenity like the red dawn. They are "enfolded in the embraces of divine ministries"—perhaps a reference to the safety and fertility of the monastery.[27] Since Hildegard refers to the Virgin Mary as the "unploughed field" from whom Jesus is born, it may be that the Abbess believes virginity, especially in the vowed religious life, is particularly verdant for giving birth to Christ spiritually on earth.

In addition to her songs, the theme of *viriditas* permeates her theology. In terms of protology, it is inherent in the divine substance itself prior to creation: "virginity preexisted in the mind of God."[28] It is embedded in the fabric of creation: "In the beginning all created things were green."[29] *Viriditas* plays a role in Hildegard's interpretation of the story of Adam and Eve. Based on a vision involving greenness, she interprets the vision as the promise of Adam and Eve's restoration and the anticipation of the "New Adam" in Christ. The heavenly paradise is green and will be, for us, the restored Garden of Eden. In a visual account of one of her visions, Hildegard emphasizes this by depicting Eve as green leaf. Barbara Newman expands on this notion of *viriditas* in the vision:

> In lieu of the conventional woman emerging from Adam's side, Hildegard envisioned Eve as a bright starry cloud to which the artist—for excellent reasons—gave the aspect of a tender green leaf. *Viriditas* for Hildegard was more than a color; the fresh green that recurs so often in her visions represents the principle of all life, growth, and fertility flowing from the life-creating power of God. In Peter Dronke's words, this *viriditas* is "the greenness of a paradise which knows no Fall," "the earthly expression of the celestial sunlight."[30]

The exile of Adam and Eve from the Garden of Eden is described as an exile from the "beautiful viridity of the field, which is the blessing of God."[31] The grace will eventually be fully restored through

---

27. Hildegard, *Symphonia*, 219.

28. Mews, "Religious Thinker," 67.

29. Mews, "Religious Thinker," 67, citing Hildegard, *Book of Divine Works*, III.5.8.

30. Barbara Newman, *Sister of Wisdom: St. Hildegard's Theology of the Feminine* (Berkeley: University of California Press, 1998), 102.

31. Mews, "Religious Thinker," 61, citing *Book of Life's Merits*, I.15.

the Son of God. This coheres with the suggestion harking back to Irenaeus, but with Hildegard's own creative stamp on it, that the return of human beings to blessing is through the greenness of the New Adam.

Viriditas permeates her theological anthropology and Christology: "The relationship of the soul to the body is like that of a sap to a tree, the intellect being the viridity of its branches and leaves." Jesus is conceived "in the deep viridity" of the Mother of God.[32] In the pursuit of religious life, the Holy Spirit brings "moisture to the green fields," solidifying and fructifying one's vocation. The greenness of the "virile mind" is the basis for true commitment.

In terms of the redemption, Hildegard sees the origin of the salvific plan in the processions of the immanent Trinity where the Son proceeds from the Father "in burning viridity." The Son is incarnate like a branch from the greenness of the Virgin, who is herself representative of "women and the earth itself."[33] Jones emphasizes that greenness for Hildegard is to be understood within the divine missions as the renewal and transformation of creation in fecundity and new life.[34] While the created order for Gregory and Hildegard is implicated equally with the fall of humanity, there is hope of their renewal in the greening action of God. Hence, we can anticipate with Revelation, "a new Heaven and a new Earth." Does this suggest that the created order will somehow be taken up in the eschaton in some new way rather than simply passing away into oblivion?[35] To the extent it does suggest a sublation of the created order into the eschatological heavenly reality, this would heighten the need for human beings to be responsible stewards of creation. Working together with God, the viridity of human intelligence and responsible action can be fruitfully applied to the amelioration of the crises.

Indeed, there is an eschatological component in Hildegard's thinking about *viriditas*. She has a distinctive interpretation of Luke 23:31: "For if [human beings] use the green wood like this, what will happen when it is dry?" Hildegard's interpretation of this passage is that Jesus is the green wood, "because he caused all the greening

---

32. Mews, "Religious Thinker," 59.

33. Mews, "Religious Thinker," 60.

34. Jones, "A Theological Interpretation of *Viriditas*," 14.

35. See Mews, "Religious Thinker," 62.

power of the virtues." Conversely, the antichrist attempts to destroy the greenness of integrity, so that the just "wither away." Hildegard views this passage both eschatologically and apocalyptically. Those of the green wood and those of the dry wood will both face judgment. There is hope in overcoming the battle, as she intuits: "In these days sweet clouds will touch the Earth with a gentle breath and cause the Earth to overflow with the power of greenness and fertility."[36]

Viridity is also invoked for healing purposes. All nature has a potential healing power since it is permeated by God's *viridity* or life force.[37] In some of her specific remedies, she mentions the healing power of the emerald because it is green.[38] She also prescribes observing green grass in order to overcome the condition of clouded or watery eyes.[39] If viridity is a sign of health, then we could easily apply Hildegard's notion to our context of climate change, especially if we consider the following passage from the *Book of Divine Works*: "In the beginning all created things were green. In the middle period, flowers bloomed, but later viridity weakened. . . . My body is weakened, my children have become weak . . . it wearies me that all my limbs have become an object of derision. See, Father, I am showing you my wounds."[40] This analogy can be easily applied to the earth and the effects of climate change analogized to the body of Christ, tortured and crucified. Of course, implied in such an analogy would be the hope of resurrection. Relatedly, Hildegard also praises those who anticipate receiving the Lord's Passion. Their desire is full of *viriditas*: "Others received the Passion of Christ with so joyful a spirit that their yearning was like the greenness of early spring when the grass and trees bring joy to people with their fresh viridity. The earnest longing of others exuded a sweet fragrance like a redolent white lily, and these people received the Lord's Passion with their whole desire, and cherished it with all possible humility, seeking not to precede others in the rush of pride."[41] Perhaps such a longing for

---

36. Hildegard, *Book of Divine Works*, 244.

37. Wighard Strehlow and Gottfried Hertzka, eds., *Hildegard of Bingen's Medicine*, trans. K.A. Strehlow (Santa Fe, NM: Bear, 1987), 144.

38. Strehlow and Hertzka, *Hildegard of Bingen's Medicine*, 38.

39. Strehlow and Hertzka, *Hildegard of Bingen's Medicine*, 7.

40. Mews, "Religious Thinker," 67, citing Hildegard, *Book of Divine Works*, III.5.8.

41. Hildegard of Bingen, *Letters of Hildegard of Bingen*, III:379

the Passion of Christ is "green" because it anticipates the resurrection like an anticipation of the viridity of springtime at Easter.

In terms of a contemporary example of the kind of witness Hildegard may have had in mind, Sr. Dorothy Stang (1931–2005) of Dayton, Ohio, a vowed religious of the Sisters of Notre Dame de Namur, comes to mind. She fought tirelessly throughout her missionary career to preserve from deforestation what has been termed "the lungs of the Earth"—the Amazon rainforest. Her protests ruffled local feathers, and she was eventually shot to death by two hired gunmen on February 12, 2005. Shortly after her death, the Brazilian prime minister placed twenty thousand acres of Amazon rainforest near the region she had served under federal protection.[42] We have no way of knowing for sure what Hildegard would have made of Dorothy Stang's sacrifice, but analogously applied, the hope for the healing of the earth flows from witnesses like Sr. Dorothy. The viridity of her faithfulness, courage, and zeal bear fruit in the hope of a restoration of viridity on our planet.

In sum, Hildegard's theology of *viriditas* is ascribed ultimately to God's creative action, as when she references God's green finger. God's greenness permeates the entire created order with its life force. Not only is it generative, but it is also regenerative with the promise of restoration. Greenness symbolizes the rebirth and re-creation of human beings brought by the incarnation of Jesus through his mother (the greenest branch).

We see here the wonderful contemporary relevance of Hildegard, *the original green campaign*. As we will see in the next section, such imagery grounds a contemporary systematic theology that supports Pope Francis's call for ecological conversion and an integral ecology.

Revisiting *Laudato Si'* in View of *Viriditas*

Laudato si' is an important contribution to and development of Catholic social teaching on the environment and ecological concerns. Pope Francis offers a comprehensive response to the ecological crises facing our world. We can think of Francis's contribution in this encyclical as a contribution to orthodoxy, in that it clarifies

---

42. See "About Sister Dorothy Stang," Sisters of Notre Dame de Namur, http://www.sndohio.org/sister-dorothy.

and develops the Church's social teaching to include the environment as part of the common good, the right of everyone to that common good, and the role of all human beings to be responsible stewards of the environment. The encyclical also includes principles of ortho-praxis, in that addressing ecological concerns should prioritize the poor. It also contains specific calls, such as making clean drinking water a right for everyone and resisting monocultural vegetation that leads to deforestation.

There is no doubt that many aspects of Hildegard's *viriditas* can complement Francis's efforts in *Laudato si'*. For example, chapter three of the encyclical bemoans the loss of biodiversity and the risk of aridity that follows from the destruction of forests, coral reefs, and glaciers. For Hildegard, barrenness and aridity reflect the loss of the original *viriditas*. This theme is consonant with her emphasis on the fecundity of *viriditas* and the abundance of God's creativity that creation should reflect.

There are two further ways in which Hildegard of Bingen's *viriditas* can complement the encyclical. First, she brings an authoritative woman's voice to the issue, a voice lacking in the encyclical. In a paper at a plenary session of the Catholic Theological Society in June 2017, Anne Clifford noted that Pope Francis made scarcely any references to women as resources for addressing the ecological exigencies of our time.[43] Second, between orthodoxy and orthopraxis, there is a need for "right theory," *ortho-theoria*. Francis's argument for an integral ecology is an advance along these lines, as he provides a methodological starting point to guide theoretical approaches. However, there is another dimension to theory, not just one that can guide the interdisciplinary and dialogical approach that an integral ecology urges, but also a component of systematic theology that can support the concerns of *Laudato si'* more broadly. Hildegard's contribution of *viriditas* can assist the latter in the construction of a systematic theology—one that accounts for the intimate relationship between God and the created order as well as the restoration of that order through the "greening" action of God in cooperation with human beings. In this way, Hildegard can supply some of the *ortho-theoria* for theology in order to integrate right teaching into right practice.

---

43. Anne M. Clifford, "Pope Francis' *Laudato Si'*, On Care for Our Common Home: An Ecofeminist Response," *CTSA Proceedings* 72 (2017): 32–46.

In order to demonstrate the ortho-theory of Hildegard's contribution, in what follows I will focus on three areas in which *viriditas* can offer theological support for Pope Francis's program in *Laudato si'*: 1) His account of the gospel of creation; 2) his call for an integral ecology; and 3) his notion of ecological conversion, and with it, a spirituality to accompany the ongoing effects of the conversion.

First, Hildegard's *viriditas* supports Francis account of the gospel of creation (re-creation in Christ). Pope Francis states that "the best way to restore men and women to their rightful place, putting an end to their claim to absolute dominion over the earth, is to speak once more of the figure of a Father who creates and who alone owns the world" (*LS* 75). The relevance of Hildegard on this account is worth repeating: "If we abuse our position to commit evil deeds, God's judgment will permit other creatures to punish us."[44] In recent years, people have become dramatically aware of the unpredictability of climate change—the result of human actions on the environment. Consequently, the theology of *viriditas* brings attention back to God as the source of creation, while human beings, as created in God's image, are to be responsible participants with a privileged role in that creation. Likewise, human beings can partake in the ongoing greening. Citing Thomas Aquinas, Pope Francis prepares the groundwork for this assertion in stating that every creature continues the creative action of God.[45] Francis maintains that the best way to transcend this notion of human domination over nature is to "to speak once more of the figure of a Father who creates and who alone owns the world" (*LS* 46).

Jesus Christ is wedded to this ecological environment in a unique and multifaceted way in that all are created through him as the second person of the Trinity, and all creation find their ultimate fulfilment in him. As incarnate, the second person shares uniquely with the created reality to which the environment we seek to preserve is inextricably bound (*LS* 99–100). This is all quite consonant with Hildegard's *viriditas*. As we have seen above, the incarnation embodies the viridity of the mind of God. Hildegard would in turn emphasize the resurrection of Christ as a transformative event, bringing "new greenness" to the aridity of the spiritually dead.

---

44. Hildegard, *Book of Divine Works*, 63–64.

45. Thomas Aquinas, *ST* I, q. 104, art. 1, ad. 4.

Francis is critical of those who espouse a superficial "green rhetoric" when it does not account for the poor, as, for example, in creating green spaces in safe neighbourhoods but not in poorer ones (*LS* 49). We find here a point where Francis can mutually complement Hildegard's *viriditas*, as her medieval context in a cloistered monastery did not readily foster an emphasis on the poor, even if she did have a heart for the marginalized.

Pope Francis also speaks about the three vital relationships between God, neighbor, and the earth that have been broken. This brokenness leads to misinterpretations of the Bible that claim human beings have dominion over the created order, instead of viewing their role as one of privileged stewardship with a grave responsibility. He points to St. Francis's emphasis on the return to "the state of original innocence" (*LS* 66).[46] Hildegard's *viriditas* offers a good complement here because of its emphasis on original innocence—the return to the green garden of paradise. The latter will entail a return to the "fresh greenness" of spring, one that echoes the virility and viridity of the Creator. Moreover, this is a theme that encompasses the three vital relationships (God, human beings and the earth), since greenness originates in God and is mediated through human beings' acts of goodwill, and the fecundity of the created order reflects this viridity as originated in the mind of God. Moreover, to further interpret Pope Francis's citation from Thomas Aquinas above, human beings prolong "God's green thumb," so to speak—they continue the work of creation (*LS* 80).

Second, Hildegard's work can complement Francis's call for an integral ecology. An integral ecology presumes that everything is interconnected. The isolation of individual parts into monads will not work; there is the need to integrate our understanding into "a broader vision of reality" (*LS* 138). For Francis, an integral ecology must consider all perspectives on ecology and the environment from the natural and social sciences, including economics, culture, psychology, and social ethics. Implied in the pope's call is a vision of reality that is capable of supporting an integral ecology that will undoubtedly be a theological vision—one that needs to be integrated into a constructive or systematic theology. *Viriditas*, as God's creative

---

46. Bonaventure, *The Major Legend of Saint Francis*, VIII, 1, in *Francis of Assisi: Early Documents*, vol. 2, ed. Regis Armstrong (New York: New City Press, 2000), 586.

sustaining action of grace and fecundity, can be an important part of this theological vision. It originates in the mind of God and extends through the greening action of the mission of the incarnate Word not only to redeem humanity, but to restore all of creation from the destructive aspects of humanity—to bring about a new heaven and a new earth. In terms of systematic theology, *viriditas* extends from the immanent Trinity into protology, theological anthropology, Mariology, Christology, redemption, ecclesiology, and eschatology. It is a thread to be woven into systematic theology, one that ameliorates strictly anthropocentric views and one that supports the integral ecology of human beings' responsible relationship with the created order. In this way, it will form an ortho-theory to support the orthopraxis for environmental stewardship. Of course, *viriditas* will also form part of that orthopraxis as it can also serve as a spirituality to support such praxis. That topic will be taken up in the next paragraph.

Third, Hildegard's *viriditas* provides a guiding analogy for fostering Francis's call for ecological conversion. Ecological conversion heals those obstacles in our development that prevent us from seeing our interconnectedness with and responsible role in the environment.[47] A proper spirituality would support and accompany the actions that follow from such a conversion. Francis admits that Christian spiritualities have not always accounted for the relationship with the created order, given the dualistic tendencies to split the life of the spirit from the life of the physical world (*LS* 216). This exigency is precisely where Hildegard can contribute. It is especially fitting when we consider Pope Francis's citation of Benedict XVI, who links the growth of external deserts throughout the world with internal deserts (*LS* 217). This barrenness is analogous to how Hildegard highlights the desolate conditions that evoke a renewal through *viriditas*. Francis calls for "a profound interior conversion" that will ameliorate the attitudes of Christians who "ridicule" environmental concerns, on the one hand, and those who take a more "passive" stance of resignation, on the other hand (*LS* 217). It also calls for a movement away from a "utilitarian mindset" that sees nature simply in terms of its use rather than for its intrinsic value and beauty (*LS* 210). Moreover,

---

47. For a creative development of this ecological conversion, see Cristina Vanin, "The Significance of Lonergan's Method for Ecological Conversion," in *Lonergan's Anthropology Revisited: The Next Fifty Years of Vatican II*, ed. Gerard Whelan (Rome: Gregorian Biblical Press, 2015), 455–458.

to be effective, the effects of the conversion have to be communal and collective rather than just within individuals. One of the fruits of such a conversion is "a health[ier] relationship [reconciliation] with creation" (*LS* 218). Again, the pope lauds Francis of Assisi as a model here, but he could have just as easily laud Hildegard of Bingen.

The conversion should foster a number of attitudes including gratitude for the gift of all life that is from God, a call to imitate God's generosity and a "loving awareness that we are not disconnected from the rest of creatures, but joined in universal communion." Finally, our God-given capacities to discern and respond creatively to problems functions as a way of self-sacrifice (*LS* 220).

In addition, convictions of the faith can help further foster the conversion. First, the faith recognizes that each creature reflects God's glory and has a meaning for us to contemplate, including a trace of the resurrected light of Christ. Second, God has put an order into the world that we cannot deny and one we should advert to and respect (*LS* 222). That order includes God's care for all creatures; therefore, we are obligated to care for all creatures. Again, St. Francis serves as the paradigm. For Hildegard, that order would also be permeated with viridity, since both the order and the viridity originate in the mind of God.

A Christian spirituality must accompany this ecological conversion and integral ecology. The spirituality emphasizes simplicity, as Pope Francis advocates that "less is more," not merely in terms of accumulation of things, but in simplifying our attention to those things. Distractions abound in the digital age that prevent us from enjoying the moment. As Pope Francis writes, "There needs to be a distinctive way of looking at things, a way of thinking, policies, an educational programme, a lifestyle and a spirituality which together generate resistance to the assault of the technocratic paradigm" (*LS* 111). Sobriety, humility, and gratitude are also essential components of this spirituality. Likewise, there is the need to intentionally contemplate beauty in the created order that reveals God's presence: "An integral ecology includes taking time to recover a serene harmony with creation, reflecting on our lifestyle and our ideals, and contemplating the Creator who lives among us and surrounds us, whose presence must not be contrived but found, uncovered" (*LS* 225). Finally, it includes a recognition of the need for one another and a community to bring about the ideal of a "civilization of love" (*LS* 231).

For Hildegard, *viriditas* facilitates conversion: "Now, in your spirit consider how long you have wandered astray in the winter of the spiritual life. And so run quickly to the viridity of the Holy Spirit, which is summer, by changing your morals. In this way, bring forth flowers of virtue, and gather your sheaves [cf. Ps 128:7] as fast as you can."[48] The Holy Spirit, as source of the greening action, can infuse the heart and so heal the obstacles that bring about aridity and dryness. The changing of one's morals is the fruit of the conversion, and the virtuous person is one that abides and mediates the greening action of God accordingly.[49] The blessings of the Holy Spirit radiate like a breeze from those who have faithfully carried out good works. The aroma (holiness) of their good virtues fills the air: "It contained all the greenness of the herbs and flowers of both paradise and the earth, and its aroma was also full of all the greenness, just as the summer has the sweetest aroma of herbs and flowers."[50]

To adopt such a notion of the life principle of viridity that originates in God, permeates the created order, accompanies those who abide in God's grace, and cooperates with God in spreading the greenness and fostering a reinvigoration of the created order, is at once to grasp the basis for a spirituality of the created order capable of meeting the exigencies of our day, as outlined in *Laudato si'*. *Viriditas* provides a vital thread to a spirituality that can accompany and sustain an ongoing ecological conversion.

Concluding Comment: *Viriditas* and Finding God in All Things

I began this essay with an image, and I would like to return to that image to support the argument I have been making: that Hildegard of Bingen provides an important complement not only to the teaching but to the implementation of *Laudato si'*. In the image, the Holy

---

48. Hildegard of Bingen, *The Letters of Hildegard of Bingen*, vol. II, trans. J.L Baird and R.K. Ehrman (New York: Oxford University Press, 1998), 88.

49. "May He anoint you with the viridity of the Holy Spirit, and may He work good and holy works in you through that devotion with which true worshipers worship God (cf. John 4.23)" (Hildegard of Bingen, *Letters of Hildegard of Bingen*, II:16).

50. Hildegard of Bingen, *Book of the Rewards of Life*, 282.

Spirit prevails upon the earth, emerging from the spiral, a symbol of the creation of the world *ex nihilo*. The earth is surrounded by a green layer and twelve green flames, symbolizing the twelve stones of the new Jerusalem (Rev 21:14) and the greening or new creation. The green flame symbolizes the action of God's life force and grace in our world. The panels to the right and left of the earth provide a closer symbolic view of the planet with the leaves symbolizing the greening of new life and the stones representing the sacredness and stability of the earth. It has been said that Gerard Manley Hopkins, who exclaimed famously that "the world is charged with the grandeur of God," was once captivated by the beauty of rocks in a puddle of water after a downpour.

In the bottom right panel, St. Ignatius holds a lifeless cross circled with leaves that indicate the greening of resurrection. His gaze is directed to the Christ child, who raises his hands in affirmation. With a hand on the Christ child and her abbess staff and a musical instrument at her feet, Hildegard of Bingen affirms the truth of the greening. She often communicates her theology of *viriditas* in her music. The rays of what Hildegard often calls the living light, the light of the Unbegotten, shines down upon them.

These images are significant because the artist brings Hildegard's theology of *viriditas* as a resource for developing a theology of creation in our time—one that complements the Franciscan and Ignatian emphases concretized in Pope Francis's *Laudato si'*. The artist also encourages us, in our imaginations, to consider the greening of the resurrection and the new life of the blood as transformed—like a red bud sprouting into a green leaf in spring. Discussing the environment, Benedict XVI once commented, "At Christmas the Almighty becomes a child. . . . The creator of the universe reduced to the poverty of the infant."[51] The child represents the vulnerability of creation and the environment. *Viriditas: Finding God in All Things*, yokes together the images necessary for a Christian theology of an integral ecology of the environment. It brings together the best of the Franciscan, Jesuit, and Benedictine traditions. But the image also calls for a systematic theology.

Hildegard's *viriditas*, inspired by Gregory the Great, was invoked, developed, and integrated throughout her thought. While her

---

51. Benedict XVI, *Environment* (Huntington, IN: Our Sunday Visitor, 2012), 17.

thought is unsystematic, it covers the major areas of systematic theology. *Viriditas* is the thread that weaves those various areas together and provides the theological category to be integrated into a contemporary systematic theology that can support an integral ecology. That ortho-theory, which flows from the orthodoxy of *Laudato si'*, can support the orthopraxis of ecological conversion, the spirituality to support and accompany the ongoing effects of such conversion, and a responsible stewardship of the environment. Eschatologically, human beings work hand-in-hand with God to ameliorate the effects of their own short-sightedness—thus making the imminent aridity of our planet green again. Pope Francis ensures that the justice for the poor and the healing of the earth go hand-in-hand.

CHAPTER NINE

Interpreting *Laudato Si'*

WHAT DOES IT MEAN TO BE HUMAN?

Thomas Hughson, S.J. (Marquette University)

Pope Francis addresses *Laudato Si': On Care for Our Common Home* to "every person living on this planet," so that readers can "enter into dialogue with all people about our common home."[1] Through dialogue, "together, we can seek paths of liberation" (*LS* 64). The encyclical stands in declared alliance with the 1972 Stockholm Declaration, the 1992 Earth Summit in Rio de Janeiro (*LS* 167), and the 2000 Earth Charter (*LS* 207). Francis issued the encyclical just before the international 2016 Paris Agreement to mitigate climate change. Like the environmental teachings of his predecessors John XXIII, Paul VI, John Paul II, and Benedict XVI as well as those of Orthodox Patriarch Bartholomew, Francis too heeds "the reflections of numerous scientists, philosophers, theologians and civic groups, all of which have enriched the Church's thinking on these questions" (*LS* 7).[2]

People from many and no religious convictions have praised *Laudato si'* and Francis for dramatically placing the ecological crisis before the conscience of humanity, situating a response within a religious framework, and exhibiting an exemplary commitment to actual, not just aspirational, cooperation toward an integral global ecology. A group of Lutheran theologians struck a bold note. They hailed the encyclical as a prophetic call summoning not only Lutherans and

---

1. Francis, *Laudato Si'* [Encyclical on Care for Our Common Home], May 24, 2015, §3.

2. See also Francis, "Address of His Holiness Pope Francis to Participants at the International Conference Marking the 3rd Anniversary of the Encyclical *Laudato Si'*," July 6, 2018, http://w2.vatican.va/content/francesco/en/speeches/2018/july/documents/papa-francesco_20180706_terzoanniversario-laudatosi.html.

Catholics but all of Christianity to an eco-Reformation that subsumes the justification by faith preached by Martin Luther into a commitment to God's care for creation.[3]

An encyclical is a literary form supple enough to have served many papal purposes over the course of Church history. The genre of *Laudato si'* follows what John O'Malley analyzed as the epideictic style of Vatican II documents. The goal of the epideictic "is the winning of internal assent, not the imposition of conformity from outside."[4] In classical literature, this literary style employed panegyric to excite admiration for an ideal. Similarly, Vatican II—as both event and text— was not canonical, minatory, or unilateral but persuasive in language and dialogical in its manner of witness and teaching. The documents presumed readers were adults of good will, not wayward children.

The epideictic style of *Laudato si'* renders the encyclical effective as a pastoral voice in religiously pluralist, international dialogue as well as within Catholicism. Pope Francis's manifest intention is to present to the Church and the world why and how the ecological crisis calls for an authentic religious response that seeks to serve global cooperation in lessening the crisis.

Moreover, the epideictic style and atypical message of *Laudato si'* have a theological premise. The style builds on and projects a world in front of the text in which God's omnipresent grace, effectively symbolized but by no means exhaustively present in the Church, enables cooperation among people of good will in coming to terms with the ecological crisis and who thereby participate in the kingdom of God. The scope of pastoral concern in *Laudato si'* includes creation, physical nature, and the cosmos on theological principle, as its second chapter highlights. Revelation transmitted by Scripture and tradition, faith, recent theology, and ecological teachings in Christian churches allows nature and the cosmos to be understood as God's creation. However, on theological principle the pope also incorporates findings from the advancing natural sciences.

The principle comes from the Thomistic and Catholic soteriological tradition. Divine grace perfects human nature. Still, the

---

3. Lisa E. Dahill and James B. Martin-Schrammm, eds., *Eco-Reformation: Grace and Hope for a Planet in Peril* (Eugene, OR: Cascade Books, 2016).

4. John W. O'Malley, *What Happened at Vatican II* (Cambridge, MA: Harvard University Press, 2008), 47.

ideal of harmony between nature and grace, reason and revelation is always partial and in flux, affected by contingent contexts whose specifics in human ignorance and sin leave the harmony never complete yet always able to commence and develop. The epideictic, dialogical style of *Laudato si'* expresses pastoral concern for the ecological crisis in a manner that benefits from and harmonizes religion and science, revelation and reason, grace and nature.

Furthermore, the pope stirs dialogue and discussion, not just compliant nods within the Catholic Church and Christian churches. Francis wrote the encyclical not least to show "how faith convictions can offer Christians and some other believers as well, ample motivation to care for nature and for the most vulnerable of their brothers and sisters" (*LS* 64). Francis continues, "It is good for humanity and the world at large when we believers better recognize the ecological commitments which stem from our convictions" (*LS* 64). Those convictions sublate ecological knowledge and values from non-theological sources into a pastoral-theological prospectus. *Laudato si'* expounds to Catholics, Christians, and other believers a this-worldly dimension of belief in Christ and God that calls for international cooperation in grappling with the ecological crisis.

Active cooperation and leadership in theory and practice mainly by laity, it seems, are how the Church can enact its witness and mission in response to the ecological crisis. *Laudato si'* invites and commissions laity and clergy alike to a new breadth of witness to the reign of God in the interaction between humanity and physical nature. The style, pastoral genre, and papal intent all combine to situate the Church, head and members, in a new horizon of solidarity that encompasses all of humanity and all of physical nature, which we understand as creation.

The Ecological Crisis as a Crisis of Meaning

This first section takes an interpretative position on *Laudato si'*: in the new horizon of solidarity, the ecological crisis is a crisis in meaning. The position leans on Bernard Lonergan's *Method in Theology*.[5] The second and third chapters of *Method* evidence the breadth

---

5. Bernard J.F. Lonergan, *Method in Theology* (London: Darton Longman & Todd, 1972).

of Lonergan's concept of meaning. The source of meaning is any conscious human activity and its content under the two aspects of the pure desire to know and categorical determinations reached through experience, understanding, judging, and deciding. Lonergan's originality surfaces in his analysis that meaning—cognitive, constitutive, effective, communicative—resides not only in individuals' thoughts, in theories, and in texts, but also "in human intersubjectivity, in art, in symbols, in language, and in the words and deeds of a person's life."[6]

It is a small step from that initial expansion to note that, according to Lonergan, a society's institutions, structures, and capacity for decisions, actions, and practices are formed by originating meanings communicated to the point of becoming common meaning. Socially, economically, and politically embodied common meaning, deteriorated to be sure, infused the prolonged human ravaging of nature whose cumulative outcome is the ecological crisis. A perspective of that sort courses throughout *Laudato si'*, but most clearly in its third chapter, "The Human Roots of the Ecological Crisis."

The crisis is a direct, yet unforeseen consequence of deliberate, misguided individual and societal thinking, deciding, and acting that modified economic institutions and work. The principal initiators and beneficiaries of the Industrial Revolution defaulted on their native drive toward self-transcendence and so shaped a primarily instrumental way of interacting with physical nature. An intellectual short circuit blanked too much cultural, personal, and religious meaning. Hence, the crisis cannot be ended without reconnecting the technological with that fuller range of meaning.

To put it another way, the family, state, and economy, besides embodying constitutive meanings, all carry meanings that guide people's action in work. This is the realm of effective meaning. People work, "[b]ut their work is not mindless. What we make we first intend. We imagine, we plan, we investigate possibilities, we weigh pros and cons, we enter into contracts, we have countless orders given and executed."[7] In industrialized countries, the technocratic paradigm colonized effective meaning and thereby became so preponderant that it displaced alternative cognitive and constitutive meanings concerning

---

6. Lonergan, *Method in Theology*, 57.

7. Lonergan, *Method in Theology*, 77–8.

human living. Thus, scientific and technical solutions that inadvertently maintain a technocratic self-understanding cannot meet the ecological crisis, as they do not heed cultural, personal, and religious thought about what it means to be human.

A conclusion is inescapable. The position on the ecological crisis as a crisis of meaning follows from combining the third chapter of *Laudato si'* on the human cause of the crisis, its fourth chapter's projected yet attainable goal of an integral ecology,[8] and its sixth chapter's presentation of ecological conversion. The ecological crisis has human roots, so meaning forms and propels the malfeasance and is the setting for its manifold corrections. In particular, an isolation from the influence of humane cultural, personal, and religious values has distorted effective meaning. The next section probes that meaning by conceiving it as the answer to the question, what does it mean to be human?

The Heuristic Question for *Laudato Si'*

Laudato si' answers a question. If an author has prepared an extensive statement to explain and to draw readers into a new perspective and congruent decisions, behind the text lies a question to which it is an answer. The main question need not be identified with an explicit passage; instead, the question is implied and pervasive throughout the whole text. In the same way, *Laudato si'* serves as an answer to a fundamental question that lies behind and forms the text. Pope Francis articulates a precise and forceful critique of modern anthropocentrism and the technocratic paradigm in the encyclical's third chapter. The critique steers attention to the main question answered by *Laudato si'*. Identifying that question is the key to the ecological crisis as a crisis in meaning, since it specifies what meaning is at stake.

The structure of question and answer has been the logic of inquiry from Socrates, Plato, Aristotle, Augustine, Aquinas, Kant, Rahner, Gadamer, and to Lonergan. Lonergan agrees with R.G. Collingwood and Gadamer that knowledge consists, "not just in propositions but in answers to questions, so that to understand the answers one has to know the questions as well."[9] The implied

---

8. As Pope Francis writes, an "integral ecology calls for openness to categories which transcend the language of mathematics and biology, and take us to the heart of what it is to be human" (*LS* 11).

9. Lonergan, *Method in Theology*, 164.

corollary is that finding the question begins the process of understanding common sense statements, theoretical explanations, and the semi-independent formation of many sorts of practices that answer the question. What main question lies behind and within *Laudato si'*?

Every question, Lonergan clarifies, seeks some definite, categorical matter of fact or value and has a transcendental aspect in actualizing the unrestricted desire to know.[10] *Laudato si'* answers, I submit, a question more basic and almost transcendental compared with those investigating the categorial content of each chapter. Each chapter responds to an important query. Chapter One answers, what natural phenomena influenced by humans constitute the ecological crisis? Chapter Two addresses, how does the act, content, and horizon of faith reconcile scientific and religious analyses of the ecological crisis? Chapter Three takes up, what has caused the crisis? Chapter Four considers, what new physical and social condition ends the crisis? Chapter Five discusses, how can the dialogical approach move toward that solution and goal? Chapter Six answers, what changes in religious and cultural self-understanding are needed for that movement actually to transpire rather than languish as an ideal?

But none of these is the main question that alone supplies the contextual starting-point and key to the meaning of the whole encyclical. What question does the encyclical as a whole answer? The question springs from the logic of inquiry in the sequence of chapters, moving from problematic effect (Chapter 1), to cause (Chapter 3), and to solution (Chapters 2, 4, 5, 6).

The third chapter of *Laudato si'* can be read as the most direct answer to the main, implied, and underlying question. Again, that chapter asks, why is there a crisis? The fault lies, dear Brutus, not with the stars (or nature) but with ourselves. Francis reflects that, "It would hardly be helpful to describe symptoms [Chapter 1] without acknowledging the human origins of the ecological crisis. A certain way of understanding human life and activity has gone awry" (*LS* 101). The "present ecological crisis is one small sign of the ethical, cultural and spiritual crisis of modernity" (*LS* 119). The cause

---

10. Bernard J.F. Lonergan, *Insight: A Study of Human Understanding*, CWL 3, eds. Frederick E. Crowe and Robert M. Doran (Toronto: University of Toronto Press, 2005), 33–34, 659–662.

of the crisis is a historically-specific understanding of the human that, especially in Western culture since the seventeenth century, has formed and guided human interaction with physical nature. It is important to remember that Francis's incisive critique of something typically modern remains within the epideictic style of *Gaudium et spes*, rather than the wholesale anti-modern position common in the Church before and during Vatican II.

Nevertheless, one influential sector in modern Western self-understanding has produced disastrous results. Francis labels that dimension the "technocratic paradigm" of "modern anthropocentrism." Anthropocentrism absolutized human autonomy instead of sustaining relative, creaturely autonomy. This absolutization forgot that God, neighbor, and nature are real, and made the modern self as individual and as a common social meaning out to be most real. By so doing, it reduced neighbor and nature to subordinate instruments while making God at most the transcendent watch-maker imagined by Deism.

Practical intelligence exercised this erroneous idea of the human through the technocratic paradigm. The technocratic paradigm, Francis explains, "exalts the concept of a subject who, using logical and rational procedures, progressively approaches and gains control over an external object" (*LS* 106). This self-understanding approaches nature "as if the subject were to find itself in the presence of something formless, completely open to manipulation" (*LS* 106). The technocratic paradigm distorts what in Lonergan's analysis is the cognitive meaning of being human. The distortion passes into the constitutive meaning of modern economies and people, becoming active in the world as the effective meaning that guides human work.

The errant modern project has not reckoned well with humans as *participants in* rather than *lords outside and over* nature. Scientists, philosophers, theologians, social-scientists and others already have contributed to a new, deeper, and more responsible participation. Francis joins them, asserting that "Nature cannot be regarded as something separate from ourselves or as a mere setting in which we live. We are part of nature, included in it and thus in constant interaction with it" (*LS* 139).

At the same time, for *Laudato si'*, the ecological crisis is indivisible from the poor suffering structural injustice. Both have the same cause: the modern, Western human self-understanding that has become influential (although not unanimous) in modern/postmodern societies. Societal "self-understanding" here roughly equates to Lonergan's "common meaning" constitutive of community. Distortion and inauthenticity in self-understanding or common meaning produced skewed social, political, and cultural outcomes, like structural economic injustice and the systematic exploitation of nature. Both ecological damage and the marginalization of the poor are effects from the libertarian, laissez-faire anthropocentrism actualized through the technocratic paradigm. The effects of the technocratic paradigm have become global in magnitude.

By putting the common meaning in the technocratic paradigm on public, international trial, Francis implies, indeed cannot avoid, the broader question about being human. The key, heuristic question answered by *Laudato si'*, then, is, "who are we?" rephrased as, "what does it mean to be human (today)?" One modern view of being human has generated the eco-crisis, demonstrating the falsity of its own presuppositions. *Laudato si'* cannot avoid the formerly settled but newly opened question about being human. The encyclical's answer is that, whatever its modern deflections, being human entails caring for the well-being of physical nature in such a way as to promote the physical well-being of the poor. While that answer does not state the whole of what it means to be human, at least this general answer cannot be omitted from any statement about humanity across disciplines.

The critique implies an alternative. That is, if we challenge the technocratic paradigm of modern anthropocentrism, then what replacement, what successor as a practicable idea of the human will be the path toward an integral ecology? What does it mean to be human? *Laudato si'* contradicts the answer predominant in modernity and introduces an alternative humanism enlightened by Christian faith. Exit from the crisis and new respect for the earth emerge only from re-asking the question about being human and re-answering in a way that involves becoming human once again but in a new way apparent to human conscience and amplified by the act and content of Catholic and Christian faith.

What does it mean to be human?[11] Today, the acute set of facts that have brought the question to the cultural forefront before,

---

11. See Lieven Boeve, Yves De Maeseneer, and Ellen Van Stichel, eds., *Questioning the Human: Toward a Theological Anthropology for the Twenty-First Century* (New York: Fordham University Press, 2014).

during, and after the publication of *Laudato si'* is not only the problem of human evil in genocide, war, oppression, racism, and sexism, not simply the search for extraterrestrial intelligent life, not only the invaluable heritage from Husserl, Heidegger, and Gadamer in philosophy, and not only investigations into human evolution. Rather, for *Laudato si'*, the preeminent provocation is the ecological crisis and its impact on the poor. All else depends on the human race appropriating a new self-understanding to guide interaction with nature. The Lutheran theologians in the volume on eco-Reformation agree that the ecological crisis is the spiritual problem of the age. So too, Neil Ormerod and Cristina Vanin estimate, "The long-term flourishing and indeed survival of our common home, Earth, is the most significant reality at stake in our time."[12]

The encyclical does not state the whole of what it means to be human. However, it does establish theologically why care for the earth and the poor cannot be omitted from any such statement. *Laudato si'* challenges the answer built into modernity's industrial and post-industrial interaction with nature. Exit from the crisis consists in a new understanding of humanity and a recovered respect for physical nature. Such respect on a wide, societal scale comes only from re-asking the question about being human and rejecting the mistaken answer of the technocratic paradigm and its assertion of absolute human autonomy. The encyclical illuminates the path of a relative, creaturely, human autonomy exercised in science and technology that cares responsibly for our common home and the poorest in the household.

The Role of Judgment in Ecological Conversion

The cultural, personal, and to some extent religious question, "what does it mean to be human?" is *sui generis*. It encompasses all sensory and conscious experience, all patterns of experience, all known meanings, all the diverse constitutions of the human good. Asking what it means to be human today, although intrinsically speculative and theoretical, seeks intelligibility in the horizon of existential decisions, both public and private. Much is at stake in the search and in its termination in some account of the human. The question accents *what* and *mean*, not *to be*.

---

12. Neil Ormerod and Cristina Vanin, "Ecological Conversion: What Does it Mean?," *Theological Studies* 77, no. 2: 328–352, at 351.

A turn to ontological matters may seem contrary to Francis's casting community with nature in affective terms, such as his conviction that ecological conversion brings about "a loving awareness that we are not disconnected from the rest of creatures but joined in a splendid universal communion" (*LS* 220). Denis Edwards also notes the role of feelings in hearing the cry of the earth and of the poor.[13] Emotions can be intentional and become a reservoir of unthematic memories. Emotions responsive to someone or something real or imagined have experiential content available to inquiry. Moreover, Lonergan considers that the pure desire to know stirs inquiry, judgment, and deliberation. So, the following discussion of judgment does not presume conflict between mind and heart, between the dynamics of knowledge and of love. After all, the pure desire to know is a desire, a mode of love. Furthermore, judgment, besides asserting what is real, often ushers in deliberation over what is good.

The question about being human anticipates what is essentially human. The patent answer in *Laudato si'* is that being human today in view of the ecological crisis means cooperative caring for our common planetary home in a way that actualizes an option for the poor. Francis's answer focuses on characteristic, essential activity rather than on the *to be* in human existence. Still, the question is properly metaphysical in the direction of essence, the *what* of being human rather than with the *that*, the human as existing. In *Insight* and *Method*, the formal act of meaning is an idea, theory, concept, surmise, or hypothesis from inquiry into experience. Judgment, however, is "the full act of meaning . . . that settles the status of an object of thought."[14]

The object of thought central to *Laudato si'* is harmed physical nature and remedial care. Care for nature includes, I will point out, human judgment about nature as an object of thought. The formal meaning of the answer on what it means to be human—cooperative caring for nature with an option for the poor—cannot be severed from the full meaning and judgment internal to ecological conversion.

In their enlightening interpretation of *Laudato si'*, Ormerod and Vanin link ecological conversion to Lonergan's moral, religious, and

---

13. Denis Edwards, "'Sublime Communion': The Theology of the Natural World in *Laudato si'*," *Theological Studies* 77, no. 2 (2016): 377–391, at 385–389.

14. Edwards, "'Sublime Communion,'" 74.

intellectual conversions and to Doran's development of psychic conversion.[15] Insightfully, they remark that "Inasmuch as the goals of control and domination are ascendant, the proper goal of complete understanding is truncated, and science promotes practices without a proper awareness of their consequences in the ecological order. Intellectual conversion can assist in clarifying the distinction between a normative understanding of science and its current empirical distortions."[16] I'd like to augment their discussion of intellectual conversion by focusing on the act of judgment. In ecological conversion, new respect for physical nature, the cosmos, and the poor hinges on a liberating, reasonable, and not necessarily scientific judgment.

Knowing comes to full term in judgment/affirmation.[17] Judgment is a reasonable affirmation of the validity or not, of ideas about fact and/or value after the pertinent questions have been answered. Affirmation or not is not only intelligent but also reasonable in the judicious assessment of these questions. Is an idea probably or surely the case, or not at all? Is this an authentic value or a passing attraction? Does something need to be done about a value or its absence? Ecological conversion, education, and spirituality overcome and correct misguided ideas and exaggerated judgments of fact and value inherent in the technological paradigm linked to modern anthropocentrism. The latter are ignorant of and hard-hearted to the reality of the poor and nature. They lack knowledge of be-ing.

Francis appreciates the importance of that lack of ontology. He professes that "where other creatures are concerned," quoting the German Bishops' Conference, "'we can speak of the priority of *being* over that of being useful'" (*LS* 69). Ecological conversion hinges on respect for the otherness of nature. Ecological conversion involves a change in something profound in cognition. Respectful philosophical affirmation completes scientific inquiry by reasonably judging that the cosmos and nature first of all simply *are* in their own right. The technological paradigm lost that simple thread. Ormerod and Vanin are right that, "Inasmuch as the goals of control and domination are

---

15. On the significance of psychic conversion in ecological conversion see Ormerod and Vanin, "Ecological Conversion," 346–349.

16. Ormerod and Vanin, "Ecological Conversion," 346.

17. See Lonergan, *Insight*, Chapters 9 ("The Notion of Judgment"), 10 ("Reflective Understanding") and 12 ("The Notion of Being").

ascendant, the proper goal of complete understanding is truncated, and science promotes practices without a proper awareness of their consequences in the ecological order."[18] Science and technology, once emancipated from their philosophical matrix, lost association with the ever-accessible judgment of nature as existing that enables careful, prudential deliberation to guide interaction with nature.

An unburdening in judgment occurs in a shift that Lonergan highlights. The shift is a crucial transition in which Aquinas moved beyond Aristotle, as Lonergan's study of Aquinas demonstrated. Frederick Lawrence points out that Aristotle and Aquinas both held the identity of knower and known in sensory and intellectual knowing.[19] Aquinas saw a weakness in positing the identity of known and knower if there is no account of otherness in intentionality, however. In Lonergan's early words, "Rational knowledge has to bear the weight of the transition from knowledge as a perfection [of the knower] to knowledge as *of the other*."[20] This transition in the act and content of judgment has a decisive ecological implication. Ecological conversion pivots on just such a judgment about nature, likely not methodical and most often pre-theoretical, but nonetheless able to be understood in the following ways.

First, by deepening the distinction between essence and existence, Aquinas identifies and opens up the recognition of otherness in natural realties conceived as substances.[21] Their otherness emerges in acts of judgment that something is or is not so—for instance, that the human species is or is not unique among animals. Affirming the otherness of natural existence stands apart from the baneful estrangement from nature due to Cartesian dualism and the technocratic

---

18. Ormerod and Vanin, "Ecological Conversion," 346.

19. On this identity, see Lonergan, *Method in Theology*, 72.

20. Frederick G. Lawrence, "Lonergan's Search for a Hermeneutics of Authenticity: Re-originating Augustine's Hermeneutics of Love," in *Lonergan's Anthropology: Revisited: The Next Fifty Years of Vatican II*, ed. Gerard Whelan, S.J. (Rome: Gregorian and Biblical Press, 2015), 28. The quote comes from Bernard J.F. Lonergan, *Verbum: Word and Idea in Aquinas* (Notre Dame, IN: Notre Dame Press, 1967), 73. Emphasis added.

21. See also John D. Caputo, *Heidegger and Aquinas: An Essay on Overcoming Metaphysics* (New York: Fordham University Press, 1982), Chapter 2 ("Heidegger's Critique of Scholasticism").

paradigm. Aquinas's substance metaphysics, when linked with his epistemology, has a principle of otherness that acclaims natural substances as actively independent of and in human knowing.

Second, Aquinas's real distinction opened space for the being-known of kinds of natural substances whose immanent form is an entelechy toward their living and surviving. The immanent plant or animal form defined as the essence of a species means that members of plant and animal species *are* in characteristic ways, and so they *are* distinct from humans knowing and using them. Substances, unlike accidents or parts, are first of all for-themselves. That belies quick and easy assumptions that plant and animal species exist solely for human use and benefit.

Aristotle and Aquinas did relate plants and animals to human use but did not ignore their immanent forms prior to and apart from human use. A substance of a specific kind exists in and on its own. The entelechy of the species and its individuals is the intrinsic tendency toward survival by eating, drinking, mating, and in some by caring for mate, offspring, and group. Human use is extrinsic and posterior to the tendency toward survival in species of plants and animals. Human use cuts short their survival, and yet the entelechy toward human survival depends on that use.

Third, the recognition in judgment that natural realities are independent in existing-toward-survival decenters modern anthropocentrism and the technological paradigm. Sweeping industrial domination as if nature was only for human use and economic profit denied in practice the respect warranted by the intrinsic entelechies in plants and animals. Human use and profit dominated effective meaning in regard to nature. Nature was not known in judgments of existence but was commodified. The captains of industry judged that they existed but bore no weight of otherness in knowledge of nature and the poor.

Again, Lonergan states, "Rational knowledge has to bear the weight of the transition from knowledge as a perfection [of the knower] to knowledge as *of the other*." The technocratic paradigm refuses the weight of transition to otherness and so offers no escape from the confines of essentialist anthropocentrism. Ecological conversion, by contrast, breaks free of essentialism confined to knowing what nature is without the liberating judgment that it *is* in all its variegated multiplicity.

Lonergan noticed that judgment is "the responsibility of the one that judges. It is a personal commitment."[22] That personal aspect of judgment is easy to miss but occurs in ecological conversion. In that regard, Pope Francis's pervasive appeal to Francis of Assisi in *Laudato si'* is instructive. Who more than the medieval saint exemplifies ecological conversion in its human fullness? His deepening love for God enveloped and drew forth love for neighbor and for nature in an ongoing, informal but powerful judgment on what is real, enlightened by attention to the Creator. Natural creatures exist as what they are. For the founder of the Franciscans, the world-wide ecological movement, and for people learning from the encyclical, the judgment of nature's existence has the quality of a commitment, no less than of a conclusion.

Fourth and paradoxically, bearing the weight of transition to otherness is not burdensome. The weight characterized Francis of Assisi's life and *Canticle of Creatures* (*LS* 3, 10–12). He experienced and exemplified spontaneous, joyous affirmations of all nature's non-human realities as God's creatures in their unique being. The ecological name for that existential affirmation is respect for nature. The baptismal name is love for all things created by divine love through the divine Word. Some manner of affirming the existence and otherness of nature figures in ecological conversion and undergirds the ecological movement.

In response to the heuristic question, "what does it mean to be human in view of the ecological crisis?", *Laudato si'* teaches the simply stated but multi-layered judgment that to be human today is to care together for our common planetary home with an option for the poorest in the household. I have argued that this caring involves an affirmation of existing-nature that comes about in the existing-person, such that one sees that nature and the poor really exist in their own right. According to the encyclical, cooperative caring for the earth and the poor belongs to what it means to be human. Such care thrives on the judgment that natural realities and the poor are real. Both exist in their own right primarily. Only secondarily does nature enable all humans to survive and flourish.

---

22. Lonergan, *Insight*, 297.

The Dialectic Between Anthropological and Cosmological Meaning

Care for nature, exercised through social and political cooperation toward an integral ecology, flows from a significant degree of cultural consensus in cognitive, constitutive, and effective meaning on being human. Robert Doran's analysis of the integral dialectic of culture provides much assistance here.[23] Cultures form, grow, and dissolve in the tension between what Doran has analyzed as poles of "cosmological" and "anthropological" meaning. The former enacts and accounts for a way of life whose measure of integrity is an attunement to the regularities of cosmic nature. The latter finds its direction and integrity in human self-transcending ideas, values and norms. Each pole tends to guide a culture in a direction opposed to the other. A culture takes place as a lengthy event somewhere along the spectrum of tension between the two poles. In an integral dialectic, both poles exert their influence. A repressed dialectic occurs when one pole monopolizes the culture.

Societies and economies shaped by modern anthropocentrism and the technocratic paradigm have repressed the cosmological pole. That view is an approximation at the level only of an ideal-type, as subaltern dissent and reaction, Catholic social teaching among them, remain cultural forces. However, these forces do not wield the power of states or major corporations that often generate distorted effective meaning. The ecological crisis is the outcome and the proof of a need for movement toward the cosmological principle described by Doran. Lonergan's concept of effective meaning pinpoints the inherent connection between the ecological crisis and work. "Underlying every form of work," states Francis, "is a concept of the relationship which we can or must have with what is other than ourselves" (*LS* 125). A more ecologically responsible alternative must replace the distorted effective meaning instantiated by the technocratic paradigm.

However, while Doran's sound thesis of a cultural dialectic has an explanatory capacity in regard to the ecological crisis as a crisis of meaning in all four functions, not least effective meaning, I hesitate to consider the integral dialectic of culture as a closed and fixed

---

23. Robert M. Doran, *Theology and the Dialectics of History* (Toronto: University of Toronto Press, 1990), 512–548.

framework. It might seem obvious that Francis's critique of modern anthropocentrism incites reacquiring an integral dialectic between anthropological and cosmological constitutive meanings. True, Doran sees that, besides transforming the anthropological principle, we need a transformed cosmological principle beginning in psychic conversion and so already internal to the anthropological principle. Still, Doran's position on the cosmological principle, whether conceived as empirically descriptive or as ideal-typical, is, I propose, open to development in light of empirical research.

Empirical paleoanthropological research on human evolution and the emergence of symbolism, language, and culture is a developing body of knowledge pertinent to the cosmological principle. There may thus be room for testing and refining the cosmological principle. To embark on this interdisciplinary path typifies theological reflection as outlined in Lonergan's specialty of "Communications."[24] Current research in paleoanthropology asks and continually, provisionally answers, what does it mean to be human? The question and answers are interwoven with pre-historic humanity's evolving interaction with physical nature and the cosmos. Interpretations of what it means to be human are prominent in biology and in culture.

Paleoanthropologists Richard Potts and Christopher Sloan authored *What Does It Mean to Be Human?*[25] Similarly, in *Becoming Human: Our Past, Present, and Future,* the editors of *Scientific American* take readers through a survey of contemporary findings on human evolution.[26] The Smithsonian Program for Human Origins titles its website, "What does it mean to be human?"[27] Summarily, in the words of John Hands, "Any explanation of where we came from—when, how, and why we evolved from primates—depends on understanding what it means to be human."[28] Theologian J. Wentzel van Huyssteen developed an interdisciplinary method in many respects compatible with

---

24. See Lonergan, *Method in Theology*, 355–368.

25. Richard Potts and Christopher Sloan, *What Does It Mean to Be Human?* (Washington D.C.: National Geographic, 2010).

26. Editors, *Becoming Human: Our Past, Present, and Future,* Special Issue of *Scientific American,* September 23, 2013.

27. Smithsonian National Museum of Natural History, Human Origins website, http://humanorigins.si.edu/evidence/human-fossils/fossils.

28. John Hands, *Cosmosapiens: Human Evolution from the Origin of the Universe* (New York: Overlook Duckworth, 2016), 427.

Lonergan's thought.[29] His answer connects Cro-Magnons to the *imago Dei*. Other approaches are also possible.[30]

Inquiry into the origins of genus *Homo*, for example, seeks and generates provisional ideas of what it means to be human. Some idea of the human serves as the criterion for distinguishing humans from other primates.[31] Does the famous bi-pedal hominin, Lucy, belong to genus *Homo*? Most but not all classify her genus *Australopithecus* and species *afarensis* as pre-human. However, Richard Potts lumps together as human all hominids from *Homo sapiens* back through genus *Australopithecus* dated 4.2–2 mya (million years ago) to genus *Sahelanthropus* that diverged from the great apes 7–6.5 mya.[32] More hold that genus *Homo* emerged from, not in, *Australopithecus afaarensis*. Where and when?

The most investigated sites are in northeastern Africa. Still, it is not known whether that is due to easier archaeological access because of geological conditions there or to an unusually large concentration of fossils. The Leakeys unearthed core-and-flake pebble tools from Olduwan Gorge in Tanzania. Dated at 2.6 mya, they were more skillfully produced and used than had been chimpanzees' pounding stones. They attributed the tools to an opportunistic, bi-pedal, meter-high species they named *Homo habilis* whose 1.9 mya fossils were, along with those of the larger *Homo rudolfensis*, the start of genus *Homo*.[33] Habilene brains were larger than chimpanzees'

29. J. Wentzel van Huyssteen, *Alone in the World? Human Uniqueness in Science and Theology* (Grand Rapids, MI: William B. Eerdmans Publishing Company, 2006); and Christopher Lilley and Daniel J. Pedersen, eds., *Human Origins and the Image of God: Essays in Honor of J. Wentzel van Huyssteen* (Grand Rapid, MI: Eerdmans Publishing, 2017).

30. See Thomas Hughson, "Neanderthal Symbolism: Neanderthal Spirituality?," Presentation at NeanderART2018, August 22–26, 2018.

31. David S. Strait, "Human Systematics," in *A Companion to Paleoanthropology*, ed. David R. Begun (Chichester, West Sussex: Wiley-Blackwell, 2013), 37–54; and Jeffrey H. Schwartz and Ian Tattersall, "Defining the Genus *Homo*," *Science* 349, no. 6251 (August 2015): 931–932.

32. Potts and Sloan, *What Does It Mean to be Human?*

33. Bernard Wood and Mark Collard, "The Human Genus," *Science* 284, no. 5411 (April 1999): 65–71; and "Defining the Genus *Homo*," in *Handbook of Paleoanthropology*, eds. Winfried Henke and Ian Tattersall (Berlin and Heidelberg: Springer Verlag, 2015), 2108–2144.

or australopithecines' but smaller than the subsequent *Homo erectus* (1.9 mya to perhaps 50 kya, even possibly to 25 kya on Java).[34] Archaeological discoveries have altered the Leakey's 2.6 mya date and sharpened the more recent estimate of an earlier start in making and using tools. Tools went back to 3.3 mya. Bernard Villmoare and associates unearthed a partial *H. habilis* mandible from 2.8 mya at Ledi-Gararu in Afar, Ethiopia. Then, an archaeological team led by Sonia Harmand discovered animal bones near Lake Turkana in Kenya with butchery marks from 3.39 mya.[35] The Harmand discovery pushed tool-using back from 3.3 to 3.39 mya. Animal bones from Dikika, Ethiopia bore butchery slashes from 3.4 mya.[36] The new dating implies that either genus *Homo* emerged 800 kya earlier than *H. habilis*, or that an australopithecine species such as *Kenyanthropus platyops* made tools, or that a still unknown early human species produced simple stone tools before *H. habilis*. Jeffrey Schwartz and Ian Tattersall underline the difficulty in establishing uniform criteria for the earliest *Homo*.[37] As Susan Antón remarks, "The origins of the genus *Homo* and the factors that may have led to its appearance remain murky."[38] Even if paleoanthropology remains an ever-evolving science, its findings can perhaps fruitfully fill out what Doran means by cosmological meaning.

Conclusion

Laudato si' addresses the ecological crisis. The crisis is a crisis of meaning. The meaning at stake is the meaning of the human. What does it mean to be human? *Laudato si'* answers: caring cooperatively

---

34. On non-*erectus* early *Homo* fossils, including *H. habilis* and *rudolfensis*, see Susan C. Antón, "Early *Homo*: Who, When, and Where," *Current Anthropology* 53, no. S6 (December 2012): S278–S298; and Susan C. Antón, "Natural History of *Homo erectus*," *Journal of Physical Anthropology*, Suppl. 37 (December 2003): 126–170.

35. Sonia Harmand et al., "3.3-million-year-old stone tools from Lomekwi 3, West Turkana, Kenya," *Nature* 521 (May 2015): 310–315.

36. Brian Villmoare, et al., "Early *Homo* at 2.8 Ma from Ledi-Geraru, Afar, Ethiopia," *Science* 347, no. 6228 (March 2015): 1352–1355.

37. Schwartz and Tattersall, "Defining the Genus *Homo*."

38. Antón, "Early *Homo*," 278.

for our common home with an option for the poor. Care involves an ontological judgment affirming the existence of evolved natural realities, including humans. Meanwhile, theology finds common ground with paleoanthropology in asking about the human in view of evolution. *Laudato si'* is open to evolution and imparts impetus to that interdisciplinary exchange (*LS* 81 and 128). Francis submits that, "There can be no ecology without an adequate anthropology" (*LS* 118). His observation recognizes the theological, philosophical, and evolutionary dimensions in an adequate anthropology. Presumably his remark also implies that such anthropology is a matter for development. Anthony Kelly advises, "An essential cultural task for a genuinely integral ecology is to provoke an uninhibited conversation on the topic of our shared humanity."[39] Both could not be more right.

Finally, *Laudato si'* does not leave *Method in Theology* unscathed. *Laudato si'* opens the door to a specific development in Lonergan studies. *Laudato si'* requires that natural values first be affirmed in their primary intrinsic be-ing and then added to Lonergan's scale of values. Their proper station is just below the vital values that natural values subtend and make possible. Natural values occupy the bottom rung in Lonergan's scale of values just beneath vital values. *Laudato si'* also touches Doran's *Theology and the Dialectics of History*. Doran's advertence to an ecological pattern of experience can be developed even beyond Gerard Walmsley's discussion of the biological pattern of experience in Lonergan and Doran.[40] Notes Walmsley, "[t]he biological pattern may also be seen as involving a recognition of ecological participation and of vital values."[41] And, as the final section of this essay intimated, it remains to be seen how interdisciplinary engagement with paleoanthropological research might test, refine, and possibly develop the cosmological principle in Doran's dialectic of culture.

---

39. Anthony J. Kelly, *Laudato Si': An Integral Ecology and the Catholic Vision* (Adelaide: ATF Publishing, 2016), 65.

40. For Lonergan, see *Insight*, 204–220; for Doran, see *Theology and the Dialectics of History*, 179–185, 545–546; and for Walmsley, see his *Lonergan on Philosophic Pluralism: The Polymorphism of Consciousness as the Key to Philosophy* (Toronto: University of Toronto Press, 2008), 96–169.

41. Walmsley, *Lonergan on Philosophic Pluralism*, 112.

CHAPTER TEN

The Glory to be Revealed

GRACE AND EMERGENCE
IN AN ECOLOGICAL ESCHATOLOGY

Benjamin J. Hohman (Boston College)

I n *Laudato si'*, Pope Francis provides the most sustained papal commentary on the relationship between humans and the environment so far.[1] While Francis's predecessors have addressed aspects of this question before, he centers their concerns in an integrated account of Catholic Social Teaching—"integral ecology"—and a needed ecological conversion. However, while Francis describes a unified ethical approach, *Laudato si'* offers more a challenge than a solution from the standpoint of a fully articulated theology. This essay suggests that an account of theological foundations developed from Bernard Lonergan's "generalized emergent probability" provides some of the necessary elements for both a more ecologically oriented theology and the promotion of ecological conversion.

This essay intends to outline a vision of theological foundations that emphasizes the unity and integrity of creation and redemption through an account of grace and emergence in relation to eschatology.[2] This eschatological approach may be surprising, as it deviates from traditional Roman Catholic emphases on purgatory, individual and general resurrection, and the Last Judgment. Beginning in the twentieth century, eschatology came to be more clearly seen as

---

1. Francis, *Laudato Si'* [Encyclical on Care for Our Common Home], May 24, 2015.

2. For an account of the conversation concerning the role of creation in relation to redemption in biblical studies, see Richard J. Clifford, "The Hebrew Scriptures and the Theology of Creation," *Theological Studies* 46 (1985): 507–23, especially at 507–508.

concerned with the way that persons are oriented according to their ultimate horizons, both in terms of their spontaneous, affective responses and their reflective, intentional decisions.[3] The ways that persons think, feel, and act in the present are shaped by their beliefs about who and what they are moving towards in their own life and in the fullness of time. A change in orientation regarding either the present or the absolute future has profound, if often overlooked, impacts on the other. Enlisting Lonergan's theology, this essay forwards an ecologically oriented eschatology in order to facilitate an ecological conversion in response to today's multiple ecological crises.

Though not always recognized for its explicitly eschatological character, Lonergan's notion of "emergent probability" can support the eschatology for which *Laudato si'* calls. The broader idea of "emergence" is hardly new to ecotheology, but many contemporary thinkers in this strain seem unaware of Lonergan's work therein.[4] Furthermore, earlier studies on Lonergan's contribution to ecotheology have focused predominantly on how emergent probability relates to a theology of creation.[5] While recognizing the importance of these

---

3. Including but not limited to the work of Albert Schweitzer, Ernst Käsemann, Ernst Bloch, Jürgen Moltmann, Wolfhart Pannenberg, and Johann Baptist Metz.

4. Emergence has enjoyed a pronounced renaissance in both evolutionary science, anthropology, philosophy, and theology in recent years. Without attempting to treat those works here, I would assert that Lonergan's account of emergent probability—especially as developed in this essay—makes a distinct contribution beyond these others. His integral, systematic locus of the concept of emergence and its development in an overtly interdisciplinary and dialogical cognitional theory, epistemology, and metaphysics provides certain advantages compared to the more Rahnerian approach taken by many of the most prominent Catholic interlocutors in theology and science and ecology. Where emergence has already been rooted in a thoroughgoing, metaphysical approach—as in the work of John Haught and Ted Peters, for instance—that metaphysics has tended towards process accounts of God and often towards faulty understandings of classical, statistical, and genetic methods in science. The unitive account I suggest here clarifies these methods and suggests their relation to dialectical methods, which are needed to ground a truly critical ecology.

5. See Cynthia S.W. Crysdale and Neil Ormerod, *Creator God, Evolving World* (Minneapolis: Fortress Press, 2013); Anne Marie Dalton, *A Theology for the Earth: The Contributions of Thomas Berry and Bernard Lonergan* (Ottawa: University of Ottawa Press, 1999); and Neil Ormerod and Cristina Vanin, "Ecological Conversion: What Does it Mean?," *Theological Studies* 77, no. 2 (2016): 328–352.

earlier contributions, this essay argues for the possibility of reframing emergent probability in relation to grace throughout the created order. By so doing, it suggests a broader foundation for a theology of redemption and eschatology that both answers Francis's call in *Laudato si'* and meets the standards of the larger ecotheological conversation today.

To articulate these foundations, this essay begins by examining the eschatological foundations of *Laudato si'* itself, as Francis's call sets the mandate for the project. However, bringing a mandate from the encyclical to bear within the larger field of theology is no simple task, and so the second section considers some criticisms theologians have posed to *Laudato si'*. Heeding this now somewhat chastised mandate, the third section presents my proposed response based on Lonergan's notion of emergent probability, especially as Patrick Byrne has framed it in relation to a Teilhardian eschatology. Finally, the fourth section suggests the larger contours of the needed constructive project, arguing that, by extending our understanding of emergent probability from its more common focus on the emergence of creation as a natural gift to an account of the emergent probabilities of grace as a gift disproportionate to nature, we may lay more adequate foundations for the eschatological and larger ecotheological vision of Pope Francis.

Laudato Si', Eschatology, and Some Guiding Themes for Development

While Pope Francis concerns himself chiefly with developing an integral ethic in *Laudato si'*, he offers some compact suggestions to ecologically reorient several traditional theological loci: sacraments (*LS* 233–237), Trinity (*LS* 238–240), Mariology (*LS* 241–242), and, finally, eschatology, in a section titled "Beyond the Sun" (*LS* 243–245). In these three short paragraphs on eschatology, Francis briefly suggests how an ecological reorientation of eschatology might broaden our understanding of God's saving action throughout God's creation.

First, Francis includes non-human creation in eschatological renewal: "Eternal life will be a shared experience of awe, in which each creature, resplendently transfigured, will take its rightful place and have something to give those poor men and women who will have been liberated once and for all" (*LS* 243). While he maintains the special place accorded to humanity in Christian theologies of creation, Francis moves away from the exclusivity that characterizes someone like Thomas Aquinas, who sees plants and animals only as food for human bodies and thus obsolete and absent from the consummation of the universe.[6] Francis affirms an independent value to these creatures when he writes, "In union with all creatures, we journey through this land seeking God" (LS 244).

Second, Francis emphasizes God's presence to all creatures, even amid their suffering: "In the heart of this world, the Lord of life, who loves us so much, is always present. He does not abandon us, he does not leave us alone, for he has united himself definitively to our earth, and his love constantly impels us to find new ways forward" (LS 245). Thus, while Francis recognizes that God calls us to a "generous commitment to give [God] our all" (LS 245), he also stresses the strength and comfort that God offers such that our "struggles and our concern for this planet [must] never take away the joy of our hope" (LS 244). In this passage, Francis echoes the theologies of hope that have recently reshaped the study of eschatology.

Still, these reflections on an ecological reorientation of eschatology, while important, remain too compact a basis for the more radical rethinking of eschatology that Francis urges. Laudato si' does say a great deal about the need for ecological conversion and its demands, however. Given the earlier assertion of a link between conversion in the present and human projections of some eschatological future, Francis's more numerous comments on conversion throughout Laudato si' provide additional insights into his vision of an ecological eschatology. Thus, in what follows, I highlight four guiding principles in the text that clarify the shape of the needed conversion.

First, Francis insists on a larger shift in worldview that synthesizes faith and reason: "If we are truly concerned to develop an ecology capable of remedying the damage we have done, no branch of the sciences and no form of wisdom can be left out" (LS 63). He warns against scientific reductionism and "the tendency, at times unconscious, to make the method and aims of science and technology an epistemological paradigm" (LS 107) and calls for an "urgently

---

6. For a discussion of Aquinas's denial of a redemptive future for plants and animals, see ST, Suppl. IIIae, q. 91, as discussed in Elizabeth A. Johnson, Ask the Beasts: Darwin and the God of Love (New York: Bloomsbury, 2014), 228–235.

need[ed] . . . humanism capable of bringing together the different fields of knowledge . . . in the service of a more integral and integrating vision" (*LS* 144) that is itself rooted in a conversion both of "lifestyle and spirituality" (*LS* 111).

Second, this humanism cannot be an unfettered anthropocentrism that espouses "a Promethean vision of mastery over the world" (*LS* 116) in which "we end up worshipping earthly powers, or ourselves usurping the place of God . . . , claiming an unlimited right to trample his creation underfoot" (*LS* 75). Francis also warns against the opposite mistake of "'biocentrism' . . . that would entail . . . yet another imbalance, failing to solve present problems and adding new ones" (*LS* 118). In other words, both excessive anthropocentrism and biocentrism displace God from the center: "Rather, all creatures are moving forward with us and through us towards a common point of arrival, which is God, in that transcendent fullness where the risen Christ embraces and illumines all things" (*LS* 83).

Third, for Francis, "an integral ecology includes taking time to recover a serene harmony with creation" (*LS* 225). This is neither a naïve Romanticism (*LS* 11, 54) nor a Luddite rejection of technology because it is a radical rather than a merely sentimental change in our disposition towards the world. As Francis submits, "[we] are speaking of an attitude of the heart, one which approaches life with serene attentiveness, which is capable of being fully present to someone without thinking of what comes next, which accepts each moment as a gift from God to be lived to the full" (*LS* 226). Far from being closed to the inbreaking of something new, this attentiveness rejects the human tendency towards quick solutions in a spirit of "rapidification" that "contrasts with the naturally slow pace of biological evolution" (*LS* 18).

Fourth, Francis insists that this larger redemptive consummation is integral to the order of creation: "The God who liberates and saves is the same God who created the universe, and these two divine ways of acting are intimately and inseparably connected" (*LS* 73). While this theme is the least developed of the four principles to be drawn from the document, it is decisive for reasons that will become clear in the next section.

To summarize, an eschatology rooted in Francis's vision of integral ecology must (1) actively integrate the insights of faith and reason (2) in relation to a proper understanding of the place of humanity within the larger created order (3) and be oriented by a subjectivity that is open to God's ongoing action in our midst, which (4) is inseparable from God's work of redemption. In relation to a fully articulated eschatology, these four principles are more aspirational than concrete solutions. Still, they are highly instructive for constructing foundations for an ecologically oriented theology that advances Francis's vision.

Some Critiques of *Laudato Si'* in Contemporary Ecotheology

While these four principles provide an important guide for constructing an ecological eschatology, some theologians worry that, on at least several occasions, *Laudato si'* betrays a relative ignorance of the current state of ecotheology. First, despite its explicit statement of the need for a unified account of creation and redemption, *Laudato si'* is said to overemphasize the role of creation to the detriment of both Christology and redemption. Denis Edwards likens this imbalance to that found in many of the earliest ecotheologies, which countered the opposite tendency of some theologies to virtually omit nature and creation within salvation history.[7] More recent ecotheologies—particularly those belonging to the "Deep Incarnationalism" for which Edwards advocates—have worked to unite both aspects in a more comprehensive account.

Second, some criticize *Laudato si'* for failing to sufficiently consider the ongoing need for evolutionary science to reorient both the method and object of ecotheological study. While Francis readily acknowledges evolution, in parts of the encyclical, his account nevertheless reflects a pre-evolutionary worldview.[8] Celia Deane-Drummond submits that *Laudato si'* remains "tantalizingly unclear" on precisely how God acts in the emergence of humanity—both

---

7. Denis Edwards, "'Sublime Communion': The Theology of the Natural World in *Laudato si'*," *Theological Studies* 77, no. 2 (2016): 377–391, at 378–379.

8. See Celia Deane-Drummond, "In Adam All Die?: Questions at the Boundary of Niche Construction, Community Evolution, and Original Sin," in *Evolution and the Fall*, eds. William T. Cavanaugh and James K.A. Smith (Grand Rapids, MI: William B. Eerdmans Publishing Company, 2017), 23–47.

collectively and as individual persons—and that Francis "fails to take into account more broadly . . . the necessity of situating ecological science in the context of evolutionary accounts, and vice versa."[9] Edwards similarly argues that *Laudato si'* would benefit from a clearer acknowledgement of the evolutionary interplay of contingency and necessity in the unfolding of the world. In particular, he adverts to the need for a theological reckoning with the messiness and suffering of evolution and, therein, with "the dark side of nature . . . [and] the theology of the cross."[10]

Finally, Deane-Drummond questions whether Francis differentiates the conceptual resources in *Laudato si'* enough to integrate the diverse kinds of knowing under the single umbrella of an integral ecology. Indeed, she argues, the term "ecology" is only a recent linguistic invention—used first by the biologist and philosopher Ernst Haeckel near the beginning of the twentieth century—and so lacks clear definition. That is, "ecology" does not effectively distinguish among the methods of investigation and verification of the diverse fields of scientific, social, and human sciences upon which it jointly relies.[11] She accordingly questions Francis's advocacy for dialogue between science and religion as his own account lacks the conceptual resources for framing this dialogue or integrating their unique contributions.[12]

These points of criticism, though not exhaustive, effectively demonstrate the necessity of a collaborative effort to develop theological foundations befitting the challenges Pope Francis sketches in *Laudato si'*. To fulfill the encyclical's specific mandate, one must confront ongoing issues concerning an ecologically and evolutionarily oriented theology. As the next section shows, Lonergan's notion of

---

9. Celia Deane Drummond, "*Laudato si'* and the Natural Sciences: An Assessment of Possibilities and Limits," *Theological Studies* 77, no. 2 (2016): 392–415, at 398 and 394.

10. Edwards, "Sublime Communion," 380.

11. Deane-Drummond, "*Laudato Si* and the Natural Sciences", 392, citing Robert McIntosh, *The Background of Ecology: Concept and Theory* (Cambridge: Cambridge University, 1985), 1–26.

12. Deane-Drummond, "*Laudato Si* and the Natural Sciences," 408–410. Deane-Drummond points especially to Donella Meadows's important work on systems theory as a helpful alternative.

generalized emergent probability can remedy these shortcomings of *Laudato si'*, while also heeding Francis's principles presented above.

Emergent Probability in Lonergan

Lonergan's notion of emergent probability first appears in a chapter of *Insight* titled, "The Complementarity of Classical and Statistical Structures."[13] Lonergan argues that when our fundamental desire to know moves from descriptions of things-in-relation-to-us to explanations of things-in-relation-to-each-other (e.g. from considering the sun as rising and setting to situating it within the solar system), our spontaneous questioning of the world employs both classical and statistical laws. Classical laws express systematic regularities in nature, all other things being equal, such as the formula, $F = ma$. Statistical laws explain non-systematic divergences from some norm by expressing an ideal frequency. For instance, statistical analysis discerns the likelihood of heads or tails on a coin conforming more closely to 50/50 over an increasing number of flips, despite the unpredictability of any single flip. Simply put, classical laws express what will happen under the proviso of all the right circumstances obtaining (i.e. if A, then B), and statistical laws express how often that proviso is met. Lonergan underscores that modern science acknowledges a complementarity between these two kinds of knowing, both as regards the cognitional operations of the human subject *and* as an objective complementarity "in the intelligibility immanent in the universe of our experience."[14] Thus, humans know things-in-relation-to-each-other according to classical or statistical formulations precisely because reality itself is constituted by both formal necessity and actual contingency and so is isomorphic with our cognitive, heuristic anticipations of these distinct kinds of intelligibility. Furthermore, reality exists precisely through the combination of these intelligibilities.

Lonergan then turns to the complementarities in the realities known, describing the intelligibility of the world in its inherently

---

13. Bernard J.F. Lonergan, *Insight: A Study of Human Understanding*, Collected Works of Bernard Lonergan (CWL) 3, eds. Frederick E. Crowe and Robert M. Doran (Toronto: University of Toronto Press, 2005), 126–162.

14. Lonergan, *Insight*, 139.

developmental, evolutionary character as emergently probable. By "emergence," Lonergan refers to the advent of something genuinely new in the world that did not exist or occur before. However, emergence does not occur *ex nihilo*. Instead, a new reality emerges from the conditions fulfilled by a concrete plurality of lower order phenomena already existing in the world. For instance, depending on the occurrence of suitable conditions on the level of physics, subatomic particles fulfill the conditions for the emergence of more complex elements and compounds operating on the distinctly chemical level. At the same time, these chemical compounds depend on the perdurance of realities whose intelligibilities are properly physical. In accord with schedules of probability, these lower order schemes of recurrence ground further schemes, from the genera of physics to chemistry, to biology, and to sensitive and rational psychologies.

The march of progress is often interrupted, and so Lonergan recognizes the possibility and reality of blind alleys in evolutionary processes. However, once a scheme of recurrence has emerged onto a new generic order, it tends toward the conservation of the lower order in a way that may lead to the emergence of even higher schemes. For instance, once living cells emerge from a chemical substrate, those cells promote the cyclical reproduction of lower order chemical processes such that the probability of the reemergence of those same life-giving chemical reactions is governed by the laws and probabilities proper to a newly emergent biological pattern of life. What was once highly unlikely to emerge becomes likelier to recur, which, in a developing universe, consequently supplies the condition for the emergence of new schemes. Thus, in his presentation of emergent probability, Lonergan provides an account of the observably intelligible and verifiably developing world order. This evinces a true dialogue between faith and reason by engaging the findings and processes of modern science and demonstrating their non-contradiction with the questions and methods of theology or other disciplines. That is, this account proposes a framework for instantiating the first principle of *Laudato si'* identified above.

Moreover, Lonergan's theory of emergent probability permits a larger revisioning of the dynamic world order in line with an evolutionary worldview. In a recent essay comparing Lonergan's emergent probability with Pierre Teilhard de Chardin's highly imaginative teleology, Patrick Byrne highlights Lonergan's explanation of the universe as an "upwardly but indeterminately directed dynamism."[15] For Lonergan, lower cycles set the conditions for the possibility of the emergence of more complex and irreducibly new phenomena, an emergence that does not depend on some *dea ex machina*.[16] The scientific account of the realization of an unlikely emergence depends squarely on time. Given enough time, the probability of something new and higher emerging increases according to both the statistical intelligibilities of their processes and the classical laws governing the lower schemes of recurrence, assuming the conditions are right. In this sense, Lonergan's more explanatory and scientific account has a distinct advantage over Teilhard's more descriptive and imaginative account. In accord with emergent probability, a lifeless physical universe can give rise to successive orders of emergence all the way up to intelligent life as we know it.

This account of emergent probability illustrates how a wide range of correlations and probabilities interact to enable the emergence of an ever more complex universe. As Byrne explains, however, Lonergan argues that two other methods of inquiry—the genetic and the dialectical— are needed to describe the ways in which human beings investigate and explain the knowable universe. These additional methods pertain to the new intelligibilities arising from the emergence of life and of intelligent life, including the distinctiveness of human forms of intelligence, which, in line with the second principle of *Laudato si'*, clarifies the unique place of humanity within creation. First, a genetic method of inquiry attends to the intelligibility of biological life, which is characterized by "embryological and other forms of development . . . [and] other forms of self-modifying processes."[17] This includes the biological growth proper to organisms, but, in higher animals and especially in humans, it also includes the "growth of self-correcting understanding in individual human beings and in human communities as well."[18] Second, with

15. Lonergan, *Insight*, 501, cited in Patrick H. Byrne, "The Integral Visions of Teilhard and Lonergan: Science, the Universe, Humanity, and God," in *From Teilhard to Omega: Co-creating an Unfinished Universe*, ed. Ilia Delio (Maryknoll, NY: Orbis Books, 2014), 100.

16. Though it does not rule out a creator. See Patrick H. Byrne, "Lonergan, Evolutionary Science, and Intelligent Design," *Revista Portuguesa de Filosofia* 63 (2007): 893–913.

17. Byrne, "The Integral Visions of Teilhard and Lonergan," 102.

18. Byrne, "The Integral Visions of Teilhard and Lonergan," 102.

the emergence of intelligence arises an "endless source of intelligible, recurring schemes" of production, cooperation, learning, and valuing.[19] However, there also arises the possibility of human unintelligence.

Thus, dialectical method examines the interplay of beings who can act attentively, intelligently, reasonably, responsibly, and lovingly, but who frequently—and, ultimately, inexplicably—do not. To account for both the biological cycles of self-regulated growth (genetic) and the impact of the misuse of (particularly human) intelligence (dialectical), we arrive at what Lonergan names "generalized emergent probability"[20] as an explanation of "the intelligible unity of the evolving universe."[21]

However, this unity is "imperfect" and "fractured" because disordered human choices against intelligent and loving action distort the range of probabilities within human consciousness and among the options for choice. From a theological viewpoint, this is the problem of evil: "Given that God is all-good, all-understanding, and all-powerful, the problem is that there has to be something more to the unity of the universe than has been envisioned so far in generalized emergent probability. Evil is the problem to which this 'something more' is the solution."[22] However, Byrne continues, this "something more" is "supernatural" in the sense that it "does not emerge from the earlier stages of evolution" but is, according to Lonergan, "principally the work of God . . . [acting to bring about] a harmonious continuation of the actual order of the universe . . . [to realize] a new and higher integration of human activity."[23] Byrne concludes with Lonergan's claim that the infusion of the "supernatural virtues of faith, hope, and self-sacrificing love . . . [to transform] the effects of evil into good" characterizes this higher emergence.[24] By acting in accord with these virtues in relation to all of creation, humans contribute to the redemption and consummation of the whole.

---

19. Byrne, "The Integral Visions of Teilhard and Lonergan," 102.

20. Lonergan, *Insight*, 533.

21. Byrne, "The Integral Visions of Teilhard and Lonergan," 103.

22. Byrne, "The Integral Visions of Teilhard and Lonergan," 103.

23. Byrne, "The Integral Visions of Teilhard and Lonergan," 103.

24. Byrne, "The Integral Visions of Teilhard and Lonergan," 103. The meaning of "self-sacrificing" does not entail self-destructive. For the most complete account of Lonergan's ethics, see Patrick H. Byrne, *The Ethics of Discernment: Lonergan's Foundation for Ethics* (Toronto: University of Toronto Press, 2016).

The foregoing account provides foundations for developing an eschatology that meets the needs of both a more ecologically oriented theology and the first two principles specified in *Laudato si'*. Lonergan's explanatory, evolutionary worldview accounts for the emergence of intelligent humanity in terms accessible to all persons irrespective of their religious creed, while elucidating the breakdown of the complete intelligibility of the world due to the inattentive, obtuse, irrational, irresponsible, and unloving behavior of human beings. Moreover, this worldview is open to an eschatology inasmuch as it acknowledges the need for a supernatural emergence within the present world order.

Still, *Insight* appeared in 1957, fourteen years before the first noteworthy papal comments on the environment in Pope Paul VI's *Octogesima adveniens* and ten years before Lynn White's "The Historical Roots of Our Ecologic Crisis."[25] Much work remains in developing and applying Lonergan's insights to a broader reorientation of theology. Other recent contributions have already clarified the relevance of Lonergan's work for understanding ecological conversion and in starting to develop a theology of emergent creation.[26] However, they do not sufficiently apply the ampler perspective of generalized emergent probability with respect to the finality of the cosmos. Without this framework, they cannot correct possible excessively anthropocentric connotations; while they properly place humans in the developmental lineage of creation, they fail to account for how non-human creation fits within the redemptive plan for the whole world order. In the next section, I will show how a more expansive understanding of emergent probability provides a set of special categories to ground a more thoroughly *theological* eschatology.

Grace and Emergence in Eschatology

In Byrne's reformulation of the overarching thrust of Teilhard's thought on the finality of the created universe, the emergence of grace

---

25. Paul VI, *Octogesima Adveniens* [Apostolic Letter on the Occasion of the Eightieth Anniversary of the Encyclical *Rerum Novarum*], May 14, 1971, §21; and Lynn White Jr., "The Historical Roots of Our Ecologic Crisis," *Science* 155, no. 3767 (1967): 1203–1207. White argues that the mounting ecological crises result from a disordered Western worldview, emphasizing especially the dangers of Judeo-Christian teleology and Christian anthropocentrism.

26. See note 5.

is the divine "something more" that overcomes the human inability to overcome the problem of sin. It is absolutely supernatural in relation to both the human incapacity to overcome moral impotence and to the proportionate being of created nature. Until this point, the theory of generalized emergent probability explains the upward thrust of an evolving world towards greater complexity by employing the understandings and concepts that are proper to created nature. Yet, from the standpoint of faith, this theory is open to an explanation in terms of the redemptive order of grace. I argue that, in accord with the principle that the differences between saving and elevating grace, on the one hand, and the culminating light of glory, on the other hand, are ones of degree, these are related to each other as developmental stages in the supernatural order.[27] It follows that emergent probability also applies to our understanding of eschatology, insofar as an emerging world order, further elevated by God's self-communication in history, reaches out towards its final consummation in the fullness of time. What, then, is the relationship between emergent probability and the order of grace?

Grace is the gratuitous gift of God's love that both heals the sinful world and elevates it to an ever more profound intimacy with God. Grace bestows upon humans disproportionate excellences that both (1) enable them to overcome their moral impotence and realize their full humanity (*gratia sanans*) and (2) bring about friendship with God (*gratia elevans*). This disproportionate character of grace grants human beings in the world a proleptic participation in the Kingdom of God that continues to unfold over time. Gracious excellence generates possibilities beyond the attainable range predicted by finite schedules of probability made possible by the intelligibility of the physical, chemical, biological, and intelligent orders of created being. At the same time, the continuation of the natural and upwardly directed dynamism of the whole world order avoids the image of an arbitrarily interventionist God so alien to contemporary

---

27. For this principle, see, for example, Aquinas in *ST* I, q. 94, art. 1, obj. 6: "We merit glory by an act of grace; but we do not merit grace by an act of nature." Aquinas argues that humans are created in grace, though grace is not merited by the order of nature, and, further, that grace is consummated in glory in the fullness of time. The commonly-repeated and condensed formulation I invoke above doesn't appear until more recent history, but the idea is found in a number of medieval authors.

ecotheology. In this view, we can apprehend the entitatively dispro-portionate activity of grace as the emergence of a radically new order integrated into nature and history and so consonant with Lonergan's foundational categories.

In one of his earliest articles, "Finality, Love and Marriage," Lonergan argues that "on each level reality responds to God as abso-lute motive and tends to Him as absolute term; but on each level it does so differently."[28] Lonergan distinguishes three kinds of final-ity operative in the dynamism of all things—absolute, horizontal, and vertical—by which all things are concretely swept up into the "upward thrust" toward higher emergent goods:

> Absolute finality is to God in His intrinsic goodness: it is uni-versal; it is unique; it is hypothetically necessary, for if there is anything to respond to motive or to proceed to term, then its response or tendency can be accounted for ultimately only by the one self-sufficient good. Horizontal finality results from abstract essence; it holds even when the object is in isolation; it is to a motive or term that is proportionate to essence. But vertical finality is in the concrete; in point of fact it is not from the isolated instance but from the conjoined plurality; and it is in the field not of natural but of statistical law, not of the abstract *per se* but of the concrete *per accidens*. . . . Vertical finality is of the very idea of our hierarchic universe, of the ordination of things devised and exploited by the divine Arti-san. For the cosmos is not an aggregate of isolated objects hier-archically arranged on isolated levels, but a dynamic whole in which instrumentally, dispositively, materially, obedientially, one level of being or activity subserves another. The intercon-nections are endless and manifest. Vertical finality would seem beyond dispute.[29]

If all three versions of finality express the order of the created uni-verse towards God, vertical finality is specifically concerned with the way that real beings are oriented towards God by their particular

---

28. Bernard J.F. Lonergan, "Finality, Love, Marriage," in *Collection*, CWL 4, eds. Frederick E. Crowe and Robert M. Doran (Toronto: University of Toronto Press, 1988), 479–480.

29. Lonergan, "Finality, Love, Marriage," 481–482.

locus within the contingently unfolding and deeply interrelated world. Whereas absolute finality describes the relationship to God as the absolute term of our longing, vertical finality recognizes the innumerable and more remote proximate relations through which all creation is lifted up in grace. Vertical finality thus clarifies the exact place of humanity among other beings in the created order. The key is to understand the relations of all things as participating in the emergent goodness of creation across time, even in the emergence of the prior conditions for the *de facto* realization of the visible missions of the Son and Spirit in history. To quote Lonergan at length:

> [It] is most conspicuous to one who looks at the universe with the eyes of modern science, who sees sub-atoms uniting into atoms, atoms into compounds, compounds into organisms, who finds the pattern of genes in reproductive cells shifting, *ut in minori parte*, to give organic evolution within limited ranges, who attributes the rise of cultures and civilizations to the interplay of human plurality, who observes that only when and where the higher rational culture emerged did God acknowledge the fullness of time permitting the Word to become flesh and the Mystical Body to begin its intussusception of human personalities and its leavening of human history.[30]

The upwardly directed dynamism that characterizes the evolutionary unfolding of nature reaches a climax in the new possibilities for divinization through the missions of the Son and Spirit in the world. Though more compact than Lonergan's later account of emergent probability in *Insight*, these comments suggest a way to extend generalized emergent probability into a theology of grace that meets the challenge of *Laudato si'*. Specifically, it grounds an eschatology that is already initiated by redemptive components that emerge, elevate, and consummate successive orders of creation. This *aperçu* heuristically anticipates the further inbreaking of contingent and improbable newness through the unfolding of redemptive grace.

Thus, while the more differentiated discussion of generalized emergent probability originated in the philosophical register of Lonergan's *Insight*, those general categories take on new meanings in relation to Christian revelation and theology, which affirms that

---

30. Lonergan, "Finality, Love, Marriage," 480–481.

God's free sending of the Son in the Incarnation changed the character of the whole world: "All creation has been groaning in labor pains until now" (Romans 8:22). Emergent probability locates God's entry into human history within a trajectory of successive higher orders of the larger world and the cosmos. Over vast swathes of time, the emergence of intelligent, rational, consciousness made possible the Second Person of the Trinity's becoming incarnate as a human being "created in God's image." This, however, is not the end of the story, for without the Incarnation and redeeming Crucifixion, Resurrection would have been impossible, as would our adoption into the intra-trinitarian life.[31] The Father's sending of the Son, who together with the Father sent the Holy Spirit of love into our hearts, grounds Paul's claim that we "are not in the flesh . . . [but] in the Spirit, since the Spirit of God dwells in [us]" (Romans 8:9) and that "because [we] are children, God has sent the Spirit of his Son into our hearts, crying, 'Abba! Father!'" (Galatians 4:6).

Notice, though, that the free offer of higher emergence through grace enables us to freely cooperate with God, who conforms us to Godself in Christ Jesus through the ongoing processes of divinization, and, thereby, builds up the Kingdom of God. Lonergan suggests that human growth in grace and wisdom through a process of divinization exists in a "harmonious continuation of the present order of the universe . . . and that its realization and development occur through acts of human acknowledgement and consent that accord with probability schedules. . . ."[32] The effects of grace become part of the larger manifold of possible and probable events in the ongoing dynamism of the universe. Thus, once the world order is leavened with the surprising effects of grace, probabilities are heightened that it will recur, both more easily and predictably. In light of this synthesis, we can conceive of creation in every moment of time rather than only a first moment in an ever-receding past. Jesus' Incarnation, Passion, Crucifixion, and Resurrection make it emergently more probable for human persons to be brought into the life of Trinitarian friendship. Nevertheless, it is the free and unmerited gift of grace itself that makes human cooperation possible and effective;

---

31. See Jen Sanders, "A Nonviolent, Trinitarian Transformation of Ecological Values," Presentation at the Catholic Theological Society of America, June 9, 2017.

32. Lonergan, *Insight*, 747–748.

thus, over time, grace actualizes the goodness both of human reality and of all created nature in its own right. By a free act of God, the Incarnation renders actual what has become emergently possible in the graced flesh of the human woman, Mary. This further enables the saving death and resurrection of Jesus so that humanity is taken up into the heart of God, and good creation, now marred by sin, is redeemed in Christ's resurrected body as the core of the New Heaven and the New Earth descending from Heaven.

In this light, we can understand that grace frees the goodness and even the holiness in humans that was emergently probable but hitherto unrealized. Moreover, theology can grasp and communicate that the operations on each level and indeed of each created thing— in the perspective of emergent probabilities, realized and unrealized— are promoted by divine grace. The God who is Lord of Nature is also the Lord of History, in which God's free grace brings hitherto unexpected and novel possibilities out of humble beginnings.

Expanding the account of grace beyond merely human contexts challenges us to rethink the place of non-human creation in God's plan, though the discussion of this implication for differing animals and ecosystems is beyond the scope of this essay. I only wish to invite a reconsideration of how divine providence perfects creation and everything in it through emergent probability. To recall the words of Henry Beston:

> We need a wiser and perhaps a more mystical concept of animals. . . . We patronize them for their incompleteness, for their tragic fate of having taken a form so far below ours. And therein we err, and greatly err. For the animal shall not be measured by man. In a world older and more complete than ours, they move finished and complete, gifted with extensions of the senses we have lost or never attained, living by voices we shall never hear. They are not brethren, they are not underlings; they are other Nations, caught with ourselves in the net of life and time, fellow prisoners of the splendor and travail of the Earth.[33]

Whether or not this theology of grace inspires the mandate to affirm that, in fact, "all dogs go to heaven," it does suggest that all dogs are

---

33. Henry Beston, *The Outermost House* (1926), as quoted in Philip Hoare, *The Whale: In Search of the Giants of the Sea* (New York: Ecco, 2010), 210.

caught up in the orders of grace and finality. Likewise, it suggests that an adequately eschatological account of creation may enrich our understanding of creation, help us transcend a merely protological account of eschatology, and open up an unlimited horizon wherein we are better able to recognize the workings of grace throughout the intelligible world.

Conclusion

It has become clear that this ecologically oriented eschatology fulfills Francis's four requirements. First, it integrates faith and reason in the verifiable continuity of emergence through progressive stages of cosmic (including human) history. This continuity is rooted in the interdependence of the higher levels of creation as more excellent and lower levels as more essential within the continued unfolding of vertical finality in the order of grace, even as the world remains liable to the surd of sin. This account accordingly transposes whatever is good in an anthropocentric account of grace and salvation into the much grander scope of God's grace at work in the whole of spatial and temporal creation. It invites us to attend to the continuity between our own existence and all the diverse elements that gave rise to our being, thereby fulfilling the second criterion gleaned from *Laudato si'*. It also fulfills the third criterion of orienting human subjectivity towards God's action in our midst, as this account stresses the irreducible newness of emergent orders in history in order to concretize the myriad ways grace builds on nature and concludes in glory beyond our imagination or doing. Finally, in relation to the fourth criterion, it specifies the continuity between the orders of creation and redemption, explaining how redemption is both disproportionate to and yet presupposes and builds on the intelligibility inherent in the finite processes of creation.

In addition to meeting Francis's criteria, this sketch of an ecologically oriented theology also answers the three challenges that Deane-Drummond and Edwards pose to *Laudato si'*. First, generalized emergent probability not only reveals the link between creation and redemption but also offers an explanatory account of the intelligibility of the divine order in creation in relation to four distinct methods of contemporary sciences. These methods—classical, statistical, genetic, and dialectical—explicitly identify the genetic reality of emergences and intelligibilities and then dialectically identify where and how the distorting effects of sin enter the world, in a new and distinctive way with specifically human intelligence and action.

Second, this account thoroughly integrates evolutionary theory into ecotheology by distinguishing between God's primary and created nature's secondary causality. Moreover, it interprets the specific way that grace moves from probability to actuality and explains the different facets of that shift in regards to diverse explanatory strata. It allows that higher-order emergences in cosmic history have depended purely on confluences of relatively unlikely events becoming more probable over long periods of time according to the interplay of classical and statistical intelligibilities. At the same time, in delineating the genetic and dialectical orders of intelligibility, this framework accounts for the novelties that are realized in the emergence of the self-correcting processes of biological life and in the tension of inquiry proper to intelligent life, respectively. Thus, God's self-communication through sanctifying grace, known as the gift of God's love poured into our hearts (Romans 5:5), is understood not only to heal the sinfulness of human persons, but also to make both possible and effective the human cooperation with God's plan that contributes to the eternal unfolding of the Kingdom of God on earth. While I cannot treat the saving power of Christ's Cross in this essay, this theoretical framework demonstrates a prior theological foundation for its place: namely, the intelligible workings of grace in relation to the other operative intelligible orders in nature through history.

Third, Lonergan's theory of emergent probability is integrated into a powerful explanatory matrix through its further grounding in a phenomenological account of cognitional theory. Lonergan's *Insight* is specifically arranged to guide the self-appropriation of the structure common to all acts of knowing through mathematics, the modern empirical sciences, and the unique forms of intelligibility that emerge in evolution. In sum, it provides a complete account of the unity and differentiation of diverse systems as well as of the unlimited possibilities of the human mind in relation to the whole of creation. Lonergan's account of a critical metaphysics argues persuasively that human beings have the potential to know and even to love all creation.

The importance of further developing this trajectory in relation to the ongoing rethinking of humanity's place in both the interconnected world and the successive ages of cosmic history is clear. It heightens our awareness of our own entanglement in the complexity of what is, as well as our responsibility to wonder about and welcome whatever we can only anticipate in the emergently probable construction of the Kingdom of God in our midst. This is reflected already in the rule of prayer and faith in the Church as seen, for instance, in the Marian dogmas. We recognize Mary's role in bringing about the pure instance of grace as operative in our own human reality in order to recognize the utter mysteriousness and greatness of the "something more" God has in store for the universe. In the doctrine of her Immaculate Conception, the Church affirms the pervasive, bodily effects of grace that reached the tip of Mary's fingers, from the moment of her conception, and this helps us appreciate the grace realized in her special role in the Incarnation. Yet, though she was full of grace from the beginning, we still marvel at the new thing God brought about in the Assumption when "the Immaculate Mother of God, the ever Virgin Mary, having completed the course of her earthly life, was assumed body and soul into heavenly glory."[34]

---

34. Pius XII, *Munificentissimus Deus* [Encyclical Defining the Dogma of the Assumption], November 1, 1950, §44.

CHAPTER ELEVEN

Ecological Conversion, Healing, and the Integral Ecology of *Laudato Si'*

Cristina Vanin (St. Jerome's University)

I n October 2018, the International Panel on Climate Change (IPCC) submitted a special report that presents the projected impacts of global warming of 1.5°C above pre-industrial level and related global greenhouse gas emission pathways. The IPCC expressed high confidence that "[g]lobal warming is *likely* to reach 1.5°C between 2030 and 2052 if it continues to increase at the current rate."[1] Indeed, the pledges to cut CO_2 emissions made at the 2015 Paris Agreement put the planet on a trajectory to reach a global warming temperature of 3°C by 2100.[2] The Panel indicated that the warming that has occurred from the pre-industrial period to the present, and that has been caused by anthropogenic emissions, will persist for centuries. The Earth will continue to experience significant changes in its climate system, such as more frequent and intense heat waves, more damaging storms, a rise in sea levels, and the bleaching of the world's coral reefs. To limit the warming to 1.5°C requires us to act immediately to cut total planetary emissions to 45% below 2010 levels by the year 2030.

However, this substantial data on climate change, along with information about species loss, habitat degradation, and loss of biodiversity,

---

1. IPCC, "Global Warming of 1.5°C," Section A: Understanding Global Warming of 1.5°C, https://www.ipcc.ch/sr15/.

2. Stephen Leahy, "Climate change impacts worse than expected, global report warns," *National Geographic*, October 7, 2018, https://www.nationalgeographic.com/environment/2018/10/ipcc-report-climate-change-impacts-forests-emissions/.

does not seem to stir human persons and communities towards the ecological conversion that the Catholic church has been urging since John Paul II's 1990 World Day of Peace Message.[3] This chapter focuses on the following questions: What are the dynamics of the breakdown and decline that we are experiencing as an ecological crisis? How are we to understand the resistance or inability of persons to acknowledge, accept, or respond to the ongoing deterioration of the earth's ecosystems? What helps us to overcome resistance at the psychic level and develop the integral ecology called for by Pope Francis in his encyclical, *Laudato si'*? It is my hope that bringing the encyclical into dialogue with the thought of Bernard Lonergan and Robert Doran on progress and decline, especially with regard to the dialectic of culture as well as the notion of psychic conversion, will help to explain how we can move toward healing the relationship between human persons and the Earth and, as a result, overcome the ecological crisis.[4]

The Analogy of Dialectic and the Integral Scale of Values

One way to begin to understand the dynamics of the ecological crisis is by turning to what Doran sees as the primary categories for understanding the structure of history, namely, the "analogy of the dialectic" and the "integral scale of values." Doran draws on Lonergan's discussion of the dialectics of the subject and of community and contributes a further dialectic of culture. Then, he relates the dialectical processes to each other according to the structure of the scale of values. Understanding these relationships and their breakdown can provide us with some insight into the dynamics of the current ecological crisis.

---

3. See Cristina Vanin, "Care and Compassion: The Need for an Integral Ecology," in *Ecotheology and Nonhuman Ethics in Society: A Community of Compassion*, ed. Melissa Brotton (Lanham, MD: Lexington Books, 2017), 179–196. This chapter provides information about the developments that have taken place in Catholic thinking about care for the natural world.

4. This chapter expands on some aspects of Neil Ormerod and Cristina Vanin, "Ecological Conversion: What Does It Mean?," *Theological Studies* 77, no. 2 (2016): 328–352.

As Lonergan states in *Insight*, each dialectic is internally constituted as a "concrete unfolding of linked but opposed principles of change."[5] In regards to the dialectic of the subject, those principles are "neural demands for psychic integration and conscious representation; . . . and the censorship over these demands [that is] exercised by dramatically patterned intelligence and imagination. . . ."[6] The dialectic of community is constituted by the principles of spontaneous intersubjectivity and the "practical intelligence that institutes the technological, economic, and political structures of society."[7] Finally, the principles that comprise the dialectic of culture are cosmological constitutive meaning and anthropological constitutive meaning.

Doran makes clear that: (i) each dialectic embodies a creative tension of limitation and transcendence; (ii) each is a dialectic of contraries, not contradictories; (iii) the integrity of a given dialectic is a function of a third principle of higher synthesis, principles beyond the ones that constitute the dialectic itself. Furthermore, both constitutive principles are important. Each dialectic is an *integral* dialectic to the degree that there is a harmonious interaction between both principles. Distortions then, are the result of the dominance of one principle over the other.[8]

How are the dialectics related to each other? To answer this, Doran turns to the integral scale of values. Lonergan speaks of five levels of value: vital, social, cultural, personal, and religious.[9] The

---

5. Bernard Lonergan, *Insight: A Study of Human Understanding*, Collected Works of Bernard Lonergan, vol. 3, eds. Frederick E. Crowe and Robert M. Doran (Toronto: University of Toronto Press, 1992), 242.

6. Robert M. Doran, "The Analogy of Dialectic and the Systematics of History," in *Religion in Context: Recent Studies in Lonergan*, ed. Timothy Fallon. (University Press of America, 1988), 38. See also Robert M. Doran, *Theology and the Dialectics of History* (Toronto: University of Toronto Press, 1990).

7. Doran, "The Analogy of Dialectic and the Systematics of History," 38.

8. Doran, "The Analogy of Dialectic and the Systematics of History," 39. There is a dialectic of contradictories that functions with respect to a third principle of higher synthesis: "either universal willingness or some blend of the biases; either authentic or inauthentic culture; either soteriological meaning and truth or . . . a one-sided vision of reality. . . ." (40).

9. See Bernard Lonergan, *Method in Theology* (New York: Seabury Press, 1972), 31–32.

higher levels of value condition the schemes of recurrence at the more basic levels so that: religious values condition the possibility of personal integrity; personal integrity conditions the possibility of genuine cultural values; cultural integrity conditions the possibility of a just social order; and a just social order conditions the possibility of the equitable distribution of vital goods.[10]

A society is healthy to the extent that the dialectic of community is healthy, that is, to the extent that there is a healthy dialectical tension between spontaneous intersubjectivity and practical intelligence. Genuine cultural values—commensurate with the proportions of the social dialectic and operative at the everyday level—ensure the integrity of this dialectic. Today, the dialectic of community is global because there are socioeconomic relations and political realities that constitute a global interdependent order. This requires us to generate cultural values that are more complex and adequate to this global reality. Such attention to the need for genuine cultural values pushes us to consider the dialectic of culture.

Drawing on the work of Eric Voegelin, Doran argues that, as with the other dialectics, the dialectic of culture is a dialectic of contraries involving two related principles: cosmological constitutive meaning (as the limiting factor) and anthropological constitutive meaning (as the promoter of transcendence). Like the other dialectics, the integrity of the dialectic of culture is a function of the concrete unfolding of *both* cosmological and anthropological insights and meaning.[11]

With the cosmological pole, meanings and values are drawn from the natural rhythms of the cosmos and the cycles of nature. The cosmic order is reflected in the order of society within which the individual finds her place. This type of meaning is rooted in one's affective and biological connections with the cosmos. We can still see cosmological meanings and values operating within various indigenous or First Nations peoples. So too are there vestiges of this culture operative in our northern hemisphere celebrations of Easter in the spring season and Christmas at the time of the winter solstice.

On the other side of the dialectic, the anthropological pole draws its meanings and values from a source of reason that transcends the world. Here, meaning is rooted in the workings of human

---

10. Doran, "The Analogy of Dialectic and the Systematics of History," 46.

11. Doran, "The Analogy of Dialectic and the Systematics of History," 53ff.

insight, reflection, and decision. The degree to which individuals are attuned to this transcendent source is the measure of the integrity of society. Individuals are to conform themselves to this transcendent reason, and societies are to conform themselves to the demands of rational individuals.

As with any of the other dialectics, the distortion of the dialectic of culture would involve, as Doran puts it, "anthropological consciousness losing affective sympathy with nature as it constitutes history, or of cosmological consciousness succumbing massively to a fatalism that it supposes is inscribed in cosmic rhythms."[12] We find ourselves today in a distorted dialectic of culture in which the anthropological culture dominates to the point that cosmological meanings and values are not simply neglected but also ridiculed.

Laudato Si'

Laudato si' confronts this cultural distortion and the significance of its impact.[13] Pope Francis challenges us with the fact that our sister, the Earth, "now cries out to us because of the harm we have inflicted on her by our irresponsible use and abuse of the goods with which God has endowed her" (*LS* 2). Because human beings regard themselves as masters of the earth, "the earth herself, burdened and laid waste, is among the most abandoned and maltreated of the poor" (*LS* 2). We maltreat the earth because we have forgotten who we really are, that we are dust of the earth as the Book of Genesis says, that the elements of our bodies are the elements of the earth and the stars, that we breathe the air of the earth, that we receive life and refreshment from the waters of the earth. The earth is lamenting. Today, the groans of the earth join the groans of all those persons most affected by this crisis.

Pope Francis decries the excessively anthropocentric nature of our culture. In his mind, the roots of this cultural crisis travel quite deep. It is extremely difficult to reshape such deeply ingrained, and very comfortable, habits and behaviors. It is especially challenging within the context of the current global market system and its primary concern

---

12. Doran, "The Analogy of Dialectic and the Systematics of History," 55.

13. Francis, *Laudato Si'* [Encyclical on Care for Our Common Home], May 24, 2015.

for its bottom line. This distorted anthropocentrism keeps us from seeing who we truly are, and so we end up acting against ourselves and compromising the intrinsic dignity of the world.

> The culture of relativism is the same disorder which drives one person to take advantage of another, to treat others as mere objects, imposing forced labor on them or enslaving them to pay their debts. The same kind of thinking leads to the sexual exploitation of children and abandonment of the elderly who no longer serve our interests. . . . This same "use and throw away" logic generates so much waste, because of the disordered desire to consume more than what is really necessary (*LS* 123).

So many of today's cultural and ecological problems stem from the centrality and pervasiveness of the "techno-economic" paradigm in which technology is seen as the "principal key" to human existence. This is a paradigm that shapes every aspect of our lives. Pope Francis critiques our uncritical reliance on the market forces that embrace every technological, scientific, or industrial advancement before any consideration of how they will affect the environment and "without concern for its potentially negative impact on human beings" (*LS* 109). As Pope Benedict XVI has stated, "by itself, the market cannot guarantee integral human development and social inclusion" (*LS* 109). Quoting one of his favorite authors, Romano Guardini, and his book *The End of the Modern World*, Pope Francis states that the technological mind "sees nature as an insensate order, as a cold body of facts, as a mere 'given,' as an object of utility, as raw material to be hammered into useful shape"; it also "views the cosmos . . . as a mere 'space' into which objects can be thrown with complete indifference" (*LS* 115).

The pope also critiques the society of "extreme consumerism" that has emerged alongside this techno-economic paradigm. The culture seduces us into believing that "[we] are free as long as [we] have the supposed freedom to consume" (*LS* 203). People are unable to resist what the market places before them. As a result of this extreme consumerism, the earth is despoiled, and billions of human persons are left impoverished (*LS* 203). It is time, Pope Francis says, to accept "decreased growth in some parts of the world, in order to provide recourse for other places to experience healthy growth" (*LS* 193).

A significant problem for us is that this paradigm is so pervasive and extensive that we cannot imagine a different way of understanding the world. Furthermore, the mindset is so dominant that it would be difficult for us to operate without its benefits and resources. When we use those resources, we cannot avoid being pulled into the logic that governs the use of the resources. We continually hear that there is no other way to order our society and that, at best, we simply need to make some adjustments within the current paradigm so that it works better for more people and the environment. And yet, as the encyclical argues, what we really need is a new "ecological culture." This would entail a new way of thinking, along with new policies, a new education, a new lifestyle, and a new spirituality—all of which can resist the dominant technocratic paradigm (*LS* 111).

A Distorted Dialectic of Culture Leads to Ecological Alienation

Like Pope Francis in *Laudato si'*, cultural historian Thomas Berry acknowledges that education, economics, agriculture, religions, global governance (e.g., the United Nations Earth Charter), and conservation has accomplished much in response to the ecological crisis.[14] All of these efforts, however, just do not seem to be enough because we continue to devastate the Earth in so many ways, whether it be climate change, deforestation, loss of biodiversity in species and cultures, pollution, or excessive waste. One reason for this is that our human alienation from the natural world is so extensive that we are not even aware of it. As Berry describes it:

> While we have more scientific knowledge of the universe than any people ever had, it is not the type of knowledge that leads to an intimate presence within a meaningful universe. . . . Our world of human meaning is no longer coordinated with the meaning of our surroundings. . . . Our children no longer learn how to read the great Book of Nature from their own direct experience. They seldom learn where their water comes from or where it goes. We no longer coordinate our human celebrations

---

14. See Thomas Berry, *The Christian Future and the Fate of Earth*, eds. Mary Evelyn Tucker and John Grim (Maryknoll, NY: Orbis Books, 2009).

with the great liturgy of the heavens. . . . We no longer hear the
voice of the rivers, the mountains, or the sea. . . . The world
about us has become an "it" rather than a "thou."[15]

Even the idea that we should have an integral and intimate relationship with the natural world lies so far outside our horizons that we
cannot contemplate it. As a consequence of this alienation, we live
our daily lives in a world of objects, not subjects. We have little contact with the natural world. We regard it as a mere backdrop to our
human undertakings. Indeed, it has little connection with what is
meaningful in life for us.

In his book, *Last Child in the Woods*, Richard Louv provides
another perspective on our alienation from the natural world in his
discussion of "nature-deficit disorder." He asks: "What happens when
all the parts of childhood are soldered down, when the young no longer have the time or space to play in their family's garden, cycle home
in the dark with the stars and moon illuminating their route, walk
down through the woods to the river, lie on their backs on hot July
days in the long grass, or watch cockleburs, lit by morning sun, like
bumblebees quivering on harp wires? What then?"[16] Will our human
children experience what Bill McKibben calls "the end of nature"?[17]

Thomas Berry similarly laments what has happened to our children: "For children to live only in contact with concrete and steel
and wires and wheels and machines and computers and plastics, to
seldom experience any primordial reality or even to see the stars
at night, is a soul deprivation that diminishes the deepest of their
human experiences."[18] He argues that, as a consequence of our alienation from the natural world, we end up teaching our children an

---

15. Thomas Berry, *The Great Work: Our Way into the Future* (New York: Bell
Tower, 1999), 15, 17. As he writes in the same work, "Everyone lives in a universe;
but seldom do we have any real sense of living in a world of sunshine by day and
under the stars at night. Seldom do we listen to the wind or feel the refreshing
rain except as inconveniences to escape from as quickly as possible" (54).

16. Richard Louv, *Last Child in the Woods: Saving Our Children from
Nature-Deficit Disorder* (Chapel Hill, NC: Algonquin Books of Chapel Hill,
2008), 97.

17. See Bill McKibben, *The End of Nature* (New York: Random House Trade
Paperbacks, 2006).

18. Berry, *The Great Work*, 82.

economic system that depends on the exploitation of life systems. If we want our children to have an attitude of exploitation, to think that the resources of the planet are there for our use, then what we need to do is make sure that they lose any feeling for and any relationship with the natural world. This is not difficult because we, ourselves, have little sensitivity for the planet. We are not even aware of the *need* for an intimate relationship with the natural world around us. As Berry puts it: "While we have more scientific knowledge of the universe than any people ever had, it is not the type of knowledge that leads to an intimate presence within a meaningful universe. . . . Our world of human meaning is no longer coordinated with the meaning of our surroundings. We have disengaged from that profound interaction with our environment that is inherent in our nature."[19]

Psychic Conversion

In Pope Francis's mind, our alienation and the roots of this distorted notion of culture reside deep within us. Let me turn to Robert Doran's notion of psychic conversion to help us understand one dimension of these strong and resistant roots and to see how this conversion is part of what is needed to overcome the alienation.[20] Doran notes that we are conscious in two ways. One is the focus of Lonergan's work: intentionality analysis, authenticity, and self-transcendence. The other has to do with the "sensitive stream of consciousness itself."[21] The psyche refers to the sensations, memories, and images that accompany our experiencing, understanding, judging, and deciding, so that there is an affective dimension to our asking and answering questions about our experience. When our questions are answered satisfactorily, the change we consciously experience is both intellectual and affective.

However, we can lose touch with this psychic flow, "the pulsing flow of life, the movement of life."[22] Moreover, there can be obstacles

19. Berry, *The Great Work*, 15.

20. See Ormerod and Vanin, "Ecological Conversion: What Does It Mean?," for a discussion of all four aspects of conversion (intellectual, moral, religious, psychic) and how they help to explain the meaning of ecological conversion.

21. Robert M. Doran, "What Does Bernard Lonergan Mean by 'Conversion'?," 2011, https://www.lonerganresource.com/pdf/lectures/What%20Does%20 Bernard%20Lonergan%20Mean%20by%20Conversion.pdf, 20.

22. Doran, "What Does Bernard Lonergan Mean by 'Conversion'?", 6.

to performing the intentional operations that arise from the sensitive stream of consciousness itself. For example, we can be hampered by a psychic censorship of the images we need to answer our questions for direct or reflective acts of insight. Further, we can experience internal resistance even to asking relevant questions. Such resistance can arise from sensations, images, desires, fears, joys, but also from the individual, group, and general biases that need to be overcome by moral and intellectual conversion.

Psychic conversion concerns the process of dealing with the connections between the two ways of being conscious, a connection all too easily lost and difficult to recover once we have lost it. As Doran writes, "[T]he reason for establishing or re-establishing that connection, in terms of authenticity, is that affective self-transcendence is frequently required if we are going to be self-transcendent in the intellectual, moral, and religious dimensions of our living."[23]

On the psychic level of the ecological crisis, as Pope Francis and Thomas Berry both grasp, we are alienated from the rhythms and flows of the natural world. We have lost the connections between these rhythms and flows and how we operate in the intellectual, moral, and religious realms. Our alienation from the natural world becomes evident in the mechanistic imaging of the natural world so ingrained in the Western psyche and in the techno-economic paradigm that dominates our culture. Both we, and the earth, pay a price for this deep-seated alienation.

The psychic component of ecological conversion moves one from alienation to a deepening relationship with the rhythms of the natural world and the other beings with whom we share this planet, not to mention with the beauty, awe, and immenseness of the story of an unfolding 13.4 billion-year-old universe. It requires recognizing how mechanistic images of the Earth impact our own psyches, and how profoundly they affect the ways we relate to the natural world, especially the ways in which we regard the natural world as a machine made up of a diversity of parts, each of which we use as we see fit.

This dimension of ecological conversion is evident when Pope Francis states that the goal of *Laudato si'* is not the amassing of information but instead helping every person "to become painfully aware, to dare to turn what is happening to the world into our own suffering . . . and thus to discover what each of us can do about it" (*LS* 19).

---

23. Doran, "What Does Bernard Lonergan Mean by 'Conversion'?", 6.

Indeed, he reiterates here what he said in his 2013 apostolic exhortation, *Evangelii gaudium*: "God has joined us so closely to the world around us that we can feel the desertification of the soil almost as a physical ailment, and the extinction of a species as a painful disfigurement."[24] It is psychic conversion that can help us to develop the depth of intimacy with the Earth and with each other that is needed if we are going to respond to the sufferings of the Earth as our own suffering and discern what we need to do to develop an ecological culture.

Ecological Attentiveness

Ecological conversion as psychic also involves becoming attentive to whatever it is that we habitually disregard. Contemporary nature writers are helpful guides for teaching us how to reconnect with the natural world and develop our capacity for intimate communion. In an article for *The Guardian,* Madeline Bunting states that nature writing shows us that "[w]e need that attentiveness to nature to understand our humanity, and of how we fit, as just one species, into a vast reach of time and space."[25] In his edited volume, *The Way of Natural History,* Thomas Lowe Fleischner states that "'natural history' is a practice of intentional, focused attentiveness and receptivity to the more-than-human world. . . . [A]ttention is prerequisite to intimacy. Natural history, then, is a means of becoming intimate with the big, wild world."[26] He furthermore insists that attentiveness to nature matters because "[i]n a fundamental sense, we are what we pay attention to. . . . Our attention is precious, and what we choose to focus it on has enormous consequences. What we choose to look at, and to listen to—these choices change the world."[27]

Lyanda Lynn Haupt, author of *Crow Planet: Essential Wisdom for Urban Wilderness*, explores how those of us who live in urban contexts can attain intimacy with the natural world. She argues that

---

24. Francis, *Evangelii Gaudium* [Apostolic Exhortation on the Proclamation of the Gospel in Today's World], November 24, 2013, §89.

25. Madeleine Bunting, *The Guardian,* July 30, 2007, http://www.theguardian.com/commentisfree/2007/jul/30/comment.bookscomment.

26. Thomas Lowe Fleischner, "The Mindfulness of Natural History," in *The Way of Natural History*, ed. Thomas Lowe Fleischner (San Antonio, TX: Trinity University Press, 2011), 5–6.

27. Fleischner, "The Mindfulness of Natural History," 9.

"it is in our everyday lives, in our everyday homes, that we eat, consume energy, run the faucet, compost, flush, learn, and *live*. It is here, *in our lives*, that we must come to know our essential connection to the wilder earth, because it is here, in the activity of our daily lives, that we most surely affect this earth, for good or for ill."[28] We are connected to the natural world in and through our everyday lives. Truly coming to know this requires us to start walking the paths of our neighborhoods and begin to know all of our human and other-than-human neighbors, "on and off the concrete, above and below the soil."[29] For Haupt, "an intimate awareness of the continuity between our lives and the rest of life is the only thing that will truly conserve the earth—this wonderful earth that we rightly love."[30]

This poem by Walt Whitman likewise expresses the belief that what we pay attention to matters and that it makes us who we are:

There was a child went forth every day,
And the first object he looked upon . . . that object
he became,
And that object became part of him for the day or a certain part
of the day . . . , or
for many years or stretching cycles of years.

The early lilacs became part of this child,
And grass, and white and red morning glories, and white
and red clover,
And the song of the phoebe-bird,
And the Third-month lambs and the sow's pink-faint litter,
And the mare's foal and the cow's calf . . . all became part
of him.[31]

---

28. Lyanda Lynn Haupt, *Crow Planet: Essential Wisdom for Urban Wilderness* (New York: Back Bay Books, 2009), 9.

29. Haupt, *Crow Planet*, 13.

30. Haupt, *Crow Planet*, 12.

31. Walt Whitman, "There Was a Child Went Forth," in *Leaves of Grass*, Comprehensive Reader's Edition, eds. Sculley Bradley and Harold W. Blodgett (New York: W. W. Norton and Company, 1973), 364.

If we are to overcome alienation and reestablish connections between our psyches and our moral/intellectual operations, we need to be deeply attentive to the natural world. Such intentional attentiveness can help to remove that difficult, often impenetrable, psychic barrier between humans and the natural world.

An Integral Ecology

The alienation overcome through psychic conversion makes it possible to develop an ecological culture in which, Pope Francis says, we understand ourselves as "part of nature, included in nature, in constant interaction with it" (*LS* 139). Central to such an ecological culture is the notion of an integral ecology, which Pope Francis regards as key for responding to the devastation of our common home. It is a new paradigm of justice, a new sense of culture "which respects our unique place as human beings in this world and our relationship to our surroundings" (*LS* 15). The word *environment* itself needs to be re-understood as entailing a relationship between the natural world and human persons: "Nature cannot be regarded as something separate from ourselves or as a mere setting in which we live" (*LS* 139). As Pope Francis says many times in *Laudato si'*, ecological conversion helps us understand that everything is interdependent and interconnected.

An integral ecology is not a religious notion but, rather, it applies to all aspects of human society: economics and politics, in different cultures (particularly those most threatened), and even in every moment of our daily lives. An integral perspective brings the ecology of our institutions into play: "if everything is related, then the health of a society's institutions has consequences for the environment and the quality of human life" (*LS* 142). What Pope Francis is talking about is nothing less than a redefinition of our notion of progress. The starting point is "to aim for a new lifestyle" that would open up the possibility of bringing "healthy pressure to bear on those who wield the political, economic, and social power" in our world (*LS* 206). He highlights and praises the good being achieved, the efforts that people are making to care for our common home.

What then, are the genuine values to which the market must pay attention? What are the values that will guide our own personal consuming? Will we ask ourselves the question that is at the heart of

Laudato si': "What kind of world do we want to leave to those who come after us, to children who are now growing up?" (*LS* 160). This is why Pope Francis says that we cannot overstate the importance of ecological education, as it can help us understand the nature of the universe and raise our consciousness. Education can open our eyes to the myths of our modern culture: individualism, unlimited progress, competition, consumerism, and an unregulated market. So too can it help us reestablish just and loving relationships with ourselves, with other human persons, with the natural world and other living creatures, and with God.

Ecological education is also able to affect our actions and daily habits. For Pope Francis, developing ecological virtues is key to the transformation of our world. There is a nobility, he says, in the duty to care for creation through all of our small daily actions (*LS* 211). It is striking that the encyclical discusses small things that each of us can do every day and that can make a real difference, such as "avoiding the use of plastic and paper, reducing water consumption, separating refuse, cooking only what can reasonably be consumed, showing care for other living beings, using public transit or car-pooling, planting trees, turning off unnecessary lights, or any number of other practices" (*LS* 211). As Pope Francis states, "An integral ecology is . . . made up of simple daily gestures which break with the logic of violence, exploitation and selfishness, which can help to create a culture in which life is shared and all beings are respected" (*LS* 230). Furthermore, "[we] must regain the conviction that we need one another, that we have a shared responsibility for others and the world, and that being good and decent are worth it" (*LS* 229).

St. Francis of Assisi

As with any dialectic, overcoming the distortions of the dialectic of culture and maintaining its integrity will require input from a soteriological culture, wherein divine meanings and values can restore their integrity. The example of St. Francis of Assisi demonstrates as much. As Pope Francis states, he is "the example par excellence of care for the vulnerable and an integral ecology that is lived out joyfully and authentically" (*LS* 10). He is the model of "just how inseparable the bond is between concern for nature, justice for the poor, commitment to society, and interior peace" (*LS* 10).

The encyclical reminds us of St. Francis's relationship to the natural world: "just as happens when we fall in love with someone, whenever [Francis] would gaze at the sun, the moon or the smallest of animals, he burst into song, drawing all other creatures into his praise" (*LS* 11). For St. Francis, "each and every creature was a sister united to him by bonds of affection. . . . His response to the world around him was so much more than intellectual appreciation or economic calculus, for to him each and every creature was a sister united to him by bonds of affection. That is why he felt called to care for all that exists" (*LS* 11).

We can utilize our intellectual knowledge to open up to the insights that we are not aliens on this earth, that we are made of the same elements, that we are part of the same family, and that we share DNA with most of the rest of creation. We can come to feel the close bonds of universal communion and know, intellectually *and* affectively, that "nature cannot be regarded as something separate from ourselves . . . we are part of nature, included in nature, in constant interaction with it" (*LS* 139). We come to know this by deep, intentional attentiveness to creation. Along with St. Francis, we can take time to contemplate creation, "to discover in each thing a teaching which God wishes to hand on to us" (*LS* 85). By "paying attention to this manifestation [of God in creation] we learn to see ourselves in relation to all other creatures" (*LS* 85).

What St. Francis models is a kinship model of relationship to the rest of creation. It starts from the fundamental notion that we human beings, all of us, are part of creation. We are not aliens on this earth but an integral part of creation. This model of relationships must permeate all aspects of our living. Pope Francis says:

> If we approach nature and the environment without this openness to awe and wonder, if we no longer speak the language of fraternity and beauty in our relationship with the world, our attitude will be that of masters, consumers, ruthless exploiters, unable to set limits on their immediate needs. By contrast, if we feel intimately united with all that exists, then sobriety and care will well up spontaneously. The poverty and austerity of Saint Francis were no mere veneer of asceticism, but something much more radical: a refusal to turn reality into an object simply to be used and controlled (*LS* 11).

This is the depth of intimacy that St. Francis models and that an emerging ecological culture requires.

Conclusion

In the end it is the self-transcending person who must commit herself to the importance of ecological conversion, education, ecological virtues, developing an ecological culture, and caring for our common home. Pope Francis is convinced that we are capable of undergoing the depth of transformation that is needed in our relationship to our common home: "Yet all is not lost. Human beings, while capable of the worst, are also capable of rising above themselves, choosing again what is good, and making a new start" (LS 205). This hopeful transformation is evident in many indigenous cultures for whom "land is not a commodity but rather a gift from God and from their ancestors who rest there, a sacred space with which they need to interact if they are to maintain their identity and values" (LS 146). It is evident in the work of so many who are striving to overcome the impacts of climate change, pollution, waste, biodiversity loss, and water shortages. It is evident in the writings of contemporary nature writers who teach about the natural world and about how to develop our capacity for intimate communion and relationship.

We can strive to understand the nature and role of all members of the cosmic family, we can affirm the whole cosmic order under the divine creator as the most comprehensive context of our being, and we can value the whole of the cosmos and allow it to shape our choices. This is the authenticity and self-transcendence that is needed to overcome today's distortions in the dialectic of culture and help restore its integrity. When we start from the perspective of understanding ourselves as an intimate part of the family of creation, then we begin to know that our care for our common home is fundamentally about love. And such deep love and care for the gift of God's creation leads us to praise God as St. Francis did in his "Canticle of the Creatures" and to live with compassion and justice as integral members of this beautiful Earth community.

CHAPTER TWELVE

Educating for Ecological Responsibility

BERNARD LONERGAN, POPE FRANCIS, AND A LOCAL CASE STUDY PROMPTED BY A GLOBAL REALITY

Jame Schaefer (*Marquette University*)

B ernard Lonergan's philosophy of knowing and Pope Francis's magisterial teachings yield a complementary trajectory toward educating for ecological responsibility, an example of which was demonstrated recently by students in the capstone seminar required for the Interdisciplinary Minor in Environmental Ethics at Marquette University. After exploring Lonergan's explanation of responsibility, his philosophy of education in which he underscores the need to integrate diverse ways of knowing, and the pope's call for "integral ecology" when addressing and acting on ecological problems, the seminar and its outcomes are described. They manifest local ways in which individuals and their religious communities can help mitigate the adverse effects of human-forced climate change when upper levels of governance fail to recognize the role human actions play in this global phenomenon and to act responsibly.

Educating for Responsibility—Insights from Lonergan and Pope Francis

In *Insight: A Study of Human Understanding*, Lonergan explains his fourth transcendental precept—responsibility—as the person's freely willing the good that emerges after having been attentive, intelligent, and reasonable.[1] Responsibility also implicitly permeates these three precepts of the cognitive process within which persons can choose to be fully attentive, fully intelligent, and fully reasonable to the best of their innate abilities. Doing so assumes openness to and consideration of data that are discovered when seeking to answer a question, recognizing what is known and unknown, and pursuing the unknown for as complete an answer as possible in order to reason to an act through which the good can be recognized. When choosing to act, decision-makers are responsible to themselves for seeking and implementing a morally good action, responsible to others, and responsible to God who is the primary good they desire when willing the good. The good that informed decision-makers seek transcends their particular interests and becomes a detached, disinterested, and unrestricted desire to know.[2] According to Lonergan, the decision-maker's failure to choose and implement a morally obligatory course of action that is consistent with what is known or to reject a morally reprehensible course of action is sinful.[3]

Responsibility for making informed moral decisions and acting accordingly to achieve the good resounds throughout the first encyclical dedicated to the ecological crisis that has grave social ramifications. In *Laudato si', On Care for Our Common Home*, the good to which Pope Francis calls all people is the flourishing of the Earth community that is currently imperiled by human attitudes toward and interactions with other species, abiota, and systems.[4] Poor and vulnerable people who are struggling to survive today are most

---

1. My reading of Lonergan's *Insight* suggests basic manifestations of these transcendental precepts: *attentiveness* as openness to discovering data and information of all types pertinent to an issue; *intelligence* by assessing the discovered; and *reasonableness* by thinking critically about the evaluations and avoiding bias and other impediments to knowing. I am grateful to Robert Doran, SJ, for leading a faculty-graduate student seminar on *Insight* from August 2012 to May 2014 that stimulated my interest in appropriating Lonergan's thinking when interrelating theology, the natural sciences, and technology.

2. Bernard Lonergan, *Insight: A Study of Human Understanding*, eds. Frederick E. Crowe and Robert M. Doran, Collected Works of Bernard Lonergan (CWL), vol. 3 (Toronto: University of Toronto Press, 1992), 659–660.

3. Lonergan, *Insight*, 689.

4. Francis, *Laudato si'* [Encyclical on Care for Our Common Home], May 24, 2015; "responsibility" is used in various forms fifty-five times.

adversely affected, and future generations are threatened to inherit a life-impoverished planetary home. Pope Francis urges Christians to recognize their duties toward the natural world and God that are, quoting Pope John Paul II, "an essential part of their faith" (64).[5] As creatures who are uniquely endowed with intellectual abilities to reason, develop arguments, interpret reality, and engage in meaningful relationships with others and with God (81, 119), Christians have a responsibility to engage in dialogue about their interconnections with other creatures, their habitats, and the biosphere of Earth and to make and execute informed decisions for their mutual well-being (68). Failing to be responsible ruins the person's relationships with one another, with Earth, and with God (70). Committed to living up to their dignity as responsible persons, the ecologically conscious are "selfless" (81, 211).[6]

For Lonergan and Pope Francis, educational opportunities are essential to facilitate the person's openness to and understanding of diverse ways of knowing[7] and integrating them for reflection and judgment about the correct course of action to achieve the good.[8] Lonergan's "generalized empirical method"[9] provides a systematic understanding of the interior dynamics of knowing that ground the differentiation of disciplines and integrate them for a unified vision from which a decision can be made.[10] The unified vision

---

5. All parenthetical references to *Laudato si'* refer to the numbered parts of the encyclical. In this reference, Pope Francis is drawing from John Paul II's, *Peace with God the Creator, Peace with All of Creation* [1990 World Day of Peace Message], January 1, 1990, §15, the first document by a pope that is dedicated to human responsibility for addressing the ecological crisis.

6. This "selfless" characterization resonates with Lonergan's understanding of "disinterested."

7. Tad Dunne illuminates this point in "Bernard Lonergan (1904–1984)," *Internet Encyclopedia of Philosophy*, https://www.iep.utm.edu/lonergan/.

8. See *Insight*, chapter 11, for a full explanation.

9. Named in *Insight*, 96, succinctly concluded in 267–269, and detailed in chapter 3, "The Canons of Empirical Method"; chapter 4, "The Complementarity of Classical and Statistical Investigations"; and chapter 6, "Common Sense and Its Subject."

10. Bernard Lonergan, *Topics in Education: The Cincinnati Lectures of 1959 on the Philosophy of Education*, CWL 10, eds. Robert M. Doran and Frederick Crowe (Toronto: University of Toronto Press, 1993), 23. For helpful discussions,

Pope Francis proffers for making decisions about the ecological crisis requires careful consideration of pertinent scientific, social, economic, cultural, political, and ethical perspectives. Embracing a theologically-grounded understanding of their intricate interconnection, he proposes "integral ecology" as the way in which to reach a unified vision that is sufficient for making decisions and bringing about changes in our thinking, attitudes, and ways of living in the world (202–203). Key to this task are religious sources that can motivate ethical behavior and take us to "the heart of what it is to be human" (11). Toward that goal, he urges "Educating for the Covenant between Humanity and the Environment" to facilitate "making the leap towards the transcendent which gives ecological ethics its deepest meaning" (210), developing an "ecological citizenship" in which good habits are manifested (211),[11] and training people in solidarity, responsibility, and compassionate care (210). He identifies various settings in which ecological education can occur with emphasis on the family's formative role (212–214).

Both Pope Francis and Lonergan view the person's opting for the morally obligatory decision as a transformation of the person. Choosing the moral route is a personal commitment that manifests the dominance of the higher aspirations of the human spirit and the human heart.[12] He poignantly describes the dynamic operation of God's gift of grace in the person who cooperates with that grace

---

see Richard M. Liddy, "Bernard Lonergan on a Catholic Liberal Arts Education," *Journal of Catholic Education* 3, no. 4 (2000): 522–532; and Jeffrey Centeno, "Learning-To-Be: Reflections on Bernard Lonergan's Transcendental Philosophy of Education Towards An Integral Human Existence," *Metanexus*, April 18, 2007, http://www.metanexus.net/essay/learning-be-reflections-bernard-lonergans-transcendental-philosophy-education-towards-integral.

11. Though Pope Francis mentions self-restraint explicitly at 105, several other virtues are implicit in *Laudato si'* that I explore in "Converting to and Nurturing Ecological Consciousness–Individually, Collectively, Actively," in *All Creation Is Connected: Voices in Response to Pope Francis's Encyclical on Ecology*, ed. Daniel R. DiLeo (Winona MN: Anselm Academic, 2018), 136–153.

12. Lonergan, *Insight*, 297; and *Topics in Education*, 62–63. Richard M. Liddy analyzes and perceptively applies Lonergan's thinking to the climate crisis in "Changing Our Minds: Bernard Lonergan & Climate Change" in *Confronting the Climate Crisis: Catholic Theological Perspectives*, ed. Jame Schaefer (Milwaukee: Marquette University Press, 2011), 253–276.

when making and sustaining this transformation.[13] For Pope Francis, the person's changes from attitudes and actions that imperil the Earth community to attitudes and actions that promote its flourishing constitute an "ecological conversion" (217, 219, 220). It is "radical" (4), "profound" (5), "impossible without motivation and a process of education" (15), "personal" (211), and "a change of heart" (218).

They also conclude that love motivates the person to choose to act responsibly. Lonergan points to the order of the universe as a good chosen by God that manifests God's goodness and perfection[14] and to God as the primary good[15] who floods human hearts with a love that operates on and cooperates with the person to achieve good.[16] A person's desire to know is ultimately a desire for God, and the person who intelligently wills the good is in love with God.[17] Urging all to ecological responsibility, Pope Francis shares Lonergan's faith-filled views about the world as a manifestation of God's love. He teaches that God "created out of love" (65), the entire material

---

13. Lonergan, *Method in Theology* (New York: Herder and Herder, 1972), 105–107, 122–123. For a presentation of how God's grace works in people collectively, see Robert M. Doran, "Social Grace," *Method: Journal of Lonergan Studies* N.S., 2.2 (2011): 131–42.

14. Lonergan, *Insight*, 721; see also 711 and 714. His discussion of perfection has affinity with Thomas Aquinas's understanding as best conveyed in *Summa theologiae* 1.73 and *Summa contra Gentiles* 2.45–46. Currently conceptualized as "the sacramentality of creation," the belief that God is manifested by the world is prevalent throughout the patristic and medieval period, a primary concept in the spirituality of the Society of Jesus as expressed by St. Ignatius of Loyola, and one that is currently being retrieved as a reason for ecological responsibility. For many examples, see Jame Schaefer, *Theological Foundations for Environmental Ethics: Reconstructing Patristic and Medieval Concepts* (Washington DC: Georgetown University Press, 2009), chapter 3.

15. Lonergan, *Insight*, 681; see his detailed explanation of the notion of God in 680–692.

16. Lonergan, *Method in Theology*, 105–107, 122–123; in 107, 122, and 123, he explicitly refers to God's love as a "gift," a term he uses interchangeably with "grace" to emphasize its dynamism. His full treatment of grace appears in *Grace and Freedom: Operative Grace in the Thought of St. Thomas Aquinas*, CWL 1, eds. Frederick E. Crowe and Robert M. Doran (Toronto: University of Toronto Press, 2000).

17. Lonergan, *Insight*, 711. Also see Dunne on Lonergan's understanding of how love functions to reverse the dynamics of moral decline in "Bernard Lonergan (1904–1984)."

universe "speaks of God's love," and everything—soil, water, mountains, and creatures—constitutes "a caress of God" with each having its own purpose (84). Human creatures are "made for love" (58), should "think deeply," "love generously" (47), and "respect" all creatures because all are dependent upon one another as constituents of our common home (42). All are called together by God's love into a "universal communion" (76). To strengthen the person's resolve to love, God offers abundant grace that is "at work deep in our hearts" (205), to which we need to be "ever open" (200), respond, and make God's grace evident in the ways we relate to other creatures (221).

Thus, Lonergan and Pope Francis provide complementary ways of thinking about, calling for, and applying the imperative of responsibility to our lives. Together they provide a backdrop from which to examine and assess a concrete example of educating for ecological responsibility.

A Locally Focused Case Study Prompted by a Global Reality

Established in 2001 by Marquette University, the Interdisciplinary Minor in Environmental Ethics requires undergraduate students to complete a capstone seminar as their culminating learning experience. It offers an opportunity for students to explore an ecological problem from a theologically based ethical perspective informed by the required courses in ecology, environmental and natural resource economics, environmental philosophy, earth and environmental physics, and religious foundations for ecological ethics. Collaboration within the capstone is required—planning, sharing drafts of research, seeking comments for revisions, assessing progress, reflecting on ethical implications, and identifying the ethical approach that should be taken to address the problem. Among the problems that have been explored in capstone seminars are the city of Waukesha's water dilemma and the Great Lakes Compact, healing the Milwaukee Estuary, water sustainability, mitigating the climate crisis through agriculture in Southeastern Wisconsin, environmental justice in the Milwaukee area, and electricity production and use in the United States.[18]

---

18. Reports generated are accessible at "Capstone Seminar Projects, Interdisciplinary Minor in Environmental Ethics," Marquette University, http://www.inee.mu.edu/CapstoneSeminarProjects.shtml.

Following is a description of the 2017 seminar and highlights of its outcomes. Though my students were not assigned to read from Lonergan's corpus, parallels of his thinking surface throughout their capstone experience. Their appropriation of Pope Francis's teachings is evident.

Description of the 2017 INEE Capstone Seminar

During the semester prior to commencing this seminar, registered students met to share their ideas for its focus. Most were enrolled in Foundations for Ecological Ethics (THEO 4440) and had pro-actively consulted with one another before our meeting. They informed me that they unanimously agreed to focus on human-forced climate change. After fleshing out why and where they wanted to orient this focus, they tentatively settled on the effects of climate change within the State of Wisconsin. They also expressed their wish for an outcome that is both practical and helpful. They agreed to research sources of information from various perspectives and come prepared to share them during the first session of our seminar. They also agreed to bring Pope Francis's *Laudato si'* that they had read in THEO 4440 as a probable source from which to identify theological motivation for addressing this global phenomenon.

The seminar opened with a review of its major purpose—a theologically based ethical response to climate change in Wisconsin. They discussed how to reach that point and committed themselves to finding sources from the perspectives of the various disciplines that are required for the capstone.[19] They anticipated having to integrate these perspectives for a comprehensive understanding of the problem in order to discern the most appropriate ethical pathway toward addressing climate change, and they readily recognized that this process requires openness to one another, individual resourcefulness, and teamwork. A basic outline for the subsequent three-hour weekly sessions was established with the expectation that they would present their outcomes to INEE faculty at the seminar's culminating session. Though most of the six students knew one another, their respective majors, and their interests in pursuing the seminar's focus, a new and welcomed addition was

---

19. Ecology, economics, political science, philosophy, and theology.

a Theology and Religion major who worked part-time in health-care and was eager to explore the health effects of climate change on vulnerable populations.[20]

When sharing the sources found between semesters, they noted the substance of the data, the organizations that provided them, and any bias requiring caution and careful consideration.[21] They discussed possibilities for categorizing these sources and settled on ecological, economic, health, political and social perspectives of fossil fuel use in Wisconsin. They began populating their findings on D2L, Marquette's online course management program, identified gaps in their data base and the types of additional sources needed, and established reasonable due dates for entering them prior to the next seminar session. Throughout the remainder of the semester, a strong sense of responsibility to one another prevailed. To facilitate their awareness of the responsibilities to which they committed, I entered detailed directions on D2L after each session.

As we began our second session, my students complained about the disappearance of data and reports pertaining to climate change from the websites of the President of the United States, the Environmental Protection Agency, and the U.S. Department of Energy. They viewed this swift elimination of data and reports—after January 20, 2017, the day Donald Trump became President—as impeding their desire to be as thoroughly informed as possible. Two students reported that the Public Service Commission of Wisconsin and the Department of Natural Resources had also removed important sources. However, they were delighted to have found non-government organizations' sites from which these and other sources could be linked into the capstone depository. Though initially frustrated, disappointed, and disgusted by these roadblocks to their learning, my students determined to find whatever they needed to proceed. Trust in government to provide credible data

---

20. The students and their majors: Wyatt Meyer—Biological Sciences, Alyx Birmingham—Global Ecology and Psychology, Lydia Melland—History, Tony Peacock—Marketing and Supply Chain Management, Eleni Eisenhart—Public Relations, and Heidi Golembiewski—Theology and Religion.

21. On avoiding impediments to understanding, see Lonergan, *Insight*, 244–267. Also helpful is Dunne's analysis of Lonergan's understanding of the working of bias and the resulting dynamics of historical decline in "Bernard Lonergan (1904–1984)."

could not have been lower as the reality of bias at federal and state levels loomed large.[22]

My students soon realized the need for sources beyond those available through the internet and Marquette's library system. They began identifying Marquette professors to share their disciplines' perspectives on the capstone topic. Among them was Ayman El-Refaie, an electrical engineering professor at Marquette, who enlightened us about the latest energy efficiency technologies that are available and at various stages of development. They also sought energy experts within Milwaukee and Wisconsin to share their respective data, perspectives, and contributions. Most agreed to consult via videoconferencing in order to avoid adding to their carbon footprints.

Our first consultant was Erick Shambarger, Director of the City of Milwaukee's Environmental Collaboration Office (ECO). He amazed my students with the many local environmentally responsible programs with which his office works, his personal energy, and his unequivocal commitment to Pope Francis's teaching about caring for Earth. He also stimulated their thinking about creating a toolkit for parishes in the Archdiocese of Milwaukee to use that would facilitate moving toward a more renewable energy future. During a subsequent seminar session, my students decided to produce a toolkit

---

22. In *Insight*, 244–267, Lonergan describes three types of bias—individual bias (244–247), group bias (247–250), and general bias (250–267). Though an analysis of reasons why federal and State of Wisconsin officials removed these data is warranted but not possible within the confines of this essay, all three biases may be suspected based on abundant publicly-available evidence of (1) denial and skepticism expressed reflexively by President Donald Trump, his appointees to head the Environmental Protection Agency and the Department of Energy, the Governor of the State of Wisconsin, and his appointee to the Public Service Commission that human activities are forcing changes in the global climate; (2) actions they have taken—especially Trump's withdrawal from the 2015 Paris Agreement with 195 other nations to minimize greenhouse gas emissions and contribute to the Green Climate Fund under the United Nations Framework Convention on Climate Change (UNFCCC), his unequivocal advocacy for coal and loosening restrictions on emissions from burning coal, and Governor Scott Walker's refusal to endorse programs that minimize greenhouse gas emissions and advance renewable and efficient energy strategies; and, (3) the 2016 Republican Party Platform that commits to eliminating the Clean Power Plan, growing a fossil-fueled economy, and shifting responsibility of environment regulations to the states.

that would feature practical ways in which people could switch from fossil fuels to efficient and renewable energy strategies. They decided to gear their toolkit for use by parishioners and parishes in the Archdiocese of Milwaukee, though they expressed hope that others in the area would find their project helpful. They aimed to create a finished product that Archdiocesan officials would want to upload to their website.

Consultations with specialists at RenewWisconsin, the American Council for an Energy-Efficient Economy, Wisconsin Energy Institute, and the State of Wisconsin's Division of Health[23] yielded data, insights, and helpful leads for the toolkit and the required research-reflection paper. Prior to each consultation, my students took turns identifying an article or report written by the consultant for all to read and from which to ask at least two questions. The fact that all consultations were lively and challenging demonstrated their preparedness and attentiveness to these experts.

While continuing to collect options for including in the toolkit, my students turned to its scholarly parallel—the research-reflection paper. Each agreed to draft key points to include in one of the sections of the paper (ecological, health, social, economic, and social ramifications of fossil fuel use at national, state, and local levels). Prior to the next session, they posted their respective points with major sources upon which to rely and reviewed each other's postings. During the session, they took turns leading discussions on their postings and seeking additional input and consensus for proceeding. Each student began to draft a chapter for the seminar paper, and a schedule was established for placing them on D2L. In subsequent sessions, assigned drafts were commented on, edits were welcomed, consensus was reached on the edited drafts, and they were revised accordingly. Opportunities were offered to footnote disparate opinions, but none of the students chose this option. Some discussions were lively with students respectfully and sometimes humorously challenging one another and suggesting edits geared toward producing a seminar

---

23. Katherine Klausing of RenewWisconsin on renewable energy sources (www.renewwisconsin.org); Seth Nowak of the American Council for an Energy Efficient Economy on energy efficient strategies (www.aceee.org); Gary Radloff of Wisconsin Energy Institute on analysis of state and federal energy policies (www.energy.wisc.edu); and staff at the Wisconsin Department of Health Services (www.dhs.wisconsin.gov).

paper that showed differentiation in the discipline-based perspectives and integrating them for moral decision-making.[24]

Identifying the most appealing theological motivation for addressing human-forced climate change became a major focus. As already mentioned, my students began revisiting Pope Francis's 2015 encyclical in preparation for the first session. They read assigned chapters for discussion during parts of four seminar sessions, consulted sources they had studied in THEO 4440 to bolster some of the pope's teachings,[25] and shared their preferred theological motivations for switching from fossil fuels to renewable and efficient energy strategies. After considering these possibilities and speculating on their potential appeal to parishioners in the Archdiocese of Milwaukee, they settled on the following:

- The *sacramentality of creation*—the belief that God is present to and manifested through the world should prompt the faithful to contemplate and respect God's creation by mitigating the emissions of greenhouse gases;
- Aquinas's concept of the *inter-cooperation of creatures* bolstered by Aldo Leopold's land ethic[26] to encourage the faithful to perceive themselves as members of the Earth community and to cooperate with one another, other species, and systems of Earth for the common good—its flourishing;
- *Self-restraint* in using the goods of Earth in ways that do not threaten the well-being of vulnerable people, future generations, and the viability of the Earth community; and

---

24. A demonstration of Lonergan's thinking about differentiating ways of knowing and unifying them as indicated, for example, in *Topics in Education*, 23.

25. Primarily my *Theological Foundations for Environmental Ethics*.

26. Aldo Leopold, *Sand County Almanac with Essays on Conservation from Round River* (New York: Oxford University Press, 1949), 237–243. The most succinct statement of Leopold's land ethic appears on 262: "A thing is right when it tends to preserve the integrity, stability, and beauty of the biotic community. It is wrong when it tends otherwise." My students especially appreciated Leopold's understanding that embracing the land ethic changes the role of *Homo sapiens* from the "conqueror" of the land community to a "plain member and citizen" of it, thereby requiring respect for other living and abiotic members of that community and accepting responsibility for cooperating with them for their mutual well-being. His land ethic resonates with Pope Francis's teaching in *Laudato si'*, especially 220–221.

- *Hope* through faith in God that people will be open to God's grace and be strengthened to switch from fossil fuels to an efficient and renewable energy future.

In the midst of this discernment process, Patxi Álvarez, SJ, the Social Justice and Ecology Secretariat of the General Curia of the Society of Jesus, visited us, shared his appreciation for *Laudato si'* and other exemplary efforts by Jesuits to reflect theologically on ecological concerns,[27] and congratulated my students on their efforts. His insights were especially encouraging to the Theology and Religion major who agreed to draft the theological section of the seminar paper, seek comments from the other students, clarify the draft during one of the seminar sessions, reach consensus, and revise accordingly.

Preparing an outline for the seminar paper proved to be the most contentious task the students subsequently tackled. After considerable discussion, they decided to modify the basic format of the Ignatian pedagogical paradigm with which they were familiar (experience/data ⟶ reflect/judge ⟶ act ⟶ evaluate) and to begin their paper with the theological motivation for addressing human-forced climate change. They hoped this approach would serve as an efficacious entry for parishioners to know about and recognize human-forced climate change as a problem that warranted their response. One student volunteered to draft the paper outline on Google Docs, other students edited and commented on it, and the edited outline was reviewed and refined in seminar until a consensus was reached.

When viewing all parts of the seminar paper together, my students proceeded to add specific recommendations for action that flowed from the theologically grounded ethical imperative to switch from fossil fuels to efficient and renewable energy strategies. They decided to list these recommendations for action following the principle of subsidiarity—individuals, families, neighborhoods

---

27. For example, "Healing a Broken World," *Promotio Iustitiae* 106, 2011/2; *Healing Earth*, the interactive online environmental science textbook commissioned by the Higher Education Secretariat of the Society of Jesus for use in Jesuit colleges and universities, and made available for use by Jesuit colleges, universities, and January 2016, https://healingearth.ijep.net/; and, *Reconciling God, Creation, and Humanity: An Ignatian Examen*, Ignatian Solidarity Network, http://jesuits.org/Assets/Publications/File/Ignatian_Ecological_Examen1.pdf.

and parishes, municipal, state, and federal governments.[28] Though strongly committed to individual responsibility, they concluded that concurrent action was needed on all levels of decision-making if the adverse effects of human-forced climate change are to be mitigated. These recommendations were submitted to the paper team for entering into D2L Discussions for commenting, suggesting edits, and assuring consensus.

Concurrently, another team focused on the toolkit. Led by the creative Public Relations major, the team designed the kit and selected from the pool of ideas some readily available efficient and renewable energy options from which parishioners and parishes can choose. The team followed the principle of subsidiarity, arranging these options according to individuals, neighborhoods, and parishes. They ended with some "simple" ways identified by the Catholic Climate Covenant in which parishes and parishioners can help mitigate human-forced changes in the global climate.[29] The completed *Flipping the Default Toolkit* was entered on D2L for discussion and completion during the last working session of the seminar.

Planning began for publicly presenting the highlights of the seminar paper and the toolkit. In addition to INEE faculty, my students decided to invite family members and friends, Marquette's Community Engagement Director, the Coordinator of the Archdiocese of Milwaukee's Social Justice Ministry, the founder of Wisconsin Green Muslims, and all experts with whom they had consulted. Each student opted to highlight key findings from the research with which they were most familiar. Some assumed additional roles—opening and moderating the program, overviewing the toolkit, recognizing guests, and fielding questions and comments. A trial run was held to assure a smooth presentation accompanied by a slide program that two of the students voluntarily prepared with input from their peers.

---

28. Presumed in Pope Leo XIII's 1891 encyclical, *Rerum Novarum*, and derived from Pope Pius XI's 1931 encyclical, *Quadragesimo anno*, 80, the principle of subsidiarity prescribes responsibility at the lower level of self-governance before moving to successive collective levels and proscribes interference by a higher level in a lower level that deprives it of exercising its responsibility but instead supports its exercise of responsibility.

29. "10 Ways Your Parish Can Make a Difference," Catholic Climate Covenant, www.catholicclimatecovenant.org/resource/catholic-climate-covenant-10-ways-your-parish-can-make-a-difference.

Outcomes of the Seminar

An excellent research-reflection paper, a useful *Flipping the Default Toolkit*, and a stellar presentation by my students were prominent outcomes of this seminar. Additional outcomes should have significance for their futures academically, professionally, and personally.

The Research-Reflection Paper

A Plan to Flip the Default that the six students carefully planned, drafted, and finalized after several iterations consists of fifty-three pages that include an introduction and seven substantive chapters. The first is "A Religious Motivation" in which they hoped to stimulate parishioners and others to want to learn about the adverse effects of climate change and options for switching to efficient and renewable energy strategies. Subsequent chapters focus on the various effects of energy use, as indicated by their titles: "The Ecological Impacts of Energy Use"; "Health of Individuals, Communities, and Future Populations"; "Societal Impacts; Political Implications Regarding Fossil Fuels"; "Economic Impacts and Benefits of Renewable Energy"; and, "A Milwaukee Study of Local Perspectives." Following these chapters are lists of recommended actions by individuals and their families, neighborhoods, parishes in the Archdiocese of Milwaukee, and Wisconsin at large to consider implementing. The paper closes with three and a half pages of consulted references.[30]

The Presentation

Opening the program, the student moderator situated the capstone project within the global context of foreboding changes in the climate that may seem overwhelming and unsolvable but must be addressed responsibly by switching from fossil fuels to efficient and renewable energy. My students described themselves as "ordinary people" who can embrace "small solutions to the large climate problem" while viewing their efforts as an entry into a movement of people throughout the world who are striving for a positive energy future. By positing themselves as "ordinary," they hoped other people would be able to identify with them, share their hope for the

---

30. A PDF is available upon request to schaeferj@marquette.edu.

future, and act responsibly by opting for small solutions that are readily available to them.

After presenting basic information about fossil fuels, renewable energy sources, and the seminar process that led to their presentation, the students took turns sharing their findings on the subtopics on which they had worked most intensely throughout the semester. The first student began with the faith-based motivations for switching from fossil fuels to renewable and efficient energy: The *sacramental creation* that attests to God's presence; *cooperation* with one another, other species, and systems for our common good— the flourishing of Earth; *restraint* when using the goods of Earth; and, *hope* through God's abundant grace for people to choose to switch from fossil fuels to renewable and efficient energy strategies. Other students followed, presenting the ecological, health, societal, economic, and political ramifications of using fossil fuels nationally, statewide, and locally. They recognized that integrating these differentiated findings and reflecting on them warrant switching to efficient energy strategies and renewable sources. They expressed their confidence that switching is possible as evidenced by the options they identified and the alternatives they discovered, and they shared their hope that efforts to switch would mean a better future if parishioners in the Archdiocese of Milwaukee and others joined them.

The student who organized and led the technical development of *Flipping the Default Toolkit* presented an overview that follows the order of the capstone research-reflection paper. Tools in the kit were accessed and explained briefly to show how easily the options can be identified.

INEE faculty, members of the students' families, friends, capstone consultants, and other guests lauded the capstone effort. Recognizing that my students' work provided practical ways in which to demonstrate ecological responsibility with sensitivity to vulnerable people and Earth, the Coordinator of the Archdiocese of Milwaukee's Social Justice Ministry stated that he would urge the Priest Council to upload the toolkit on the Archdiocesan webpage. The Director of Marquette's Office of Community Engagement welcomed a PDF of the toolkit for uploading on its website as an example of the type of community outreach his office encourages. The Director of the City of Milwaukee's ECO complimented my students and said he would add the toolkit to ECO's web site. Speaking on behalf of Wisconsin Green Muslims, Huda Alkaff, its founder and director, congratulated my students on their fine work from a religious perspective and joined them in hoping others would choose to convert to energy efficiency and renewable sources.[31]

Toolkit for Flipping the Default from Fossil Fuels to Efficient and Renewable Energy Strategies

Currently accessible from the website of the Interdisciplinary Minor in Environmental Ethics,[32] the Archdiocese of Milwaukee,[33] the City of Milwaukee,[34] Marquette's Office of Community Engagement,[35] and other sites,[36] *Flipping the Default Toolkit* begins with the religious motivation for switching from fossil fuels to renewable sources and energy efficiency strategies. The synopses of the theological concepts that most profoundly motivated my students appear first: the *sacramentality* of creation; *cooperation* with others for our common good; *restraint* when using the goods of Earth; and, *hope* through God's grace for switching from fossil fuels. Links to sources of information

31. Alkaff was one of twelve recipients in 2015 of President Barack Obama's "Champions of Change," for her exemplary efforts in protecting the natural environment and human communities from the effects of climate change.

32. INEE Capstone Seminar, *Flipping the Default Toolkit*, Interdisciplinary Minor in Environmental Ethics, Marquette University, May 2017, https://www.inee.mu.edu/documents/INEEFlippingtheDefault.pdf.

33. Archdiocese of Milwaukee, https://www.archmil.org/ArchMil/Resources/SOLJUS/INEE4997. When announcing the Social Justice Committee of the Priest Council's decision to include the toolkit on the Archdiocesan website, the Social Justice Ministry Coordinator wrote that the priests were impressed with the "strong theological reflection" it contained and were amazed "that college students had that strength" (E-mail from Rob Shelledy, May, 16 2017).

34. Environmental Collaboration Office, City of Milwaukee, https://city.milwaukee.gov/ImageLibrary/BBC/images/MarquetteUFlippingtheDefaultToolkit.pdf.

35. INEE Capstone Report, *Flipping the Default Toolkit*, Office of Community Engagement, Marquette University, https://www.marquette.edu/community-engagement/documents/INEE4997FlippingtheDefault-CommunityBasedProjects.pdf.

36. For example, Forum on Religion and Ecology, Yale University, http://fore.yale.edu/news/item/flipping-the-default-from-fossil-fuels-to-renewables-and-energy-effici/.

include Pope Francis's *Laudato si'* and statements by Popes John Paul II and Benedict XVI on the ecological crisis.[37]

Subsequent pages in the kit include sources that individuals, neighborhoods, and parishes can access. For individuals, my students included links to voter education, information on voting available through the Wisconsin Elections Commission, and four Milwaukee programs that aim to help people choose and adapt to a renewable energy lifestyle. At the neighborhood level, they included links to assessors of energy efficiency in buildings, renewable energy training, sustainable investments, and support for organizations that practice and advocate "green energy." Parishes are alerted to efficient and renewable energy services offered by the City of Milwaukee, homily helps collected by the Catholic Climate Covenant for priests, and Catholic Energies that works with dioceses and parishes to reduce energy use in buildings. Another page provides links to Christian, Muslim, Jewish, and local and regional interfaith organizations that provide religiously motivated sources for conserving energy and using renewable sources as ways to protect "Mother Earth." At the state level page, corporations are encouraged to invest in renewable energy by contacting Renew Wisconsin and Midwest Environmental Advocates, and Wisconsin lawmakers are urged to develop a renewable energy portfolio standard for future investments and a flourishing planet. The last page of the toolkit consists of the Catholic Climate Covenant's "10 Simple Ways to Make A Difference Today," thus encouraging others to participate in seemingly small ways that can cumulatively contribute to achieving an energy future in which the Earth community can flourish.

More Meaningful Outcomes

The most profound outcome was my students' commitment as individuals to be ecologically responsible as Pope Francis urged and as Lonergan explained generally as his fourth transcendental precept. After reflecting on their research findings and discussing in depth how to act, each concluded with a personal decision to switch from

---

37. John Paul II, *Peace with God the Creator, Peace with All of Creation* [1990 World Day of Peace Message], January 1, 1990; and Benedict XVI, *If You Want to Cultivate Peace, Protect Creation* [2010 World Day of Peace Message], January 1, 2010.

reliance on fossil fuels to efficient and renewable energy. They also realized the need for collective action at successive levels of governance beyond themselves as individuals. Though they considered their individual responsibilities essential, they realized the need to demonstrate responsibility among themselves, the people with whom they live and work, and their families, parishes, neighborhoods, and communities. The fact that they discovered early in the semester that federal and state governments had removed data pertaining to human-forced climate change prompted them to realize that local action is vital and may be the only realistic hope at this time. Their decisions demonstrated a transformation in themselves that Lonergan envisions and parallels the ecological conversion that Pope Francis urges. The fact that they presented themselves to others as "ordinary people" was a conscious decision within which to welcome others who thought of themselves as ordinary to identify with them. Their decision is admirable. How they characterized themselves is cherishable.

Another related outcome was their ability to integrate their diverse knowledge, skills, and interests to achieve a comprehensive understanding of the harmful effects of relying on energy sources that threaten the flourishing of the Earth community. From this comprehensive view of the adverse ecological, health, economic, social, and political effects from reliance on fossil fuels, my students discerned that the only ethical path to take was switching to renewable and efficient energy strategies. They deliberately chose that pathway. This outcome manifests Lonergan's understanding of knowing that prompts decisions to act responsibly and Pope Francis's call for an integrated ecological approach to addressing the ecological crisis.

Other outcomes have significance for my students. The teamwork skills they developed and refined will be helpful during their graduate studies, professional lives, and social relationships. They recognized and respected each other's specified knowledge and skills, and they built on their differences when working in teams to tackle many multi-dimensional tasks—finding credible sources of information, presenting assigned reports in-seminar, commenting on drafts of parts of their research-reflection paper, and submitting tools for the toolkit. They expanded these skills when collaborating on their research-reflection paper, public presentation, and toolkit that they offered to the Archdiocese of Milwaukee. Surely, they are well prepared to work with others after an arduous but stimulating, productive, and meaningful capstone seminar.

Conclusion

Lonergan's explanation of responsibility that follows when a person is attentive, intelligent, and reasonable and his emphasis on integrating different ways of knowing to discern the ethical imperative for acting meshes well with Pope Francis's teachings about the need for an integrated ecological approach to address and act responsibly toward other people, species, systems, and Earth. They also share a similar understanding of the transformation that individuals experience when they discern, choose, and follow the ethical pathway that surfaces. And, both emphasize the dynamic role of God's love for motivating, strengthening, and sustaining care for Earth—our common home.

Students in the 2017 Capstone Seminar for the Interdisciplinary Minor in Environmental Ethics at Marquette University demonstrated responsibility generally and specifically. They demonstrated responsibility generally when identifying and committing to the ethical imperative they discerned individually and agreed upon collectively after having been attentive, intelligent, and reasonable. They demonstrated responsibility specifically when discerning the ethical imperative to mitigate the adverse effects of human-forced climate change and committing to be ecologically responsible as Pope Francis urges. They advanced their individual commitments when collaborating to produce a practical set of "tools" for switching from fossil fuels to renewable and efficient energy strategies and a seminar paper that provides scholarly support for their *Flipping the Default Toolkit*.

The overall structure of this seminar provided a framework within which students could exercise their diverse ways of knowing that Lonergan describes and an opportunity to focus on an ecological issue that Pope Francis urges all to address. By explicitly requiring students who are seeking this minor to integrate the knowledge and skills they learned in various disciplines to address one ecological issue and conclude to an ethical response, they were able to demonstrate integrated learning as envisioned by the current pope and one of the twentieth century's most eminent systematic theologians. That my students embraced this opportunity wholeheartedly is exemplary and gratifying.

CHAPTER THIRTEEN

Cities as Learning Ecosystems

LONERGAN'S EMERGENT PROBABILITY IN URBAN SPACES

Edward Dunar (Fordham University)

I n his 2015 encyclical, *Laudato si'*, Pope Francis develops his notion of integral ecology alongside references to the city as a habitat for community. In doing so, he conveys a shift in papal teaching toward a more positive regard of the potential for the design of city spaces to contribute to human flourishing, community life, and solutions to the global ecological crisis. Francis's description of urban issues as connected to humans' embeddedness in broader ecological systems parallels a long-standing conversation among urban theorists regarding how to conceptualize the city and the impact of underlying metaphors about urban form on policy.

In this chapter, I will use Francis's treatment of the city as a point of departure for examining how urban designers and theorists have advocated an interpretation of the city as an ecosystem. This model offers a means of analyzing how urban places are constituted simultaneously by intentional decision-making and processes that cannot be fully controlled by individuals or governments. The church has a stake in these conversations as it discerns its role as a community of disciples in neighborhood contexts and seeks possibilities for grace and redemption in settings marked by poverty and violence. Next, I will turn to Bernard Lonergan's account of "emergent probability" as a helpful framework for adding analytical depth to the model of the city as ecosystem. Emergent probability accounts for the possibility of cumulative processes of increasing complexity and higher orders of justice in social life. I argue that it can illustrate the regard of the city as ecological in ways that can help us recognize urban places as the result of multiple contingent processes and as human habitats where God's grace is revealed in cooperation with human deliberation and agency.

The City in Papal Teaching

Francis advances a long-term development in papal teaching that has gradually come to recognize urban places not only as sites of suffering but also as settings for redemption. *Laudato si'* refines an attentiveness to the urban built environment within Catholic Social Teaching that began with Paul VI's treatment of urbanization in *Octogesima adveniens* (1971).[1] At an early stage, papal encyclicals judged urban life pessimistically. Paul describes urbanization as a symptom of the disruption caused by the modern economy, which weakens the social bonds and human agency present in agrarian life (*OA* 8). He observes how urbanization fosters an instability in economic life that threatens human dignity and creates a materialistic lifestyle that warps social relations. City life tempts people to forget their nature and their purpose. Paul explains,

> While certain enterprises develop and are concentrated, others die or change their location. Thus new social problems are created: professional or regional unemployment, redeployment and mobility of persons, permanent adaptation of workers and disparity of conditions in the different branches of industry. . . . While very large areas of the population are unable to satisfy their primary needs, superfluous needs are ingeniously created. (*OA* 9)

By disrupting traditional forms of community, urban life frays the forms of relationship necessary for human fulfillment, leading to transience, loneliness, and alienation.

Paul's solution is for Christians to create new forms of neighborliness by reweaving traditional community bonds into local neighborhoods. He writes, "There is an urgent need to remake at the level of the street, of the neighborhood or of the great agglomerative dwellings the social fabric whereby man may be able to develop the needs of his personality" (*OA* 11). The parish and the neighborhood association

---

1. Paul VI, *Octogesima Adveniens* [Apostolic Letter on the Occasion of the Eightieth Anniversary of the Encyclical *Rerum Novarum*], May 14, 1971.

must animate such work. Although he concludes his remarks on urbanization with a note of hope and an appeal to the image of Jerusalem as a holy city, Paul primarily casts the city as a sinful Nineveh or prideful Babel. He continues, "The city is in fact often the place of sin and pride—the pride of man who feels secure enough to be able to build his life without God and even to affirm that he is powerful against God" (*OA* 12). Redemption of the wicked city will therefore require bold and prophetic forms of community life.

Subsequent popes continue to characterize the city as a place where the pathologies of modern life are most obvious while simultaneously opening the door for more optimistic readings of urban life. In *Centesimus annus* (1991), John Paul II introduces an association of urban suffering with the ecological crisis.[2] In the encyclical, he develops the notion of a "human ecology," a reality of interdependence and relationality that requires protection from economic forces in the same way that the natural world does (*CA* 38). In articulating this concept, he emphasizes the *form* of the urban environment needed for flourishing. Indeed, he affirms "the need for urban planning which is concerned with how people are to live" (*CA* 38). John Paul uses the notion of human ecology to argue that, while human beings have the ability to transcend their circumstances "so as to move toward truth and goodness," they are conditioned and shaped by their society and environment. Because sin is concretized in human environments, bold action is required for the redemption of these spaces. He writes, "The decisions which create a human environment can give rise to specific structures of sin which impede the full realization of those who are in any way oppressed by them. To destroy such structures and replace them with more authentic forms of living in community is a task which demands courage and patience" (*CA* 38). John Paul links the experience of dehumanization in the city to humans' act of forgetting that they too are creatures whose flourishing is linked to that of the rest of creation.

Most recently, in *Laudato si'*, Francis treats the design of the city as a component of an integral ecology that further joins together environmental integrity and human well-being.[3] While still

---

2. John Paul II, *Centesimus Annus* [Encyclical on the Hundredth Anniversary of *Rerum Novarum*], May 1, 1991.

3. Francis, *Laudato Si'* [Encyclical on Care for Our Common Home], May 24, 2015.

acknowledging the challenges of urban life, he also affirms the potential of the city. Francis marvels at the beauty of a skyscraper (*LS* 103). He refers to "our rooms, our homes, our workplaces and neighborhoods" as sites where "we use our environment as a way of expressing our identity" (*LS* 147). He recognizes the witness of neighborhoods where love, creativity, and community overcome poverty, crime, and overcrowding (*LS* 149). Echoing John Paul's exhortation to urban designers, he urges these practitioners to take into account "people's thought processes, symbolic language, and ways of acting" in their work (*LS* 150). For Francis, an integral ecology must take the city seriously, both as the context of the most economic production and consumption that strains "our Sister, Mother Earth" (*LS* 1) and as the place where billions of people live out their daily lives.

Catholic Social Teaching has its roots in an interpretation of natural law that originally focused upon small-scale property rights as an extension of individuals' ability to cultivate creation to provide for their families.[4] It is therefore unsurprising that the tradition would suspect urban life, with its heightened mobility and distinctive land use patterns. The urban environment threatens a worldview that regards deep, stable community as most reflective of the human telos toward God. Therefore, Francis's relative optimism toward urban life represents a noticeable shift. While he continues to view cities as sites of immense suffering, particularly given the displacement, pollution, and poverty of the contemporary global economy, he does not reiterate the belief of his predecessors that urban life is inherently dehumanizing and unnatural. Rather, cities can serve as human habitats that reflect community values of solidarity and interdependence if they are understood in the context of broader cultural and ecological systems.

Metaphors for the City

Over the past two decades, a dynamic theological conversation around urban space has emerged among theologians, activists, and pastors concerned about the economic inequality and environmental devastation that commonly accompanies accelerated global urbanization.

---

4. Leo XIII, *Rerum Novarum* [Encyclical on Capital and Labor], May 15, 1891, §47.

One thread of this conversation relates Christian convictions of community to the principles of the "New Urbanism" movement, a political coalition that promotes the cultivation of human-scale, walkable, mixed-used, and socioeconomically-diverse urban neighborhoods.[5] One representative of this project is Presbyterian pastor and theologian Eric Jacobsen. Jacobsen argues that the church has much to learn from the New Urbanism movement about the relationship between the built environment and the health of human society.[6] In turn, the church offers a distinctive articulation of human flourishing that can counterbalance the tendency of urbanists to focus on technical principles of design at the expense of recognizing how community life helps define a place. He asserts that Christians must bear witness to "the built environment [as] ultimately a setting for people. It is a setting that has the potential to engage you as a whole person, and it is a setting where you can meet and interact meaningfully with other people. Life takes place within the built environment."[7] He observes that the majority of urban design conversations revolve around individual buildings or isolated elements of a neighborhood. Christians, with a commitment to the identity of a place as a setting for community, must instead emphasize the way in which the built environment facilitates the enactment of community and relationship in the space between buildings. We construct streets and buildings not as ends in themselves, but as means for opening new possibilities for human development.

Jacobsen asserts that models of conceptualizing cities can either highlight the integrity of human agency and community or obscure the bottom-up enactment of place. He cites the study of cognitive scientists George Lakoff and Mark Johnson concerning the role of root metaphors in human reasoning to argue that we must uncover

---

5. Congress for the New Urbanism, "What is New Urbanism?," https://www.cnu.org/resources/what-new-urbanism.

6. By "built environment," theorists mean the constructed elements of human places. For example, the built environment includes streets, sidewalks, buildings, parks, and gardens. The term is intended both to differentiate the constructed aspects of particular places from the natural environment and to enable analysis of the ways in which settlement reflects shared values. See Eric Jacobsen, *The Space Between: A Christian Engagement with the Built Environment* (Grand Rapids, MI: Baker Academic, 2012), 11–18.

7. Jacobsen, *The Space Between*, 25.

the underlying theoretical assumptions about cities that are implied in the operative images that design professionals and policymakers employ. Lakoff and Johnson demonstrate that root metaphors shape how individuals perceive and order their sense of reality. More than merely reflecting thought, metaphors play a central role in conceptualization. They write, "Our ordinary conceptual system, in terms of which we both think and act, is fundamentally metaphorical in nature."[8] Metaphors structure our ways of understanding and applying specific ideas in ways that are both helpful and limiting.

When applied to questions of urban policy, metaphors for the city contain implicit assumptions about what is valuable, natural, and achievable within certain places.[9] To explain this point, Jacobsen conducts a comparison between activist Jane Jacobs's description of the city as a body and architect Rem Koolhaas's suggestion that cities are lead-like in being malleable only through the exertion of power. For Jacobs, the city is a complex system that is capable of self-repair through the daily rhythms of the lives of the people who collectively inhabit a place. The life of a street is a common achievement of the people who build trust and take responsibility for the well-being of the place through quotidian interactions and habitual relationships. Jacobs employs the metaphor of the body to support her argument that the city exhibits organized complexity, in contrast to the assumptions of designers who understand the city in terms of simple physical laws or principles of disorganized complexity that require a top-down imposition of order.[10] The practical insight of this metaphor is that cities, like organisms, operate according to numerous interlocking processes. Jacobs writes, "They are always made up of interactions among unique combinations of particulars, and there is no substitute for knowing the particulars."[11] Cities might operate according to generalizable laws that can inform decision-making, but, to best understand them, we need to begin with their unique cultural and physical contexts.

---

8. George Lakoff and Mark Johnson, *Metaphors We Live By* (Chicago: University of Chicago Press, 2003), 3.

9. Jacobsen, *The Space Between*, 172.

10. Jane Jacobs, *The Death and Life of Great American Cities* (New York: Vintage Books, 1992), 430.

11. Jacobs, *The Death and Life of Great American Cities*, 441.

In contrast, Koolhaas primarily views the city as an expression of the power of the social elite and the inexorable momentum of the logic of modernity. He criticizes urbanism as a profession that engages in "illusions of involvement and control" over a phenomenon that defies human control.[12] Jacobsen characterizes Koolhaas's vision as asserting that "the city, like lead, is inert and somewhat malleable and, perhaps most important, can be taken as a kind of abstract medium for the working out of power relationships."[13] The dynamics of such a city are out of the control of its everyday inhabitants. Instead, it is the creative architect who can shape a place by marshaling the resources of power to erect buildings that creatively convey the contradictions and alienation of modern life. Even such architects are confined by limited resources and contingent power, however, so the best they can hope to achieve is an expression of transgressive honesty. Jacobsen prefers Jacobs's description of the city as a body because it is compatible with a theological recognition of urban areas "as orders of creation that God is using to prepare people for the life of shalom that we are to experience in the eschaton."[14] Koolhaas's metaphor of the city as lead severely limits the recognition of voices that can shape a place.

The metaphors used to offer diagnoses of and prescriptions for urban life have long been contested among urban design theorists. Kevin Lynch concludes that even helpful metaphors often fail to consider the complex tensions and contradictions of urban life. Cities contain some elements that are planned and others that arise spontaneously. They generate prosperity and perpetuate poverty. They are resource-intensive but also enable ecologically low-impact lifestyles. Metaphors for the city tend to simplify these tensions or smuggle untenable assumptions into analysis. For example, the image of city as body or organism might help analysts note their patterns of self-regulation, growth, and rejuvenation as Jacobs does in lauding the bottom-up order of street life. However, this metaphor understates the importance of procedural decision-making and supports assumptions about urban life that are empirically discredited but

---

12. Rem Koolhaas, "Whatever Happened to Urbanism?," *Design Quarterly* 164 (1995): 28–31.

13. Jacobsen, *The Space Between*, 175.

14. Jacobsen, *The Space Between*, 179.

nonetheless persistent in political rhetoric, such as the characterization of crime and poverty as spreading like a contagion.[15] Another common metaphor is that of the machine. Urbanists who approach cities as fundamentally mechanical often assume that virtue and well-being can be engineered. A notable proponent of this approach is French-Swiss architect Le Corbusier, who holds that design according to geometric principles can offer solutions to class tensions, crime, and poverty. He describes a house as "a machine for living in" and urges the architect to instill order in dwellings and other buildings.[16] In line with his understanding of built places as mechanical, he excitedly predicts, "We shall arrive at the 'House-Machine,' the mass-production house, healthy (and morally so too) and beautiful in the same way that the working tools and instruments which accompany our existence are beautiful."[17] A sense of the city as mechanical does helpfully highlight the technical dimensions of the city that can benefit from intervention from engineers, such as traffic patterns, health codes, and infrastructure. However, Lynch cautions that it oversimplifies human behavior and risks justifying practices of social and political domination.[18]

In light of these risks, Lynch proposes a model of the city based on "performance dimensions" or "metrics" that measure the extent to which cities support certain aspects of human well-being. His performance dimensions include vitality (supporting biological health), sense (allowing for easy mapping and navigation by inhabitants), fit (matching the environment to what inhabitants want to do), access (connecting individuals to other people, resources, and information), and control (distributing decision-making in a way that maintains transparency and respects subsidiarity). Because tradeoffs between these dimensions are unavoidable, Lynch offers two meta-criteria: efficiency and justice. A city must make effective use of limited resources and distribute its benefits equitably.[19] Recognizing the need for some sort of general metaphor to tie these metrics together, he provisionally

---

15. Kevin Lynch, *Good City Form* (Cambridge, MA: MIT Press, 1981), 96.

16. Le Corbusier, *Towards a New Architecture*, trans. Frederick Etchells (New York: Dover Publications, 1986), 4.

17. Le Corbusier, *Towards a New Architecture*, 7.

18. Lynch, *Good City Form*, 88.

19. Lynch, *Good City Form*, 224.

proposes a loose sense of a city as a "*learning ecosystem*" in which the human as "the dominant animal consciously restructures materials and switches the paths of energy flow."[20] Ultimately, Lynch is not fully convinced by his own proposal. He judges that his performance dimensions have practical use and believes that the metaphor of a learning ecosystem integrates them into a cohesive model. Nevertheless, he yearns for a theory that has "the ability to evaluate form and process together, as they vary over a span of time."[21]

Lynch's evaluation of his own proposal implies that a productive model of the city needs to meet two criteria. It must (1) recognize the manifestation of human values in the built environment through form and (2) account for the dynamism of evolving processes over time. As we consider suitable frameworks for understanding urban places from a Christian perspective, I argue that Francis's articulation of integral ecology in *Laudato si'* poses the need for two additional criteria. (3) An effective model must recognize the city's dependence on broader ecosystems beyond itself. The idea of a learning ecosystem can mistakenly imply that the city is a bounded and autonomous reality. In fact, it depends on resources beyond its own borders and it imposes externalities on broader local and global human and natural ecosystems. A city's physical boundaries do not represent the full ecological footprint needed to support its energy and resource usage. Furthermore, individual cities depend upon regional, national, or international infrastructures to maintain connections to other places and broader legal and economic systems. (4) From the standpoint of Christian hope, any understanding of the urban built environment must leave room for the workings of God's grace. If city life presents unique human and ecological challenges, any model of conceptualizing urban space that is suitable for practical use by Christians and the church must clarify the call to discipleship and mission in the city as well as the ways in which God is present in places constructed by human hands.

Lynch's model of the city as a learning ecosystem can incorporate these criteria, but only if we elaborate the mechanics behind how learning takes place. If human beings can improve their techniques for managing material space and the flow of energy based on shared

20. Lynch, *Good City Form*, 115.

21. Lynch, *Good City Form*, 324.

values, what is the nature of this learning? How can human learners and builders understand their relationship with the contexts in which they are embedded but seek to change for the common good? What role can faith play in this process?

Emergent Probability as a Background for a Learning Ecosystem

I argue that we can begin to work out the implications and possible usefulness of a model of the city as a learning ecosystem that meets all four of these criteria by turning to Bernard Lonergan's notion of "emergent probability." This framework leaves room for recognizing both the potential and the challenges of urban places while also clarifying the ways in which human decision-making can and cannot support community flourishing in particular settings. In *Insight*, Lonergan introduces emergent probability as a worldview that recognizes "the complementarity of classical and of statistical investigations from the viewpoint of knowing."[22] A classical heuristic seeks constant and abstract laws, whereas statistical investigations recognize variable yet probabilistically-measurable outcomes. Lonergan asserts that we can combine these heuristics by recognizing that processes in the world unfold through distinct cycles, or "schemes of recurrence," that repeat based on probability. A given scheme or series of schemes sets the grounds of possibility for new schemes of recurrence emerge.[23] For example, the processes of planetary formation make possible the emergence of atmospheric systems, which in turn provide conditions conducive to the emergence of life. Emergent probability offers an explanatory framework that accounts for the appearance of new phenomena while also recognizing that such development is subject to limits and laws. In Lonergan's words, the "world process is open" but "increasingly systematic."[24] Processes and realities unfold successively but contingently.

As it applies to their intersubjective systems of shared meaning, human beings participate in emergent probability through

---

22. Bernard J.F. Lonergan, *Insight: A Study of Human Understanding*, Collected Works of Bernard Lonergan, vol. 3, eds. Frederick E. Crowe and Robert M. Doran (Toronto: University of Toronto Press, 2005), 137.

23. Lonergan, *Insight*, 145.

24. Lonergan, *Insight*, 149.

self-transcendence, the accumulation of insights and judgments, and the application of new knowledge to the social order. For example, the existence of a physical telecommunications infrastructure and social practices of the service industry made possible the extension of the Internet to consumers, which in turn facilitated the emergence of cultural communities that had not been previously possible. For each of these steps, human inquiry and judgment rather than natural processes drive the unfolding of progress. Human society and culture develop when individuals in community take responsibility for their own self-transcendence to advance in understanding and preserve the authenticity of shared social meaning.[25]

One dimension of development in society is the extension of goods from individual attainment to collective access. The numerous intersubjective processes involved in society give rise to systemic sharing of desired goods, which Lonergan terms the "good of order." He explains,

> The good of order . . . is not merely a sustained succession of recurring instances of the particular good. Besides that recurrent manifold, there is the order that sustains it. This consists basically in (1) the ordering of operations so that they are cooperations and ensure the recurrence of all effectively desired instances of the particular good, and (2) the interdependence of effective desires or decisions with the appropriate performance by cooperating individuals.[26]

For example, one person's desire for education and intellectual growth is an individual good. The good of order consists of institutions, processes, and cultural meanings that support widespread access to literacy and educational opportunities.

This progress is not inevitable. Processes and goods can take an unexpected turn toward harm, a reality that we cannot help but recognize in the pathologies of some of the aforementioned Internet cultures. The possibility of development depends on the functioning of the schemes of recurrence that set the conditions for the emergence of a process in the first place. An economic system that

25. Lonergan, *Insight*, 234.

26. Bernard J.F. Lonergan, *Method in Theology* (Toronto: University of Toronto Press, 1971), 49.

depletes or pollutes natural resources diminishes its own long-term sustainability. Furthermore, when human beings exercise agency over certain schemes of recurrence, insights and judgments of individuals and groups can be and often are tainted by bias that judges egotistically rather than according to the drive for intelligibility. Consequently, "the group is prone to have a blind spot for the insights that reveal its well-being to be excessive or its usefulness at an end."[27] Lonergan associates such bias with social evil. The effects of bias on shared common sense accumulate, dragging societies into cycles of decline that are difficult to correct. The good of order deteriorates to the point that injustices are tolerated and social order "becomes to a greater or less extent the instrument of a class."[28] Blinded by bias, human beings can distort systems around bias to the point of unintelligibility, threatening the sustainability of shared order and closing meaningful possibilities of further development. In the realm of meaning, emergent probability depends on human adherence to intelligibility and authenticity.

Toward the end of *Insight*, Lonergan describes the divine solution to the problem of bias, evil, and decline as likewise operative through the mechanisms of emergent probability. These problems can be solved through the range of possibilities of human life as "a new and higher integration of human activity," but only "in accord with the probabilities."[29] The criteria by which society might be saved from evil clearly points to the identity and ministry of Jesus Christ, a point Lonergan later makes explicit in his formulation of the "Law of the Cross" in *De Verbo Incarnato*.[30] According to this precept, God reveals the solution to evil through the life, death, and resurrection of Jesus Christ. Mark Miller notes that Lonergan interprets the paschal mystery as communicating two powerful truths. First, Jesus' willingness to undergo suffering for human sin reveals God's love for humanity and God's intention to redeem evil not through force but through persuasion. God chooses this means of salvation to initiate friendship with humanity on terms that human

---

27. Lonergan, *Insight*, 248.

28. Lonergan, *Method in Theology*, 54.

29. Lonergan, *Insight*, 719–720.

30. Bernard J.F. Lonergan, *De Verbo Incarnato*, third ed. (Rome: Pontifical Gregorian University, 1964).

beings can understand and respond to. Miller explains, "An act of satisfaction performed out of divine charity for one's enemy may soften this person's heart and inspire her/him to return this love, thus forming a friendship."[31]

Second, Jesus' life, death, and resurrection teaches humanity how to overcome evil with good. In this way, the Cross serves as instruction for disciples who seek to cooperate with God's grace in redeeming the world. Lonergan writes, "Divine wisdom has ordained and divine goodness has willed, not to do away with the evils of the human race through power, but to convert those evils into a supreme good according to the just and mysterious Law of the Cross."[32] According to the Law of the Cross, redemption takes place when human beings freely respond to the suffering of others with love, repentance, and self-sacrifice. Because human beings can embrace this option only through God's grace, acts of loving redemption in the world not only imitate or are inspired by, but also participate in Jesus' original sacrifice. Miller summarizes, "Christ's friendship revealed on the cross inspires us, with the help of the Spirit, to respond with love, to repent for our own sins, to become friends with Christ, and to bear each other's burdens out of charity."[33] Christians take up the Law of the Cross in appropriating the life of discipleship, an event that takes place within the probabilities of human society and context. Cynthia Crysdale explains further how the realization of the Law of the Cross by human beings demonstrates the logic and possibility of emergent probability. She explains that shifts in human meaning that increase the probability of reversing decline arise from higher integrations of human experiences and judgments.[34] This requires loving sacrifice because such higher integrations require the dismantlement of distorted schemes of recurrence through interventions that take place at the level at which the problem of evil emerges. In this way, "it is

---

31. Mark T. Miller, "Imitating Christ's Cross: Lonergan and Girard on How and Why," *Heythrop Journal* 54, no. 5 (September 2013): 859–879, at 864.

32. Lonergan, *De Verbo Incarnato*, 550. The translation is taken from Miller.

33. Miller, "Imitating Christ's Cross," 864.

34. Cynthia Crysdale, "The Law of the Cross and Emergent Probability," in *Finding Salvation in Christ: Essays on Christology and Soteriology in Honor of William P. Loewe*, eds. Christopher D. Denny and Christopher McMahon (Eugene, OR: Pickwick Publications, 2011), 209.

precisely through allowing the evil embedded in [these distortions] to be exposed for what it is that this dismantling can occur."[35]

Theoretical and Practical Applications to Urban Design and Ministry

Emergent probability is a helpful framework for understanding the mechanics of city as a learning ecology, as a human invention that depends upon broader ecosystems, and as a setting in need of redemption. As a heuristic for understanding the complex factors of development in natural and human life, it underscores the combination of intentional decision-making and natural processes that form the ground of possibility for healthy communities that support flourishing and ecological balance. Vibrant and humane urban environments are a good of order that emerges based on physical infrastructure, healthy natural ecosystems, and systems of responsive decision-making that empower individuals and communities to assume agency in their own environments. Maintaining stability and justice in a city thus requires stewardship of the natural, social, and economic prerequisites for urban life. Urban policies that undermine the natural settings, community modes of decision-making, and everyday uses that give places vitality undermine the processes that set the conditions for vibrant urban places in the first place. By recognizing that the emergence of as-yet unforeseen possibilities of good depends on sustainable and authentic processes, an awareness of emergent probability also challenges policymakers to avoid sacrifices in democratic process in pursuit of expediency. Future developments will unfold through processes of democracy and respect for the integrity of human beings and nature, processes that demand consistent maintenance and preservation. For both city officials seeking further improvements to their neighborhoods and churches discerning their mission in the communities around them, an attentiveness to the cultural and natural processes of a place will avoid well-intentioned efforts that hurt a place. New possibilities successfully emerge in places only in continuity with the community's history.

To the model of the city as a learning ecosystem, Lonergan's thought also offers a path for redemption in settings that bear the

---

35. Crysdale, "The Law of the Cross and Emergent Probability," 210.

scars of social sin. Cities can serve as sites of redemptive possibility and schools for virtue, but also as settings for chaos and suffering. Theological engagements with the urban built environment frequently point out that the predominant vision of redeemed humanity, the heavenly Jerusalem, is a holy city rather than a restoration of the Garden of Eden. T.J. Gorringe detects such a process in scripture. He writes, "The Bible begins in a garden but ends in a city. Eden is not so much the site of primitive innocence as of temptation and fall, and the new creation will take the form of a city."[36] He refers to Irenaeus of Lyons in observing that "rather than think in a sin–fall–redemption pattern we might rather think of redemption as a *process*. Human beings were made in God's image . . . but had to grow into God's likeness, a process in which they were nurtured by God the Spirit," a trajectory that includes the gradual redemption of the physical environments that shape human experience and identity.[37] However, we are still undergoing this journey; God's unfolding plan of redemption is incomplete on this side of the eschaton. The fact that Catholic Social Teaching has primarily focused on cities as sites of suffering bears witness to the reality that the vision of the city as a place of virtue, fellowship, and redemption has not yet been fully realized.

Lonergan's argument for the efficacy of loving sacrifice, implied in his initial articulation of emergent probability and developed further in his account of the Law of the Cross, offers a counter-witness to simplistic solutions to urban challenges that, in reality, require adaptation and sacrifice. It stands as a prophetic challenge to technocratic approaches that either circumvent local democracy by imposing top-down policies or holding a naïve trust in the market as it is currently constituted, which contributes to unjust patterns of gentrification and displacement. From the standpoint of the church as a participant in the learning ecology of the city, emergent probability presents a frame in which acts of ministry might be oriented toward loving engagement within local processes. In doing so, the local church lives up to Pope Francis's call to ecological conversion in *Laudato si'*. In reference to humans' relationship with the natural world, Francis writes, "Rather than a problem to be solved, the world

---

36. T.J. Gorringe, *A Theology of the Built Environment: Justice, Empowerment, Redemption* (New York: Cambridge University Press, 2004), 119.

37. Gorringe, *A Theology of the Built Environment*, 114.

is a joyful mystery to be contemplated with gladness and praise" (*LS* 12). As an ecological reality constituted in part by the rhythms of community life, the city also requires a sense of humble and loving service on behalf of its shapers and guardians. The call to join acts of incarnational charity and discernment with an eye toward justice requires an understanding that this mission is linked with the contexts of specific cities, neighborhoods, and streets. Situations of suffering and injustice require not only technical reasoning, but also a conversion to the neighbor and the environment that may require loving sacrifices on the part of those seeking renewal. Francis argues that such conversion will require leadership that is "capable of striking out on new paths and meeting the needs of the present with concern for all and without prejudice towards coming generations" to avoid the risk that "new power structures based on the techno-economic paradigm may overwhelm not only our politics but also freedom and justice" (*LS* 53). Within the framework of emergent probability, such conversion grounds the possibility for restored and new social goods.

Both of these aspects of emergent probability—the dependence of new possibilities on current healthy schemes of recurrence and healing social sin and bias through loving sacrifice—indicate the need for both caution and commitment on the part of local governments, organizations, churches, and residents. When a neighborhood or city faces entrenched problems, intervention by various actors is necessary, but overly ambitious large-scale action risks undermining the processes and relationships that make human flourishing possible. Therefore, a perspective informed by emergent probability must recognize the need for local policies and actions that embrace incremental experiments that might set the conditions for the emergence of new realities and leave room for the exercise of agency by the inhabitants who know a place best. Recognizing the city as an ecological and emergent reality goes hand-in-hand with a cautious approach toward large-scale, top-down planning that presumes an ability to engineer solutions to economic and social problems. Urban policymakers must instead trust grassroots and local forms of knowing and community. Top-down modes of planning not only fail to take into account the myriad complex factors that determine the health of a place, but also risk introducing bias into urban design projects by confining decision-making to experts or powerful interests.

In an explicit appeal to the image of an ecosystem, Charles Marohn, the founder of the urbanist community-building organization *Strong Towns*, contrasts a cornfield with a rainforest to argue for an approach toward city planning that respects local relationships and agency.[38] While the monocultural cornfield is designed for maximum efficiency at the expense of adaptability and resilience, the rainforest contains a complex, adaptive system involving a multitude of interdependent species. For Marohn, the disciplines of city planning and economics have depended on a simplistic focus on economic growth. The results of planning interventions that have not respected local culture and relationship have been devastating. Marohn points specifically to the urban renewal programs of the twentieth century that involved massive demolition and rebuilding to demonstrate the dangers of a design approach that neglects local complex systems. He writes that, although neighborhoods eventually demolished by urban renewal programs often experienced high rates of poverty, "they were also vibrant. They were full of strong social connections, the kind that makes a place resilient. The great injustice that was done in these places had economic ramifications, for sure, but the worst aspect was social. We tore apart the complex fabric of the community. That we would now out of fear resist the restoration of this fabric, in poor and affluent neighborhoods alike, defies all that we have learned."[39]

There are many historical and contemporary examples of the sort of displacement described by Marohn. For example, historian Douglas Rae describes the demolition of the dense and diverse Oak Street Neighborhood during the redevelopment of New Haven, Connecticut, in the 1960s. City government officials promoted and justified the project employing a rhetoric of urban vitality and racial justice, but the project ultimately displaced nearly a fifth of the city's households, most of them families of color.[40] Geography theorist Katherine McKittrick describes how such programs of demolition often served racialized cultural narratives that sought to erase the presence of people of color, a dynamic evident in the demolition of

---

38. Charles L. Marohn, "Understanding Growth, Part V," *Thoughts on Building Strong Towns* (Strong Towns, 2017), 42.

39. Marohn, "Understanding Growth, Part V," 47.

40. Douglas Rae, *City, Urbanism and Its End* (New Haven, CT: Yale University Press, 2003).

Africville, Nova Scotia.[41] Many of the most harmful and disruptive failures in urban design throughout the twentieth century resulted from officials assuming the epistemological privilege of experts while discounting local histories, meanings, and relationships. In emphasizing the need for careful interventions that reflect trust for local knowledge, I do not intend to minimize the role that wisely-discerned, large-scale city or regional plans can play in generating new possibilities for urban life. Indeed, such plans can serve as essential instruments for achieving the good of order in distributing the benefits of city life. Rather, we must heed Lonergan's assertion that goods of order depend upon the ordering of cooperations between independent agents.[42] The scaling of healthy city settings depends upon respect for the agency of the various people and institutions involved in governance and community-building. An effective policy, whether exercised on the level of the neighborhood block or the region, recognizes the exercise of judgment on the part of inhabitants and everyday decision-makers as part of the schemes of recurrence that may lead to unexpected benefits and possibilities in urban life.

A theological engagement with the built environment can offer distinctive insights to activists, policymakers, and designers who make decisions about infrastructure, zoning, and governance. This discernment must consider impacts on the schemes of recurrence upon which the very possibility of the healthy city depends. Furthermore, a sense of the city as a learning ecosystem, interpreted through the lens of emergent probability, calls attention to the fact that the decisions and commitments made today might set the grounds of possibility for future realities. Urban life around the world continues to surface stark contradictions in our economic systems and ideologies. By thinking about the city as a learning ecosystem that develops and finds strategies of correction in the face of decline through the workings of emergent probability, we can find a starting point for a method for thinking through urban issues that unites Francis's call for an integral ecology and Lynch's hope for an understanding of city life that illuminates how the places where we live, work, and love express and shape our values.

---

41. Katherine McKittrick, *Demonic Grounds: Black Women and the Cartographies of Struggle* (Minneapolis, MN: University of Minnesota Press, 2006).

42. Lonergan, *Method in Theology*, 49.

CHAPTER FOURTEEN

Water Ethics Under Development

HELP FROM LONERGAN'S METHOD

Thomas C. McAuley (St. Paul University, Ottawa)

A water ethics literature has been developing over the past several decades. In a world that faces increasing water scarcity, competition for resources, and water poverty, the question arises: how do we evoke a more ethical governance and use of water? Water is both local and global. There are some 276 transboundary or international river basins. About 3 billion people live within 145 countries that share these rivers. Examples include the African and the Laurentian Great Lakes as well as rivers such as the Mekong, the Nile, the Amazon, the Indus, the Brahmaputra, and the Columbia River. Water is most often mediated to people through water governance and management institutions. Such institutions cannot avoid value decisions, whether local, regional, or international in scale. There exists a tension between anthropocentric and ecocentric approaches as natural systems suffer pollution and loss of biodiversity. For water ethics, what kind of normative foundations are being used or proposed? Are they adequate? How might the method and opus of Bernard Lonergan help water ethics and governance? How can it help in the long-term move towards a new water ethic? This essay examines these matters more closely.

Water Crises in the Anthropocene

Water is irreplaceable in supporting all species and ecosystems of the earth's community of life. It is fundamental for human well-being and underpins agriculture, energy, and economies, from local to global. Throughout history, water has been central as powerful civilizations emerged along major rivers like the Yangtze, Indus, Nile,

Tigris, and Euphrates. In our times, however, water poses a problem. A creeping and multi-faceted water crisis increasingly affects our interdependent world. Over the course of the twentieth century, world population tripled, and water use grew sixfold. Water scarcity now affects more than a third of the world's population, and two-thirds of the globe live in areas that experience water scarcity for at least one month per year. Some 845,000 dams have already been constructed worldwide—mainly for energy production, agricultural irrigation, and urban water supplies. Agriculture is the largest user of freshwater globally, taking on average 70% of water use. Pollution can affect both surface and groundwater, including irrigation water and its resultant food products. Biodiversity is likewise moderately to highly threatened in 65% of continental river discharge, according to a major global study.[1] Throughout the world, withdrawals of water for irrigation exceed natural aquifer recharge rates, causing continual decrease in groundwater levels. According to a 2015 NASA satellite study, a third of the world's 37 largest groundwater aquifers are in distress.[2] In the face of these water crises, concerns are growing about the ability to feed the world by the year 2030. Around the world, just access to clean water and the sustainability of water resources are critical to human security, development, and peace.

Water poverty affects several billion people. There are over 800 million people lacking sufficient access to safe water, and two and a half billion people lack sanitation facilities.[3] Elevated rates of child death due to water-borne diseases are found among the water-poor. Women and children miss opportunities for education because of the large amounts of time they spend fetching water. Community development also suffers from this lost time. Water poverty likewise

---

1. C. J. Vörösmarty, et al., "Global Threats to Human Water Security and River Biodiversity," *Nature* 467 (September 2010): 555–561.

2. NASA, "Study: Third of Big Groundwater Basins in Distress," June 16, 2005, www.nasa.gov/jpl/grace/study-third-of-big-groundwater-basins-in-distress.

3. Figures from the UN differ according to definitions of "safe" and "access." A higher figure is found in the 2017 UNU-INWEH ("United Nations University Institute for Water, Environment and Health") Water Crisis Report, which states that 1.8 billion people use drinking water sources contaminated by feces. See Lisa Guppy and Kelsey Anderson, *Water Crisis Report* (Hamilton, Canada: UNU-INWEH, 2017), available at http://inweh.unu.edu/wp-content/uploads/2017/11/Global-Water-Crisis-The-Facts.pdf, 2.

affects millions of people living around the peripheries of major cities in the developing world. Many of the poor disconnected from a city infrastructure pay a much higher price when purchasing water from standpipe operators, tanker truck operators, or collecting water from untreated sources.[4] Responding to these exigencies, the United Nations Sustainable Development Goals (SDG) for 2015–2030 includes a goal specific to water. The sixth goal aims for universal access to safe and affordable drinking water and sanitation facilities for all by 2030. Access to safe and affordable water can be said to underpin the other 16 SDGs because of water's radical connectedness to all human activities.[5] As the report states, "'Not having access' to water and sanitation is a polite euphemism for a form of deprivation that threatens life, destroys opportunity and undermines human dignity."[6]

While humans suffer considerably from today's water crisis, they also bear much of the blame. The term "Anthropocene" names our era as a new geologic time period beginning in the mid-twentieth century marked by an overwhelming evidence of increasing impacts of human activity on our planet's continents, oceans, and ecosystems. The previous epoch—the Holocene—was a period of relatively stable climate under which civilizations and agriculture developed for over 10 millennia following the retreat of the last major glaciation. Those conditions, however, are now changing at an unnaturally rapid rate under human-caused climate change. We are now facing unprecedented threats. Among these, the hydrologic cycle, already dynamic and variable, has revealed a tendency towards greater extremes in both rainfall and droughts. Water has been called the "hammer" of climate change since increasing ocean temperatures can fuel hurricanes and tropical storms bringing exacerbated flooding, while droughts also increase in scale and become more persistent.

---

4. United Nations Development Programme, *Human Development Report 2006: Beyond Scarcity: Power, Poverty, and the Global Water Crisis* (New York: UNDP, 2006), available at www.undp.org/content/dam/undp/ library/corporate/ HDR/2006%20Global%20HDR/HDR-2006-Beyond%20scarcity-Power-poverty-and-the-global-water-crisis.pdf.

5. United Nations, "UN Sustainable Development Goals," available at https:// sustainabledevelopment.un.org/? menu=1300.

6. United Nations Development Programme, *Human Development Report 2006*, 5.

Water Ethics: The Quest for Ethical Water Use and Management

There are numerous scientific papers, UN reports, and books by experts on global water issues. In the past several decades, there has also appeared a body of literature on water ethics. Water ethics literature critically examines the human role in these problems, highlighting the values and ethics that underlie the governance and use of freshwater. Sandra Postel, for example, argued cogently about the need for a new water ethic in her 1992 book, *The Last Oasis, Facing Water Scarcity*, and in a later article "The Missing Piece: A Water Ethic."[7] For Postel, "our stewardship of water will determine not only the quality but the staying power of human societies."[8] She asks, "Why has so much of modern water management gone awry? Why is it that ever greater amounts of money and ever more sophisticated engineering have not solved the world's water problems? Why, in so many places on this planet, are rivers drying up, lakes shrinking, and water tables falling?"[9] Postel urges a historic shift away from approaches to water management that are guided by a utilitarian ethics akin to prevailing market-based socio-economic paradigms. A new water ethic needs to see people and water as interconnected parts of a greater whole, and it must make the protection of freshwater ecosystems a central goal. For Postel, what is needed is "a set of guidelines and principles that stops us from chipping away at natural systems until nothing is left of their life-sustaining functions, which the marketplace fails to value adequately, if at all."[10]

Although water ethics involves individual attitudes, the literature seeks principally to bring moral or ethical inquiry into the arena of freshwater governance and policy. David Groenfeldt, a well-known water ethicist, argues that "getting the ethics right" is

---

7. Sandra Postel, *Last Oasis: Facing Water Scarcity* (New York: W.W. Norton, 1992), 3; see also Postel, "The Missing Piece: A Water Ethic," in *Water Ethics: Foundational Readings for Students and Professionals*, eds. Peter G. Brown and Jeremy J. Schmidt (Washington, DC: Island Press, 2010), 221–226.

8. Postel, "The Missing Piece," 222.

9. Postel, "The Missing Piece," 221.

10. Postel, "The Missing Piece," 224, 222.

the first step to better water governance.[11] For Groenfeldt, we have mistakenly assumed that water management is a technical subject that should be left to the experts. However, technical management choices are full of embedded assumptions. He writes, "the *governance* of water, the laws, policies and institutions which set the context for technical water management, is anything but technical. Water governance is all about values. . . ."[12] Groenfeldt echoes Postel in identifying a default, strictly utilitarian, divide-and-conquer ethic operative in water management. This tacit ethic, according to Groenfeldt, is covered by "the fiction that decisions about water are made through objective logic unencumbered by subjective values."[13]

The book, *Water Ethics: Foundational Readings for Students and Professionals* appeared in 2010. In it, co-editors Peter Brown and Jeremy Schmidt argue that water ethics entails more than simply avoiding past mistakes in making decisions about water. It also concerns the persons making those decisions, their attitudes and virtues, and the realization that they are one part within many complex socio-ecological systems. For Brown and Schmidt, "a water ethic must be seen as constitutive of, and complementary to much broader social and moral obligations."[14] The anthology includes a range of perspectives—utilitarianism, ecofeminism, ecocentric ethics, communitarian ethics, pragmatism, and religious ethics. None of them are foundational in the sense of providing a metaethics or epistemology, however. Rather, they start with principles and insights most often related to justice, human dignity, intrinsic environmental value, and sustainability. The readings reflect the intersection of water needs and choices with broader social and moral obligations to aboriginal peoples, women, children, the poor, future generations, and the living environment.

UNESCO sponsored work on water ethics between 1997 and 2004, along with the "World Commission on the Ethics of Scientific

---

11. David Groenfeldt, *Water Ethics: A Values Approach to Solving the Water Crisis* (London, U.K.: Routledge, 2013), 161.

12. Groenfeldt, *Water Ethics*, 3.

13. Groenfeldt, *Water Ethics*, 4.

14. Brown and Schmidt, "An Ethic of Compassionate Retreat," in *Water Ethics: Foundational Readings*, 280.

Knowledge and Technology" (COMEST).[15] An overview of this work by Jerome Delli Priscoli and a team of scholars summarized a number of important principles for water ethics practice. These include: human dignity, participation, solidarity, human equality, the common good, stewardship, transparency, inclusiveness, and empowerment. Human rights and human dignity were considered foundational. In the summary, Priscoli and his team recognized that the world's diversity of cultures and values present an important challenge for water ethics. Ethical values take different forms in different cultural groups, and cultural diversity must be considered. The study thus raises the question of how to account for value differences between individuals, groups, and societies. UNESCO more recently sponsored an Asian and Pacific working group on water ethics. This group examined, updated, and built on the earlier COMEST work, while also critiquing it for remaining too anthropocentric. It suggested that future reflections on water ethics should take a more ecocentric approach.[16]

In 2011, Martin Kowarsch reviewed the existing water ethics literature as part of a German project on "Sustainable Water Management in a Globalized World."[17] The literature reviewed also included the earlier UNESCO work. Kowarsch concluded that a sufficiently coherent and comprehensive water ethics is missing and that existing work is inadequate for the complexity of the water crisis and all its interconnecting factors. Kowarsch proposed another solution—a pragmatic tri-modal concept of justice based on basic needs fulfillments, sufficient opportunities, and fair procedures. Kowarsch attributes foundational status to his triangle of justice, calling it "a general moral standpoint."

---

15. Jerome Delli Priscoli, James Dooge, and Ramón Llamas, *Water and Ethics: Overview* (Paris: UNESCO, 2004), available at https://www.internationalwaterlaw.org/bibliography/articles/Ethics/Overview.pdf. See also World Commission on the Ethics of Scientific Knowledge and Technology, *Best Ethical Practice in Water Use* (Paris: UNESCO, 2004), available at http://unesdoc.unesco.org/images/0013/001344/134430e.pdf.

16. Jie Liu, et al., *Water Ethics and Water Resource Management* (Bangkok: UNESCO, 2011), http://unesdoc.unesco.org/images/0019/001922/192256E.pdf.

17. Martin Kowarsch, *Diversity of Water Ethics: A Literature Review* (2011), available at http://dialog.hfph.mwn.de/Members/m_kowarsch/nawama-2nd-working-paper-igp/view.

Missing Foundations and Incomplete Methods

This review of water ethics literature indicates its missing foundations. Still, the literature does supply valuable principles and objectives. These include the concept of sustainable development as well as UN declarations concerning the human right to water and the rights of indigenous peoples. More recently, there are the Bellagio Principles on Valuing Water.[18] The field of water ethics also proposes several frameworks or procedural methods. A "framework of water ethics construction" is found in the 2011 UNESCO-sponsored report, *Water Ethics and Water Resource Management.*[19] The framework calls for an interdisciplinary collaboration of representatives from central and local governments, the water affairs department, researchers in the natural, human and social sciences, and stakeholders for municipal, ecological, agricultural, and industrial water use.[20] According to Jie Liu's framework, these diverse groupings are used to discuss ethical assumptions and make sound water judgments. The framework mentions the need for education and aims for a contribution from different views of value "to seek for a ground in practical water ethics and lifestyle change."[21] The report states that it has no intention to provide a meta-ethic. The framework remains incomplete, however, given the need to bridge a diversity of cultures, religions, and philosophical approaches usually present in large and international river basins.

Another method is the "values approach" Groenfeldt and Schmidt proposed in 2013. The authors argue that "values are central to ordering water for the purposes of governance" and that,

18. High Level Panel on Water (U.N.), "Bellagio Principles on Valuing Water," 2017, available at https://sustainabledevelopment.un.org/content/documents/15591 Bellagio_principles_on_valuing_water_final_version_in_word.pdf.

19. Liu et al., *Water Ethics and Water Resource Management*, 18.

20. This cast of proposed participants parallels similar groupings that have been engaged by the International Joint Commission (IJC) in its Canada-US transboundary water studies where boards and binational working groups came from all stakeholder groups, all levels of government, and often tribes and First Nations. There are differences in that IJC studies brought forth options to the Commission for deliberation and decisions that took place without explicit calls for a discussion of values and ethics.

21. Liu et al., *Water Ethics and Water Resource Management*, 33.

"[w]hen values are not explicitly considered, governance norms lack orientation."[22] In a world of polycentric water governance with three principal perspectives—management, institutional capacity, and social-ecological systems—one must sufficiently grasp operative inherited and implicit values. The three steps of the values approach are: 1) identify inherited values; 2) reason about values; and 3) order water anew. Still, Groenfeldt and Schmidt caution, "[a] values approach to water governance does not resolve ethical dilemmas, but it improves our understanding of how and why ethical issues are central to the task of adapting technical and political issues to changing patterns of water governance."[23]

One year later, Schmidt and Christiana Peppard highlighted the complexity of the space in which water ethics is emerging. It is an "interdisciplinary yet distinct space at the juncture of philosophical norms, social practices, hydrological constraints, and practical demands."[24] They argue that a Western model of rationality based on universality and necessity cannot meet the contextual complexity of evolving social and ecological systems. For Schmidt and Peppard, a viable water ethic can be articulated "[o]nly in the interplay of grounding principles and their pragmatic mobilization in specific contexts," and water ethics will "continue to be characterized by moral and ethical *bricolage* and ongoing discernment of how norms and context intersect."[25]

But what is "moral and ethical bricolage"? Bricolage involves crafting or tinkering with things. How is this mysterious process performed with multiple ethical perspectives? Water decisions and policies need justifiable moral reasoning. These same questions apply to the framework proposed in the 2011 UNESCO report on Water Ethics and Water Resource Management. Missing is *how* the different views of values are combined and what the normative ground should

---

22. David Groenfeldt and Jeremy J. Schmidt, "Ethics and Water Governance," *Ecology and Society* 18, no. 1 (2013): 14, available at http://www.ecologyandsociety. org/vol18/iss1/art14/.

23. Groenfeldt and Schmidt, "Ethics and Water Governance," 14.

24. Jeremy J. Schmidt and Christiana Z. Peppard, "Water Ethics on a Human-Dominated Planet: Rationality, Context, and Values in Global Governance," *Wiley Interdisciplinary Reviews: Water* 1, no. 6 (2014): 533–47, at 533.

25. Schmidt and Peppard, "Water Ethics on a Human-Dominated Planet," 540.

be. Similarly, in the "values approach" proposed by Groenfeldt and Schmidt, what is the ground of those who reason about values and then reorder them?

Despite appeals for "embodied" experience and epistemology in place of abstract rationality,[26] the water ethics literature surveyed above neglects the human subject. Articles and books on water ethics are all turned towards the objects of concern, whether they are unjust social water distribution, water scarcity, pollution, poor water management, or threatened ecosystems. If we hope to arrive at normative judgments about water usage and management, however, we must begin with the subject and what she is doing as a knower and chooser.

Along with the missing subject, the field of water ethics finds itself without a cognitional theory and an intentionality analysis. This lacuna is evidenced in apparent struggles with modernity's turn to the subject and by misunderstanding the roles of logic and deduction in ethics. For instance, Schmidt and Peppard claim that a Western model of rationality grounded in universality and necessity is inadequate for a world where social and ecological systems are characterized by change rather than stability. Water ethics instead needs to be adaptable and flexible and thus cannot be a "rote application of pre-established ethical algorithms."[27]

German philosopher Simon Meisch criticizes Schmidt and Peppard on this point. He writes,

> Schmidt & Peppard . . . argue against ethical and epistemological foundational approaches to water that, according to their view, have dominated human water handling since the Enlightenment. . . . [They] seem to argue for a cognitivist ethics, they are ambiguous with regard to ethical relativism that they regard as a promising pathway to deal with water issues in the 21st century.[28]

---

26. Christiana Peppard, *Just Water: Theology, Ethics, and the Global Water Crisis* (Maryknoll, NY: Orbis Books, 2014), 16–17.

27. Schmidt and Peppard, "Water Ethics on a Human-Dominated Planet," 542.

28. Simon Meisch, "Water Ethics: Reflections on a Liquifying Topic," in *Ethics of Science in the Research for Sustainable Development*, eds. Simon Meisch, Johannes Lundershausen, Leonie Bossert, and Marcus Rockoff (Baden-Baden: Nomos, 2015), 364.

For Meisch, "dealing with water is an interdisciplinary and trans-disciplinary business—and water ethics needs to be part of it when it comes to implicit and explicit normativities and moral judgements."[29] When ethical judgments are inevitably connected to cultural and historical contexts, relativistic positions run into self-contradictions in their metaethical and normative assumptions due to the conflicting moral stances of different communities. Metaethics, according to Meisch, is "the epistemology of ethics. It explores the language and logic of moral discourses and the methods of moral arguments."[30] Such is the extent of his epistemological reflection. Meisch contends that a basic ethical framework is already provided by the broadly accepted concept of sustainable development, a concept whose "normative core is the idea of inter- and intragenerational justice in the face of decreasing natural resources, the ecosystems' limited capacity to absorb human emissions, and the ongoing environmental destruction."[31]

Water ethics literature ignores not only the subject but also a foundation that can anchor epistemology, objectivity, and normative judgments. Those who might attempt to look further into solving this water ethics dilemma are quite likely to encounter the large-scale abandonment of the quest for epistemological and metaphysical foundations across both the Anglo-American Analytic tradition and the Continental tradition.[32] This surrender is connected to a problematic conceptualism, perceptualism, and myth of the "already-out-there-now-real" alluded to by Lonergan. As he argues, modernity has generated too many subject-neglecting accounts of objectivity, and that philosophy has been dominated by those who "have thought of truth as so objective as to get along without minds."[33]

Recovering the subject entails understanding how the subject knows and chooses. But how can we come to know reality and

29. Meisch, "Water Ethics: Reflections on a Liquifying Topic," 370.

30. Meisch, "Water Ethics: Reflections on a Liquifying Topic," 357–358.

31. Meisch, "Water Ethics: Reflections on a Liquifying Topic," 368.

32. See, for instance, Michael McCarthy, "Pluralism, Invariance, and Conflict (Bernard Lonergan on Invariants of Intentional Subjectivity)," *Review of Metaphysics* 51, no. 1 (Sept. 1997): 3–21.

33. Bernard Lonergan, "The Subject," in *A Second Collection*, Collected Works of Bernard Lonergan (CWL), vol. 13, eds. Robert M. Doran and John D. Dadosky (Toronto: University of Toronto Press, 2016), 62.

make pronouncements about it in a way that is objective? To treat of truth and objectivity in any sound and thorough fashion, according to Lonergan, it is first necessary to settle the issues of cognitional theory, epistemology, and assumed metaphysics.[34] Lonergan offers "non-foundationalist" foundations that are quite different from problematic conceptualist notions of epistemology and metaphysics. We shall examine these below.

Foundations and a Generalized Empirical Method

One of the challenges of multidisciplinary collaboration is the different methods found within the natural and human sciences, methods all necessary for participatory water governance and ethics. For Lonergan, "[m]athematics, science, philosophy, ethics, theology differ in many manners; but they have the common feature that their objectivity is the fruit of attentiveness, intelligence, reasonableness, and responsibility."[35] Lonergan's "Generalized Empirical Method" (GEM) elucidates the common core of related and recurrent operations extant in both natural science and human studies.

The interrelated operations in human consciousness involved in knowing and doing are both intentional and conscious. They are intentional in that they make objects psychologically present to the subject. They are conscious in that they make the performing subject present to herself, not as an object, but as a subject. The operations of consciousness—experiencing, understanding, judging, and deciding—are performed by all people. They may be used well or badly, explicitly or not. Lonergan contends that operations of consciousness are universally human and challenges readers in *Insight* to become conscious of and appropriate their own use of the operations of consciousness. These operations serve as internal dynamic norms, as a capacity that promotes us towards truth, reality, and decisions for value. These are the internal norms that are the common core of the natural sciences and the human sciences, along with all human

---

34. Bernard Lonergan, "Philosophy and the Religious Phenomenon," in *Philosophical and Theological Papers: 1965–1980*, CWL 17, eds. Robert C. Croken and Robert M. Doran (Toronto: University of Toronto Press, 2004), 22.

35. Bernard Lonergan, *Method in Theology* (New York: Herder and Herder, 1972), 265.

knowing and doing. The operations of consciousness are the normative pattern of related and recurrent operations that yield ongoing
and cumulative results. This inner pattern is what Lonergan means
by GEM. As a "metamethod," it underlies all the specific methodol-
ogies of the natural and human sciences, philosophy, and theology.
As universal to humanity, it also provides a common ground for both
transdisciplinary and transcultural collaboration.

The fundamental unity of consciousness includes our agency in
the world. This agency comes out of the existential level, the level of
freedom and responsibility. At this level, our consciousness expands in
a new dimension when a judgment on the facts is followed by deliberation on what we are to do about them.[36] Lonergan writes, "Further, as
a metaphysics is derived from the known structure of one's knowing,
so an ethics results from knowledge of the compound structure of one's
knowing and doing; and as the metaphysics, so too the ethics prolongs
the initial self-criticism into an explanation of the origin of all ethical
positions and into a criterion for passing judgment on each of them."[37]
Proper use of these internal norms of consciousness carries us beyond
ourselves in self-transcendence. Objectivity is the fruit of attentiveness
at the empirical level of experience, of intelligence in questioning and
understanding, of reasonableness in judgments of fact, and of responsibility in deliberations, decisions and actions. The transcendental
precepts enjoin fidelity to these norms: *Be attentive! Be intelligent!*
Be reasonable! Be responsible! These precepts highlight the exigence
towards cognitive and moral self-transcendence. Objectivity accordingly cannot be separated from the knowing and deliberating subject,
as it is the fruit of authentic subjectivity.

How Generalized Empirical Method Could Help in Water Ethics

The use of GEM in water governance and water ethics is promising. A first benefit involves adjudicating values. Water governance
institutions make decisions and policy regarding water, people, and

---

36. Lonergan, *Method in Theology*, 9.

37. Bernard Lonergan, *Insight: A Study of Human Understanding*, CWL 3,
eds. Frederick E. Crowe and Robert M. Doran (Toronto: University of Toronto
Press, 2005), 23.

nature in an already value-laden field. Thus, there exists an unavoidable need to adjudicate between competing value and ethical systems. This unexplained process has been described as "bricolage" and as "reordering" values within the field of values from various perspectives. How are such decisions justified? What is the normative basis for final judgments of value? Large and international river basins populated by different cultures and religions only complicate the question. GEM offers a normative basis in theory and practice for the adjudication of such water decisions. It is especially valuable since the operations of consciousness are universal and can handle transcultural questions and deliberations. Employing GEM still requires all pertinent scientific and socio-cultural data as well as their representation in a non-biased way. Those involved can learn together, especially about the natural science and hydrology of the river basins, aquifers, or water concerns in question. All involved in ethical deliberations—having backgrounds in engineering, science, law, economics, ethics, politics, or theology—must commit to seeking the good together by using a common method that respects the transcendental precepts for attentiveness, intelligence, reasonableness, and responsibility. This commitment includes seeking further information and using dialectic and dialogue to rectify potential contradictions.

A second benefit involves institutions. Water institutions are created and operated by means of the operations of conscious intentionality. It is possible to examine such institutions to discern how their modes of operating, and even their founding charters, may or may not be well-aligned with the metamethod of human intentionality. The International Joint Commission of Canada and the United States (IJC) provides a good example. Widely recognized as a successful water institution, the IJC has, on all but two occasions in over a century, successfully settled questions and disputes in the transboundary waters along the Canada-US border. These waters include the Laurentian Great Lakes, along with approximately 350 streams. One reason for this success is the effective freedom to deliberate and to objectively advise the two governments, as is guaranteed by the 1909 Boundary Waters Treaty (BWT). The IJC was founded as a unitary binational organization under the treaty. As a creation of a treaty and not of national governments, it is relatively free from political interference. The same cannot be said for many international water institutions whose members represent their governments and whose ability to function is stymied by political interventions, especially in periods of tensions between states. In the case of the IJC, the necessary essential freedom that was arranged in the founding BWT allows for the freedom to continue engaging the fourth level of intentional consciousness, that of deliberation and decision. This aspect of the founding treaty is thus aligned to GEM.

Another reason for its success is the Commission's mission to pursue the common good of both countries in preventing and resolving disputes over shared waters. Seeking the common good of both countries is further supported by the IJC's Guiding Principles of "joint fact-finding" and consensus-seeking in decision-making. The IJC has six Commissioners—three Canadians and three Americans—supported by staff and boards from both countries. Joint fact-finding serves as a check against group bias and competing nationalisms. Without this principle, one risks the common game of "your facts" versus "our facts." Seeking consensus is sometimes more arduous than simply voting. However, where voting can leave issues unresolved between voting parties, consensus-seeking promotes dialogue to find the root of different lines of reasoning and value positions. The consensus exercise can also foster authenticity in dialogue partners such that it facilitates relations of respect and closure on decisions. The Guiding Principles enjoin the IJC to work as "a single integrated body working collegially in a spirit of openness, mutual trust and confidence, and in the common interest of both countries."[38] The Commission has maintained a collegial culture through today and has inculcated this culture in its many binational boards that work within the major transboundary basins from the Atlantic to the Pacific.

Joint fact-finding, working collegially, and respecting each person's "personal and professional capacity" implicitly favors the proper use of intentional cognitive operations. With the IJC, collaborative experiencing, understanding, and judgment of facts ground deliberations. Thus, the four interdependent levels of operations of GEM can be recognized as implicitly operative in the IJC. Authentic performance of members and participating individuals cannot be guaranteed, however, for any institution. This is where education in GEM along with commitments to self-appropriation of the operations of

---

38. The Mission and Guiding Principles of The International Joint Commission are available at www.ijc.org/en_/IJC_Mandates.

consciousness could be embraced to enhance results. Using GEM could promote the formation and transformation of the very institutions that mediate water to humans and the rest of our common home. Similar and more extensive studies of GEM-alignment in water institutions present promising avenues of research.

A New Water Ethic and a New Ecological Culture

Besides GEM, there are several other dimensions of Lonergan's work that could benefit water ethics and water governance. First, regarding the increasing recognition to move from an anthropocentric to a more ecocentric water ethics, Lonergan's heuristic model of world process grounds humans and human agency within a universe of "emergent probability." Lonergan situates humans and human agency as dependent on natural systems in an already value-laden natural world. The intelligible orders of nature precede, underlay, and condition the orders of human invention. As an intelligible, emergently probable universe becomes intelligent, humans are responsible for the emergence of history.[39] Conscious human intentionality cannot be bypassed, however, even when solutions such as legal rights for nature and rights for rivers are proposed. For Lonergan, self-transcendence is the basis of all ethics. We are called to be self-and-species transcendent.[40] Beyond the level of concepts and laws, nature and rivers require human spokespersons. "Rivers with rights" debates show that native peoples and ecologists are more fitting for this role than lawyers and bureaucrats.

Second, for Lonergan, living and operating on the level of the times is essential and not doing so is backwardness.[41] This means acknowledging connections between past, present and future issues, rather than having the latest smartphone. Being on the level of the times today requires considering all the pertinent data. This includes

---

39. Lonergan, *Insight*, 628, 656, 497.

40. I credit this term to Gordon Rixon, S.J. I interpret it as the broader range of self-transcendence for humans between earth and nature of which we partake and the uncreated Divine.

41. Bernard Lonergan, "Dialectic of Authority," in *A Third Collection: Papers by Bernard J. F. Lonergan, S.J.*, ed. Frederick E. Crowe (Mahwah, NJ: Paulist Press, 1985), 8.

the ways humans are changing and harming the earth. It also means participating in the challenge of the great turning towards ethical and sustainable living in the era of the Anthropocene. Lonergan scholars should explicitly integrate Lonergan's compact and rich work on "the human good" into its pre-established roots in the natural world of emergent probability. The "human and global good" should replace "the human good." Thus, the objective of morally transcending existential consciousness is the intention, the promotion, and the active pursuit of the human and global good.

Third, water ethics and governance must deal with diverse values. Participatory governance approaches have been encouraged for many decades now as global standards. But how can non-commensurate values be compared and related in order to make judgments of value for decisions on water policy and contentious issues and projects? Lonergan's integral scale of values can help here. The integral scale places vital, social, cultural, personal, and religious values in ascending order, relating their levels through "sublation."[42] In sublation, all proper features and properties of what is sublated are carried forward to a fuller realization within a richer context. Sublation does not interfere with what is sublated, rather, it introduces something new and distinct, putting everything on a new basis.[43] Cultural values, for example, sublate social values. The higher function of culture is to "express, validate, criticize, correct, develop, improve" the meanings and values operative at the social, economic, and political level.[44] Cultural values exist because of the underpinning of vital and social values, but they rank higher. Authentic cultural meanings and values are the condition of a just social order. Religious values sublate the cultural into a fuller horizon. This is evident in the encyclical *Laudato si'*,[45] which sublates vital, social, and cultural values, carrying them forward into a richer context and fuller horizon of religious love. The integral scale of values thus offers differentiation and relational clarity for the inevitable encounter with diverse values in ethical deliberations over water.

---

42. Lonergan, *Method in Theology*, 31–32.

43. Lonergan, *Method in Theology*, 241.

44. Lonergan, *Method in Theology*, 32.

45. Francis, *Laudato Si'* [Encyclical on Care for Our Common Home], May 24, 2015.

Appeals in the literature for a new water ethic are part of this great turning towards a sustainable future. These appeals converge with Pope Francis's call to renew dialogue on the future of this planet in *Laudato si'*. The objectives of a new water ethic and a "new ecological culture" (*LS* 111) are too closely related to be simply in parallel. Section two of the first chapter of *Laudato si'* concentrates on water issues (*LS* 27–31), while water is mentioned specifically in over two dozen other locations. Links between poverty, water, and ecology are acknowledged as well as the moral imperative towards the water poor. "Our world has a grave social debt towards the poor who lack access to drinking water, because they are denied the right to a life consistent with their inalienable dignity" (*LS* 30). These water poverty references echo and support the sixth UN Sustainable Development Goal.

The water sector can learn much from *Laudato si'* regarding the longer way forward towards a new water ethic. The road to a new ecological culture goes beyond mere change in response to problems. As Pope Francis describes that culture: "[I]t is not merely change in certain sectors in response to problems. Rather, it is a distinctive way of looking at things, a way of thinking, policies, an educational program, a lifestyle, and a spirituality; these altogether in a way that can redress the deepest problems of the global system" (*LS* 111). That is, problems cannot be solved on their own without understanding their connectedness and underlying causes (*LS* 16, 70, 93, 138). Such underlying causes are political, economic, and ideological in nature. On the ideological level, *Laudato si'* indicates the need to get beyond the "myths of modernity." These myths are "grounded in a utilitarian mindset (individualism, unlimited progress, competition, consumerism, [and] the unregulated market)" (*LS* 210). The water ethics literature critiques these same underlying problems.

In other words, applied to water ethics, water managers and decision-makers need to discover their own implicit values. Frequently, these implicit values can reflect the myths of modernity and may neglect values higher than vital and social. Some might even prefer to ignore values other than those that economists can reduce to cost-benefit ratios. Such blind spots are symptoms of a larger historic trend in modernity that involves a distortion and truncation of the integral scale of values. Fred Lawrence, reflecting on Lonergan's integral scale of values, argues that today's advanced technology and efficiency in providing multiple particular goods can verge on the elimination of cultural, personal, and religious values. He writes:

> When this happens, two distortions result; first, values come to be equated with needs and desires on the level of appetite; and second, social goods of order come to be conceived as efficient means to the satisfaction of self-interested covetousness. Then, the end of human living is conceived as an unlimited and disoriented satisfaction of needs and capacities disguised as freedom.[46]

Implications of such a distorted scale of values for society are enormous and far-reaching according to Lawrence. The normative order of civil society is turned upside down. The polity becomes the servant of the economy and technology, and a triumphant technocracy organizes human living around economic value and through competing egoisms of persons and groups. A new water ethics, one fulfilling the calls of *Laudato si'* and aided by Lonergan's work, must present a genuine alternative to such distortions.

Conclusion

The developing field of water ethics can gain much from appropriating the method and work of Bernard Lonergan. Most importantly is the need in water ethics and governance for normative foundations and a method that employs these foundations. Symptomatic of this need is the avoidance to date of the human subject and of the internal cognitional and existential operations involved in knowing and choosing. GEM explicitly appropriates the internal human norms that promote truth, objectivity, and the pursuit of the human and global good.

Self- and species-transcendence is fundamental to overcoming the anthropocentric-ecocentic conundrum that faces humanity in the Anthropocene. While concepts and laws that protect nature can help, these are the product of human intentionality. In a universe of emergent probability, we depend on the intelligible orders of nature that

---

46. Frederick Lawrence, "The Ethics of Authenticity and the Human Good," in *The Importance of Insight: Essays in Honour of Michael Vertin*, eds. John J. Liptay and David Liptay (Toronto: University of Toronto Press, 2007), 146.

precede, underlay, and condition the human project. Heeding the transcendental precepts of GEM means taking unbiased responsibility for knowing and acting in the world. This means that anthropocentrism must be transcended in the greater scheme of an emergently probable world. Protection of sustaining ecologies will not happen through the use of concepts alone, but rather through the proper use of the normative operations of conscious intentionality.

Institutions that govern and manage water have much to gain in appropriating GEM. As seen in the brief analysis of the International Joint Commission, water institutions can be ethically effective inasmuch as their founding principles and operative cultures authentically reflect the inner norms of human consciousness. The explicit adoption of GEM with commitments to self-appropriation could enhance these results even more. Similarly, the crafting of treaties, institutional charters, and collaborative agreements can benefit by being more closely aligned to the metamethod of human consciousness.

Finally, bringing about a new water ethic can be considered as a differentiable component within a much-needed overarching "integral ecology" called for by Pope Francis in *Laudato si'* (*LS* 137). The way forward includes the cultural and educational challenge of recognizing and moving beyond the ideologies and myths of modernity. Progress in this direction will require the authentic use of the inner norms of GEM. Adoption of GEM in water ethics and governance could be tailored to the needs and challenges of acting institutions, government agencies, policy makers, and water diplomacy and peacemaking. Inasmuch as the norms of conscious intentionality are appropriated and authentically used, persons and institutions are directed towards the active pursuit of the human and global good. Attentiveness, intelligence, reasonableness, and responsibility will all be engaged on the way towards a new water ethic and a new ecological culture.

CONTRIBUTORS

Nicolas Baumgartner is finishing a Ph.D. in Theology and Religion at Durham University (UK). His thesis explores how and if moral theology can engage with empirical economics, using the phenomenon of trust as an example. Nicolas is also an impact investment professional, with experience raising and investing capital for social and economic development both in the UK and in Emerging Markets. He holds a B.A. in Economics from the University of St. Gallen (Switzerland) and a M.A. in Theology and Religion from Durham University. He is based in Amsterdam.

Lucas Briola is assistant professor in theology at Saint Vincent College (Latrobe, PA). He recently finished a dissertation at The Catholic University of America entitled, "Integral Ecology, Eucharist, and the Scale of Values: A Contribution of Bernard Lonergan" and is currently revising it for publication. His most recent article, "The Integral Ecology of *Laudato Si'* and a Seamless Garment: The Sartorial Usefulness of Lonergan and Doran's Turn to Culture," appeared in the *Lonergan Review*. His work has also appeared in the *Journal of Moral Theology* and the *Downside Review*, and he has contributed to dailytheology.org, catholicmoraltheology.com, the *Church Life Journal*, and *America Magazine*. He is coordinator of the "ecological culture" section of the International Institute for Method in Theology.

John Dadosky, Ph.D., S.T.D., is professor of theology and philosophy at Regis College/University of Toronto. He is author of *The Structure of Religious Knowing* (SUNY Press, 2004), *The Eclipse and Recovery of Beauty* (University of Toronto Press, 2014), and *Image to Insight* (UNM Press, 2018). He is co-editor of three volumes of the Collected Works of Bernard Lonergan, including *Method in Theology* (2017) and is currently working on the final archival volume (CWL 25) with Robert Doran. He was a founding member of the Lonergan Consultation that meets annually at the annual meeting of the Catholic Theological Society of America (CTSA). He has several forthcoming articles on Lonergan's thought in refereed journals. He is also treasurer to the CTSA and the American Theological Society.

Edward Dunar is a Ph.D. candidate in Systematic Theology at Fordham University in New York City. He received his Master of Divinity from the Harvard Divinity School. His dissertation research focuses on the church's call to challenge racism in the context of the urban built environment. In particular, he is interested in how local churches can draw on their theological traditions to promote well-being and democratic decision-making in their neighborhoods and cities.

Benjamin J. Hohman is a Ph.D. candidate in Systematic Theology at Boston College. His dissertation brings Bernard Lonergan into dialogue with contemporary evolutionary theology, focusing specifically on the role of grace in ongoing evolutionary processes. His publications include "Toward a More Eudaimonistic Scientia" in *Heythrop Journal* (2016), as well as book reviews for *Horizons* and the *Journal of Moral Theology*. His forthcoming publications include "Prolegomena to Any 'Metaphysics of the Future': A Critical Appraisal of John Haught's Evolutionary Theology" in *Horizons* (December 2019) and "Gender and Metaphysics: Judith Butler and Bernard Lonergan in Conversation" in *Theological Studies* (March 2020).

Thomas Hughson, a member of the Society of Jesus, is professor emeritus at Marquette University. His research has recently turned—in light of themes in Lonergan—to paleoanthropology and archaeology. He is interested in the question, "What may be inferred from Neandertal material culture and physiology about possible religious experience?" He presented "Neandertal Symbols: Neandertal Spirituality?" at the NeanderArt2018 conference at the University of Turin last August. Its more developed form will appear in the conference Proceedings. The organizer of the conference solicited a book that is outlined and tentatively titled, *Neandertal Symbols: Neandertal Religion? An Interdisciplinary Study*. Hughson contributed a chapter, "Roman Catholic Pastoral Theology" to a principally Anglican book, *The Study of Ministry: Theory and Best Practices* (2019). He edited *The Holy Spirit and the Church: Ecumenical Reflections with a Pastoral Perspective* (2016), contributing a chapter on "Life After Liturgy: The Paraclete and Social Mission." He also recently authored "Kenotic Ecclesiology: Context, Orientations, Secularity," in *Seekers and Dwellers: Plurality and Wholeness in a Time of Secularity*, ed. Philip Rossi (2016).

Thomas C. McAuley is a professional water resources engineer who served the International Joint Commission (IJC) from 2000–2012 as a senior engineering advisor where he had responsibility for boards and studies in nine major watersheds straddling the Canada-US border between the Columbia River basin in the west and the St. Croix River in the east. He recently completed a Ph.D. in theology and ethics in 2018 at St. Paul University in Ottawa, Canada. Tom has a degree in Geological Engineering from the University of Toronto and an MSc in Civil Engineering-Water Resources from the University of Manitoba. Though semi-retired, he actively follows global water, environmental, and climate developments and continues to research, write, and teach part-time at St. Paul University.

Joseph Ogbonnaya is Associate Professor of Systematic Theology at Marquette University. He specializes in systematic theology, with a particular emphasis on the theology and philosophy of Bernard Lonergan and Robert M. Doran, African Theology, and World Christianity. His books include *African Perspectives on Culture and World Christianity* (2017), *African Catholicism and Hermeneutics and Culture* (2014) and *Lonergan, Social Transformation and Sustainable Human Development* (2013).

Nicholas Olkovich is Assistant Professor and Marie Anne Blondin Chair in Catholic Theology at St. Mark's College in Vancouver, Canada. Nick teaches foundational, systematic and pastoral theology at the undergraduate and graduate levels. He was co-editor of *The Promise of Renewal: Dominicans and Vatican II* (ATF Press, 2016) and has published articles in *Political Theology*, *The Heythrop Journal*, *Pacifica: Australasian Theological Studies*, and *Method: Journal of Lonergan Studies*. His ongoing research focuses on the relationship between ethics, politics and religion and on human rights theory and practice in particular. He is especially interested in bringing Lonergan's work into dialogue with contemporary political philosophy and theology.

Jame Schaefer (Ph.D., Marquette University, 1994, Systematics/Ethics) focuses on constructively relating theology, the natural sciences and technology with special attention to religious foundations for ecological ethics. Her publications include *Theological Foundations for Environmental Ethics: Reconstructing Patristic and Medieval*

Concepts (Georgetown University Press, 2009), *Confronting the Climate Crisis: Catholic Theological Perspectives* (Marquette University Press, 2011), *Environmental Justice and Climate Change: Assessing Pope Benedict XVI Ecological Vision for the Catholic Church in the United States* (Lexington, 2013), essays in several edited volumes, articles in *Cistercian Studies Quarterly, Environmental Ethics, Geosciences, The International Journal for Climate Change Strategies and Management, The Journal of Religion, Nature, and Culture, The Journal of Moral Theology, Theological Studies,* and *Worldviews: Religion, Culture, Science,* and the inaugural "Animals" entry in *New Catholic Encyclopedia* (2013). She collaborated with other scholars in drafting *Healing Earth,* the online environmental science textbook commissioned by the Higher Education Secretariat of the Society of Jesus, spearheaded the three-year Best Practices Project of the Society for Conservation Biology, and serves as the Handling Editor of manuscripts submitted to *Conservation Biology* that incorporate faith, ethics and/or values.

Paul St. Amour received his B.A./M.A. in philosophy from Boston College, and his Ph.D. from Fordham University. He is currently an Associate Professor of Philosophy at Saint Joseph's University, in Philadelphia. His scholarly and teaching interests include Philosophy of Religion, Ancient and Medieval Philosophy, Aquinas, Contemporary Thomism, Kierkegaard, Ethics, and Philosophy of Economics. He has written numerous articles applying the thought of Bernard Lonergan to a wide range of philosophical issues. His recent research has focused on Lonergan's macroeconomic theory. His articles have appeared in *The Thomist, Analecta Hermeneutica: International Institute for Hermeneutics, Lonergan Workshop, Method: Journal of Lonergan Studies, The Lonergan Review, Theoforum, Contemporary Philosophy,* and *Proceedings of the American Catholic Philosophical Association.*

Cristina Vanin is an associate professor of theology, associate dean, and director of the Master of Catholic Thought theology program, at St. Jerome's University in Waterloo, Ontario. She received her B.A. from St. Jerome's University, her M.Div. from St. Michael's College, Toronto, and her Ph.D. in theology from Boston College. Influenced by the thought of Bernard Lonergan and Thomas Berry, she focuses on the role that theology can have in helping us respond adequately to the ecological crisis. She has worked with the Jesuits of Canada on its Mission and Ecology Committee, and helped to prepare a guidebook on *Laudato Si'* for the Canadian Conference of Catholic Bishops. Recent publications include: "Ecological Transformation through Attentiveness and Intimacy," in *Encountering Earth: Thinking Theologically With a More-Than-Human World,* (eds. Trevor Bechtel, Matthew Eaton, and Timothy Harvie, 2018), "Care and Compassion: The Need for an Integral Ecology," in *Ecotheology and Nonhuman Ethics in Society: A Community of Compassion* (eds. Melissa J. Brotton, Lexington Books, 2017), and "Ecological Conversion: What Does It Mean?" in *Theological Studies* (2016), co-written with Neil Ormerod.

Kate Ward (Ph.D., Boston College; M.Div., Catholic Theological Union; B.A., Harvard College) is Assistant Professor of Theological Ethics at Marquette University. Her research focuses on economic ethics, virtue ethics, and ethical method. She has published articles on wealth, virtue, and economic inequality in journals including *Theological Studies, Journal of Religious Ethics, Heythrop Journal,* and *Journal of the Society of Christian Ethics.* She is completing a monograph exploring the impact of wealth, poverty and inequality on the pursuit of virtue.

Gerard Whelan is an Irish Jesuit and Professor of Fundamental Theology at the Pontifical Gregorian University. He is author of *Redeeming History: Social Concern in the Thought of Bernard Lonergan and Robert Doran* (2013) and *A Discerning Church: Pope Francis, Bernard Lonergan and Theological Method in Changing Times* (Paulist Press, 2019).

INDEX

A

analogy of dialectic, 85, 200, 201, 202, 203

anthropocentrism, xii, 98, 163, 165, 166, 169, 171, 173, 174, 183, 204, 271

antirepresentationalism, 60, 66, 68, 69

B

Berry, Thomas, 138–139, 205–208

bias, xvi, 7, 30, 39, 43–56, 75, 90–95, 106–115, 130, 13, 208, 222–223, 246, 250, 265–266, 271

biodiversity, 100, 104–105, 150, 199, 205, 214–215, 254

Byrne, Patrick, 91–93, 181, 187–190

C

capital market liberalization, 20

capstone seminar, xx, 215, 220, 233

Catholic social teaching, xi–xv, 26, 29, 35, 38, 96, 119–120, 123–125, 129, 135, 149, 173, 179, 236, 238, 249

classical laws, 186, 188

cognitional theory, xviii, 197, 261, 263

common good, xi, 12, 13, 25, 26, 29, 33, 45, 51, 60, 63, 72, 77, 78, 96, 103, 150, 225, 229, 230, 244, 258, 266

communitarianism, 101, 108, 109–111, 115

communitarian vision, 101

cosmological and anthropological constitutive meanings, 85, 87, 89, 202

crisis of meaning, 71, 72, 73, 78, 161–163, 173, 176

D

dialectic of community, 85, 89, 201, 202

dialectic of culture, 85, 88, 89, 173, 177, 200–205, 212, 214

dialectic of the subject, 85, 88, 201

Doran, Robert M., ix, xii, xiv–xix, 53, 79–95, 97, 106–107, 109, 114, 116, 120, 129–132, 135, 173, 177, 200–203, 207–208

E

ecological conversion, xviii–xix, 142, 149, 151, 153–155, 157, 163, 167–172, 179–182, 190, 199, 208, 211, 214, 219, 232, 249

ecological crisis, xi, xvii, 97–100, 108, 114, 119–121, 127, 159–168, 172–173, 176, 200, 205, 208, 216, 218, 231–232, 235, 237

ecological responsibility, xx, 137, 215, 219–220, 229

ecology, xiv, xx, 97, 98, 100, 107–108, 112, 114–115, 120, 122, 124, 128, 130, 159, 177, 180, 182, 185, 220, 226, 248–249, 269

economic inequality, 4, 17, 39, 93, 112

economic-technical junction, xv, 15, 19

ecotheology, 120, 180, 184, 192, 197

emergent probability, xv, xviii, xx, 7, 22, 26, 111, 179, 180–181,

186–190, 193–197, 235, 244, 246–252, 268, 270

empirical paleoanthropological research, xviii, 174

Enlightenment, 34, 57, 59, 61–62, 68, 98–100, 102, 106, 108, 261

environment, xvi, 4, 7, 14, 17–19, 21, 61, 80, 95, 98, 99, 114, 121–124, 126, 138, 139, 149–153, 156–157, 179, 190, 204, 205, 207, 211, 213, 236–239, 242, 243, 249, 250, 252, 257

environmental sustainability, 4–5

epideictic, 160–161, 165

eschatology, xviii, 65, 153, 179, 180–184, 190, 191, 193, 196

evil, xxi, 28, 91, 116, 151, 167, 189, 246–248

F

Francis, Pope, xi, xii, xvii–xxi, xviii, xix, xx, 28, 43, 47, 49, 51, 54, 120, 124–128, 131–135, 137, 139, 142, 149, 150, 151–157, 159–169, 172–174, 177, 179, 181–186, 196, 200, 203–205, 207, 208, 211, 212–214, 215–225, 231–233, 235–238, 243, 249, 250, 252, 269, 271

G

generalized empirical method, xx, 217, 263–264

global human rights, xvi, 57

globalization, xi–xxi, 3–7, 12–22, 23–24, 39–40, 47, 49, 51, 53–56, 57–58, 75, 78, 79–80, 84, 87, 94–95, 97, 107

globalization of solidarity, xvi, 39, 53–56

global warming, 100, 199

good of order, 4, 12, 15, 32, 70, 90, 245, 246, 248, 252

grace, xvi, xviii, 32, 24, 28, 31, 32, 38, 79–80, 87–92, 141, 160, 179, 190–198, 218, 235–236

nature and, 161

greenhouse gas, 100, 199, 225

H

heuristic, xiv, xv, xvii, 3, 5, 8, 14–15, 22, 73, 74, 78, 91, 114, 120, 163, 166, 172, 186, 244, 248, 267

Hildegard of Bingen, xviii, 137–138, 150, 154–156

Hollenbach, David, 58, 69, 72–78

human ecology, 121–127, 237

humane development, 26, 28, 35

humane globalization, xii, xvii, xix, 23, 36–38, 54, 80, 120

human flourishing, 43, 54, 77, 235, 239, 250

human good, 19, 59, 69, 70, 75, 95, 167, 268

human intersubjectivity, 162

I

Incarnation, 89, 144, 151, 194, 198

Industrial Revolution, 99, 162

inequality, xvi, 39–43, 45–56, 80, 94–96, 238

Institute for Method in Theology, ix–x

integral ecology, xii, xiv, xvii–xxi, 119, 120, 124, 126–127, 132–133, 135, 142, 149, 150–157, 163, 166, 173, 177, 179, 183, 185, 200, 211–212, 215, 218, 235, 237–238, 243, 252, 271

integral scale of values, xiv, 80, 81, 83, 90, 93, 95–96, 128–131, 200, 268–269

J

Jacobs, Jane, 104, 240

L

Laudato si', xi, xvii–xx, 120, 124–128,
131–135, 137–139, 149–151,
155–157, 159–168, 172, 176–177,
179–182, 184–188, 190, 193, 196,
200, 203, 205, 208, 211, 212, 216,
221, 226, 231, 235–237, 243, 249,
268–271
Law of the Cross, 88–90, 246, 247, 249
Lawrence, Frederick, 31, 34, 170,
269–270
Lonergan, Bernard, ix, xii–xxi, 7–10,
15, 22, 25, 29, 39, 43, 53, 56, 58,
69, 80, 91–93, 97, 105, 120, 128,
135, 161, 163, 174, 179, 186, 200,
207, 215, 231, 235, 244, 253, 263,
270

M

MacIntyre, Alasdair, 58, 99, 103
macroeconomic circulation analysis,
xv
market, xiii, xv, 5, 7, 11, 17, 20, 23–38,
51, 57–59, 94–96, 130, 203–204,
211–212, 249, 256, 269
market mechanisms, 23–24, 26,
30–31, 34, 36, 58
McNichols, William Hart, 137–138
Melchin, Kenneth, 109–111, 115
multinational corporations, xv, 3–4,
16–18, 21, 29, 85, 100

N

neoliberal ideology, xv, 11, 17, 23, 26,
36, 38, 59
neoliberalism, xvi, 7, 12–13, 23, 26,
34, 38, 58, 67, 78
Northcott, Michael, xvii, 97–115
Novak, Michael, 23–38

O

operations of consciousness, 263–265

P

Piketty, Thomas, 42, 45, 52, 93, 112
political-economic junction, xv, 15, 17
populism, 107–109, 115
practical intelligence, xv, 8, 30,
75, 83–85, 89, 95–96, 129, 165,
201–202
psychic conversion, xix, 130, 169, 174,
200, 207–209, 211

R

Rawls, John, 76, 110–111, 115
religious freedom, 74–75
Rorty, Richard, xvi, 58, 60–69, 73–78

S

scale of values, xvi–xviii, xx, 80–82,
90–93, 95, 119–120, 129–131, 135,
177, 200, 270
scotosis, xvi, 39, 44, 45, 47, 49–53, 56
self-transcendence, 73–74, 77–78, 81,
162, 207–208, 214, 245, 264, 267
social grace, 77, 80, 90–91
solidarity, xvi, 53, 55, 57, 58, 61,
63–64, 66–69, 76–77, 161, 218,
238, 258
soteriological culture, 130, 212
statistical laws, 186
Stiglitz, Joseph, 3, 22, 93, 95

T

technical-natural junction, xv, 15, 21
technocratic paradigm, xii, xvii, xix,
126, 154, 162, 163, 165–167, 171,
173, 205
Theology and the Dialectics of History,
xiv, 129, 177
theology of *viriditas*, 139, 145, 149,
151, 156
transcendental precept, xx, 111, 215,
231, 264–265, 271
trickle-down theories, 28

U
United Nations Sustainable Development Goals, 255
universal willingness, 88

V
values approach, 259–261
vertical finality, 192, 193, 196

Voegelin, Eric, 85–87, 129, 202

W
water ethics, xix, xx, 253, 256–262, 264, 267–271
water poverty, xx, 253, 254, 269
world-cultural community, xvii, 91
world-cultural humanity, 107, 109